I0812752

IMAGES
of America

ST. LAWRENCE COUNTY PORTRAITS

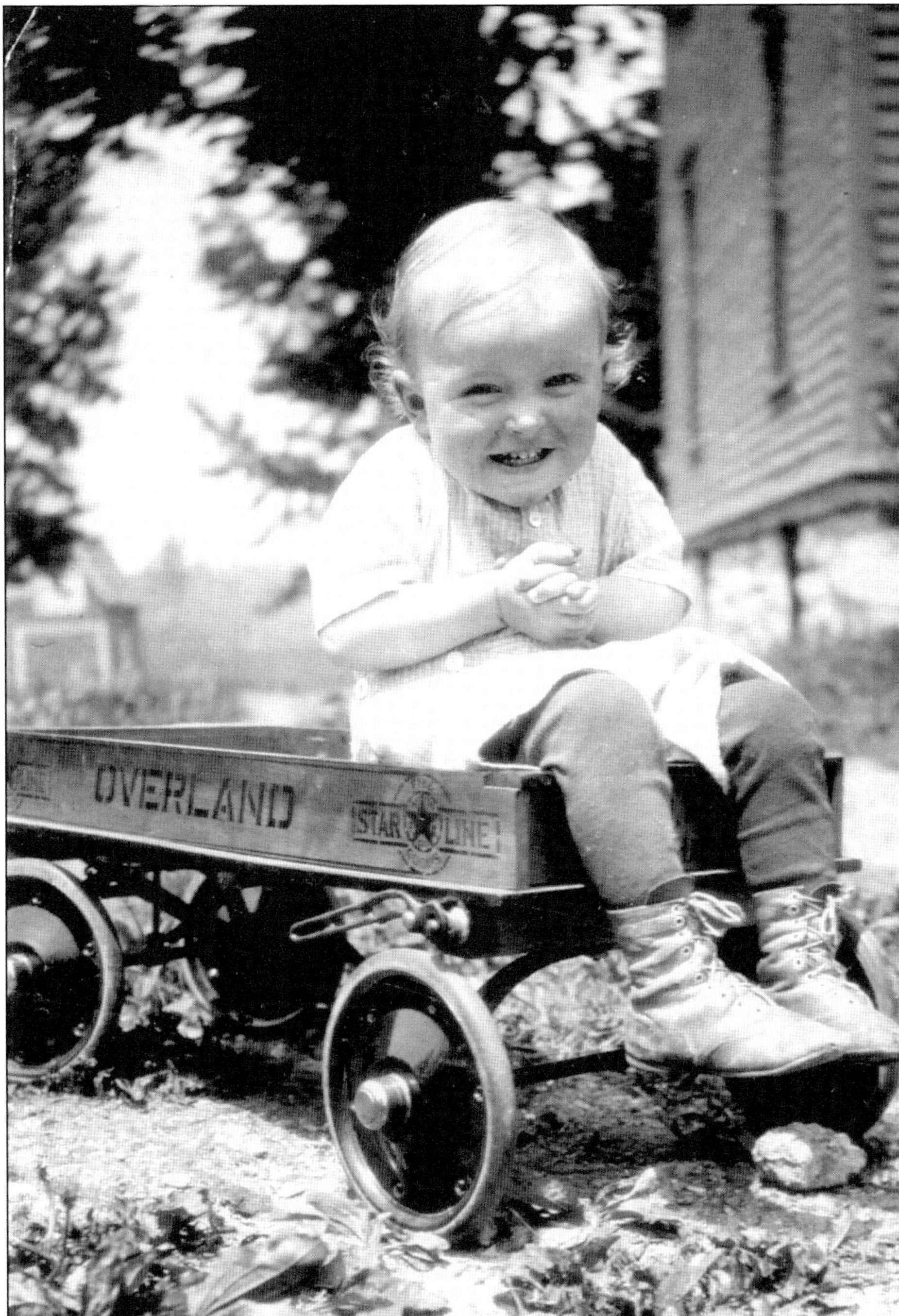

PENNY FOR YOUR THOUGHTS! Looking happy as can be, as well as a bit mischievous, is James McCormick Jr. He was born in Canton in 1921. His father, at one time, sold Hudson cars where today's bowling alley is located, and his mother was a teacher. Jim is remembered as a gifted musician and for his service in the U.S. Air Force in Europe during World War II. His letters home described his war experiences, and were published in the *Canton Plaindealer*. He was killed in an in-flight air collision in 1945.

IMAGES
of America

St. Lawrence County Portraits

Patricia Harrington Carson
and E. Anne Mazzotta

ARCADIA
PUBLISHING

ISBN 978-0-7385-3863-1

Published by Arcadia Publishing
Charleston, South Carolina

Printed in the United States of America

Library of Congress Catalog Card Number: 2005925732

For all general information, please contact Arcadia Publishing:
Telephone 843-853-2070
Fax 843-853-0044
E-mail sales@arcadiapublishing.com
For customer service and orders:
Toll-Free 1-888-313-2665

Visit us on the Internet at www.arcadiapublishing.com

This book is dedicated to David E. Martin of Ogdensburg, whose know-how, dedication, and his untold hours of scanning photographs have made this book a reality

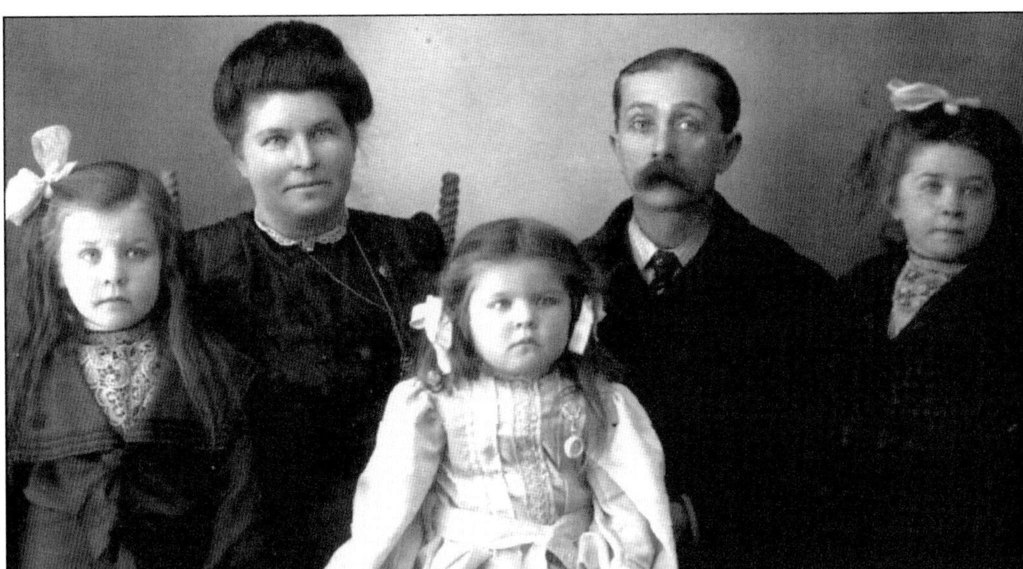

BROOKDALE, 1907. Jenny and Joseph Curtis are shown here with their three daughters, from left to right, Belle, Thelma, and Mildred. Mildred married Earl Stickney from Jenkins Neighborhood, near Winthrop, and ran a small dairy farm. Belle received her nursing degree from the State Hospital School of Nursing and later married Harold Nichols from Louisville Landing. Thelma pursued a degree in nursing from A. Barton Hepburn Hospital and married Carl Lewis from North Stockholm. (Courtesy of Carlton Stickney.)

Contents

ACKNOWLEDGMENTS

We want to thank the St. Lawrence County Historical Association (SLCHA) Museum and Archives, the St. Lawrence University Archives, the St. Lawrence County historian's office, county historians, and the many people who have so generously allowed us to use their family photographs in this book.

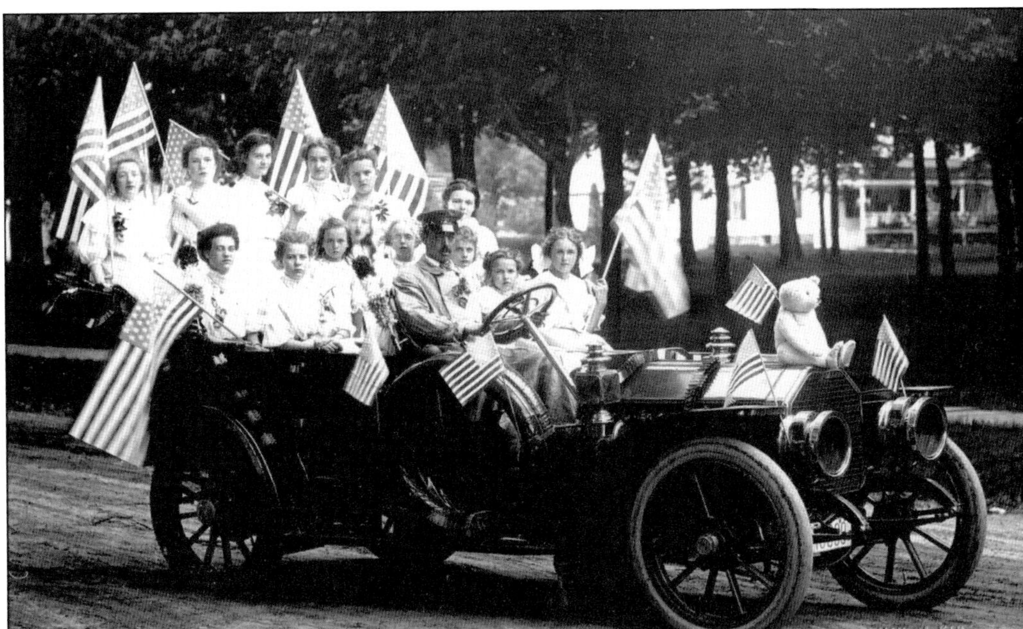

FOURTH OF JULY CELEBRATIONS. From the Civil War on, Independence Day has been for the community what Christmas has been for the private family. Waving flags, bunting-draped buildings, and marching bands filled one and all with patriotism. These fourteen, flag-waving Canton girls are ready to celebrate in a 1915 Model T Ford with a neatly dressed chauffeur. Note the teddy bear on the front of the car. (Courtesy of SLCHA.)

INTRODUCTION

Between 1840 and 1850, the first daguerreotype studios were opened, making the family image available to all. It was the way to immortalize the family and to preserve memories for times to come.

Before the camera was invented, nobody knew what other people's families, besides possibly some neighbors, looked like. Oftentimes the only community that parents and their children knew was their own.

Rich families were the only ones able to have their portraits painted, and those were not always of the full family group. One variation was the primitive, when the itinerant limner (artist) would appear in the village with the canvases already painted except for the faces, which would be added later. Although the clothes and background were not authentic, when the faces were added to the portrait, the family had a cherished heirloom.

With the advent of photography, proud and loving parents from all walks of life were able to have formal studio portraits of their children as well as the complete family.

Family albums covered with velvet and filled with pictures adorned parlor tables in American homes everywhere, preserving the past and providing a model for the future.

The rich and the poor, the young and the old, the farmer and the townsfolk are all included in this book, shown in the glory that was once theirs.

We hope to have portrayed the formality of the Victorian Era, with the elaborate backgrounds and the elegant clothing of both children and adults. The fine photographic studios located in many of the towns were responsible for the settings and décor that defined the era.

In contrast, the warmth and simplicity of the less formal pictures of children playing, family picnics and outings, holidays, and home-life on the farm, show the everyday joys captured by a loving relative with a Kodak camera.

The photographs included here date from the mid-1800s, when one traveled by horse and buggy, read by the glow of an oil lamp, and sat around wood-burning stoves for warmth. We then travel through the years ending with the era known as the Roaring Twenties. The 1920s were a time when the world was alive with the peace and prosperity that followed World War I. It was the era of the flapper, the Charleston, and bathtub gin.

These people have left a part of themselves on the photographer's film. This is a history book by itself, telling volumes about a county and its people.

Interspersed among the portraits are some of the more notable figures of the time. Included in these pages is Frederic Remington, born in Canton, who was a world-renowned artist and sculptor. He is best known for his bronze sculpture *Broncho Buster.* Henry Rushton, born in Edwards, built small boats and canoes of the finest quality. He became world-famous after showing his boats at the Chicago World's Fair in 1893. Most famous was his canoe "Indian Girl." The Pickins twins, Bessie and Jessie, who were born in Heuvelton, can also be seen in these pages. They began their singing careers in vaudeville and performed at Windsor Castle for King Edward VII and Queen Alexandra. Bessie later became a famous opera star.

In conclusion, we, the authors, are proud of these pictures and want to sincerely thank the people who so kindly offered them for our use. We feel that these portraits most accurately exemplify our title, *St. Lawrence County Portraits.*

The people in the book, looking out at the world with awe and wonder, tell a story in pictures entitled "The Way We Were."

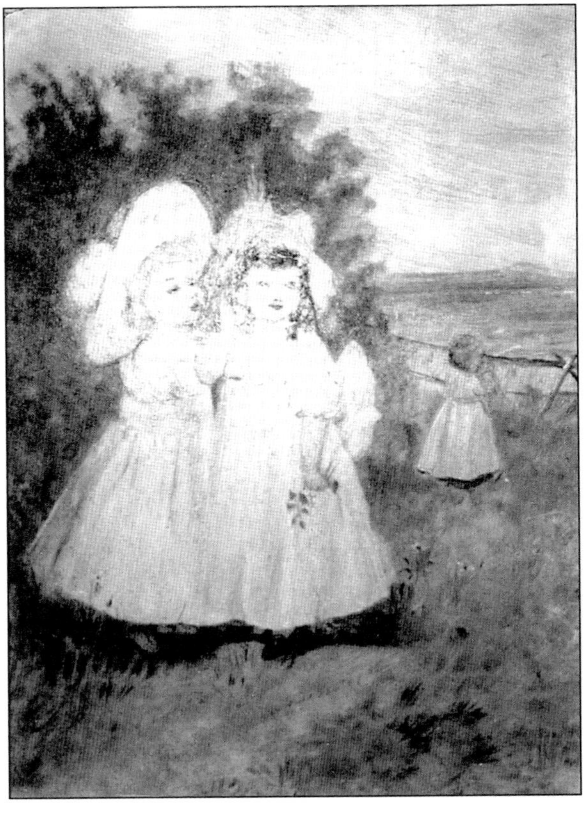

PRIMITIVES. This is an example of a primitive. Itinerant artists would appear in a village with paintings that were already complete. The only things that needed to be added were the faces. (Courtesy of Patricia Harrington Carson.)

One

Portraits of Children

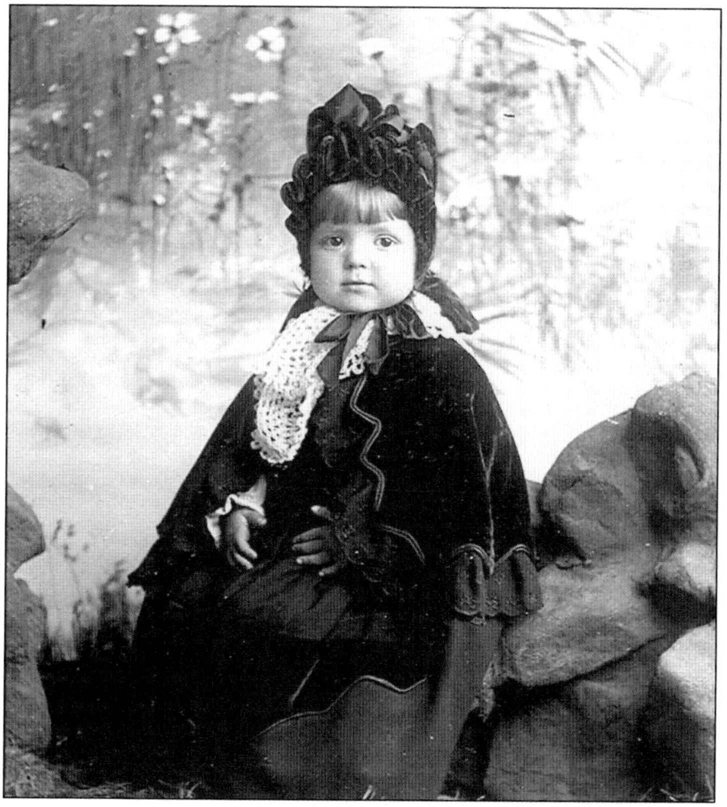

First Teaching Job in Eben. Clarice M. Brown is dressed in the height of fashion. She was born in Pierrepont on September 3,1891. She was a daughter of Donald and Margaret Brown. Her father was born in Scotland and her mother in England. She attended Canton Schools and was a graduate of Potsdam Normal School in 1915, whereupon she took a teaching job in Eben. Clarice was an elementary teacher in New Jersey and Hawaii. At one time she operated an elementary school in Ogdensburg. She was named "Pierrepont Citizen" of the year in 1987. Clarice died at the age of 99. (Courtesy of SLCHA.)

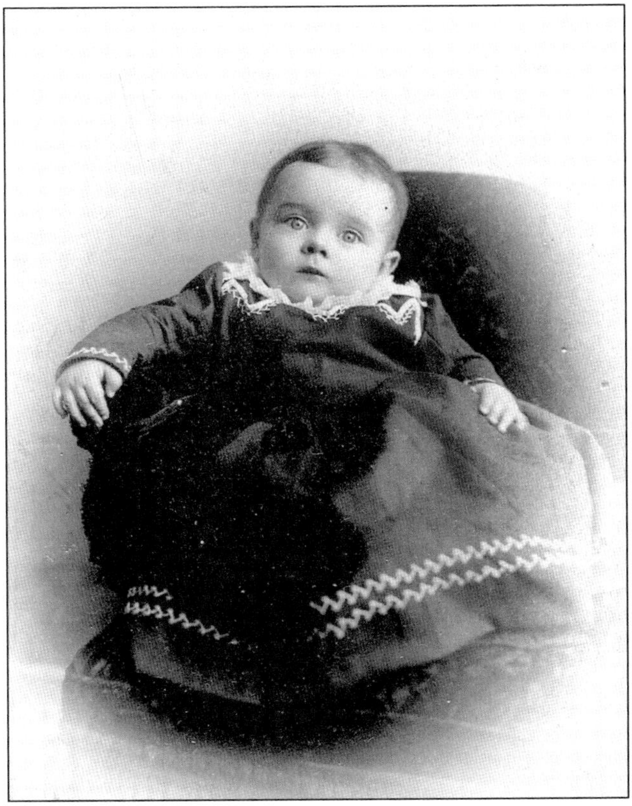

A 1915 St. Lawrence University Graduate. This photograph of Beatrice Reynolds was taken at the Stone and Wilcox Studio in Malone in 1891. Beatrice graduated from St. Lawrence University in 1915. She married Daniel Beaman, who was a St. Lawrence University classmate. The family lived in Richville, Waddington, and Ogdensburg. They were the parents of five children. Her dress, so ornately trimmed, was probably made by her mother. (Courtesy of Mary Ruth Judd.)

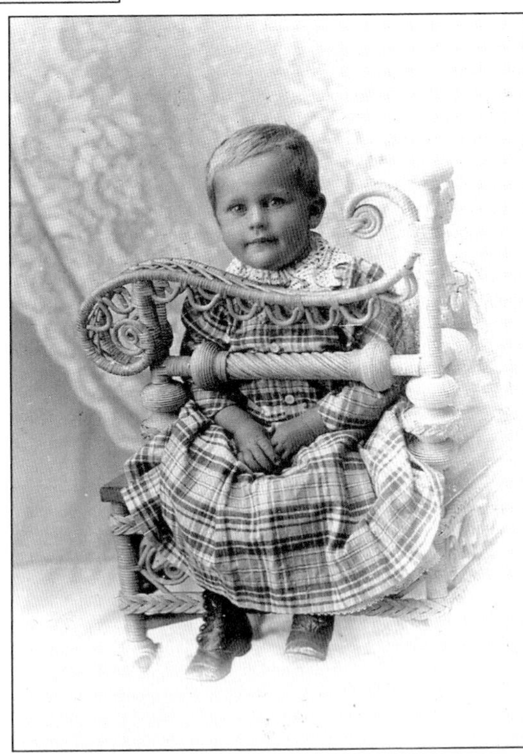

Early St. Lawrence County Family. Almeron Clark Judd was born in May 1891 in the family homestead on Farnes Road in Canton. He looks quite fetching here in his little plaid suit. His parents were Franklin and Zettie Shipman Judd, who were life-long farmers. On the farm they had horses, cows, pigs and chickens. They grew popcorn, which they sold, and they made maple syrup from their woods. An early Judd ancestor, Daniel Judd, ran a gristmill for Stillman Foote (Canton's founder) and was a Revolutionary War veteran. (Courtesy of Herb Judd.)

HAPPY ON THE FARM. Mina Freeman was born in her country home on State Street Road in Canton. The first two-story house in the area, it was built in the late 1830s. The property was originally part of the Van Rensselaer Tract. The farm was bought by Velourus Freeman and his wife Elmina in 1867. The property passed through four more generations including Mina Freeman. She married Herbert Eggleson Sr. and the farm has remained in the Eggleson family ever since. (Courtesy of Peggy Eggleson.)

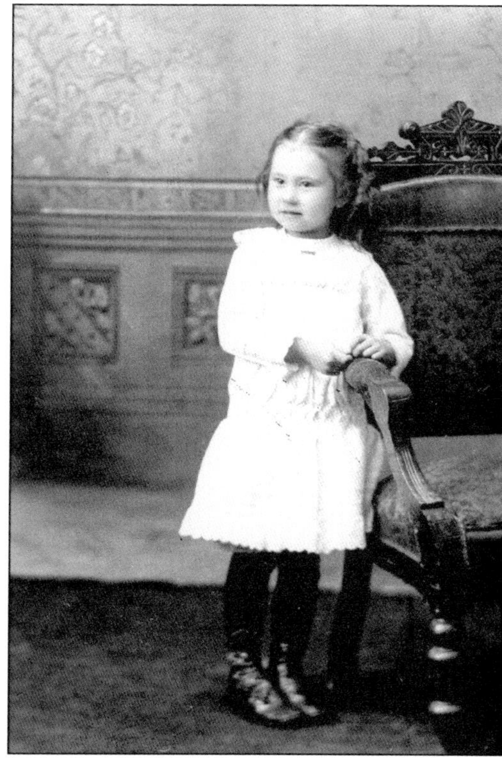

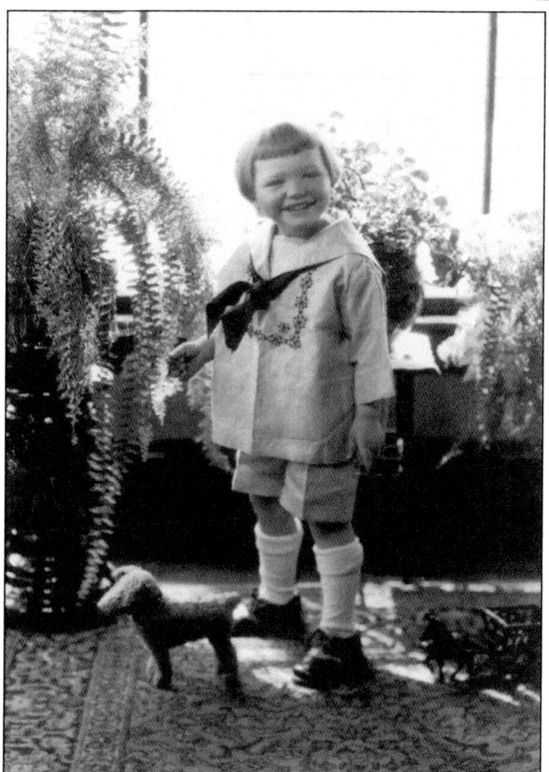

GREW UP TO BE AN ARMY PILOT. Robert James, pictured with his toys, was born on a farm in Massena in 1922. He was the first-born son of Leonard Nelson and Ruth Balch Beylea. The suit he is wearing was hand-sewn and embroidered by his mother. Robert was a World War II army pilot and in later years worked at the New York State School of Agriculture at Canton. Today he lives with his wife Shirley on Route 22, Potsdam. Robert's interest at the present time is building a full-size birch bark canoe. He has recently completed a four-foot replica of one of Henry Rushton's canoes. (Courtesy of Shirley Beylea.)

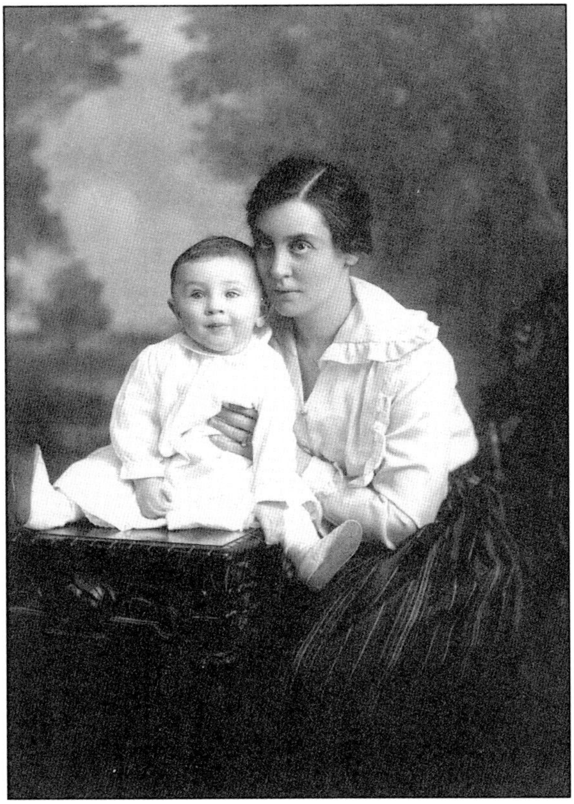

MOTHERLY LOVE. This sweet baby girl, so content in her mother Ella's arms, is Margaret Newell. She was the daughter of Ella Waterman and Albert P. Newell. Her father was the secretary of the Newell Manufacturing Company in Ogdensburg. Margaret was educated at the Emma Willard School and Smith College. She later became the wife of Alfred Wild. (Courtesy of Allan Newell.)

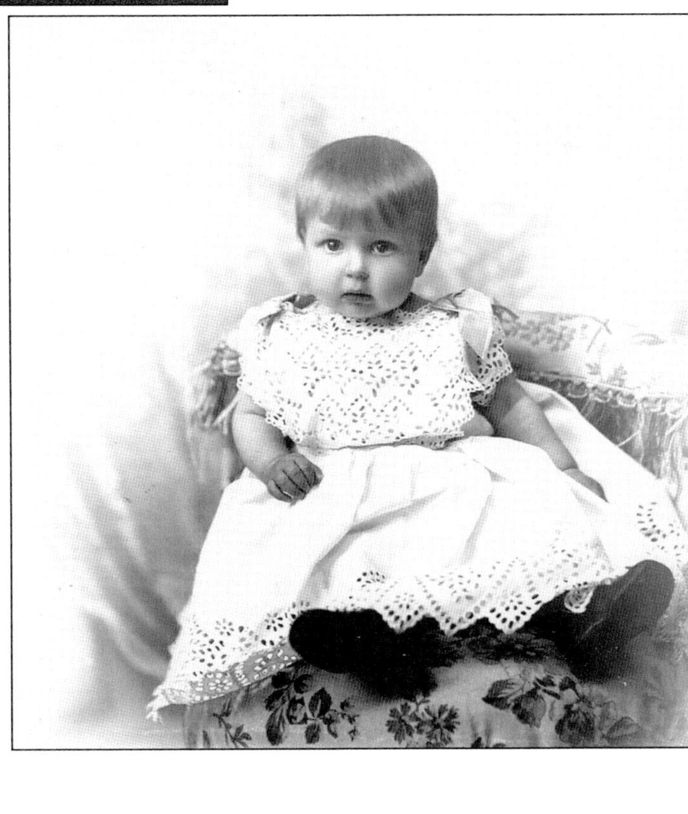

FRENCH TEACHER. Dressed in white lace is Ruth Brown, one of the daughters of Margaret and Donald Brown. Donald was a Civil War veteran, who later prospected for silver and gold in Colorado. The Brown family owned a farm in Pierrepont. Ruth and her sister Clarice both became school teachers. Ruth taught French in high school and Clarice taught elementary school. Together, they visited their father's native Scotland and their mother's native England. Their last trip was to Hawaii where they both taught at Iolani, an Episcopal mission school in Honolulu. (Courtesy of SLCHA.)

MASTER'S IN SCIENCE FROM NEW YORK UNIVERSITY. Edyth Marshall was born on March 27, 1905, on Cream of the Valley Road, outside Gouverneur, New York. In this picture she is six months old and staring intently at the camera. She attended Gouverneur High School and John Hopkins School of Nursing. Later she received a B.S. from St. John's University and an M.S. from New York University. She married George R. Elmer of Canton. Her last employment was superintendent of the E. J. Noble Hospital in Gouverneur. Her later years were spent living on Pierrepont Road in Canton. (Courtesy of the Elmer family.)

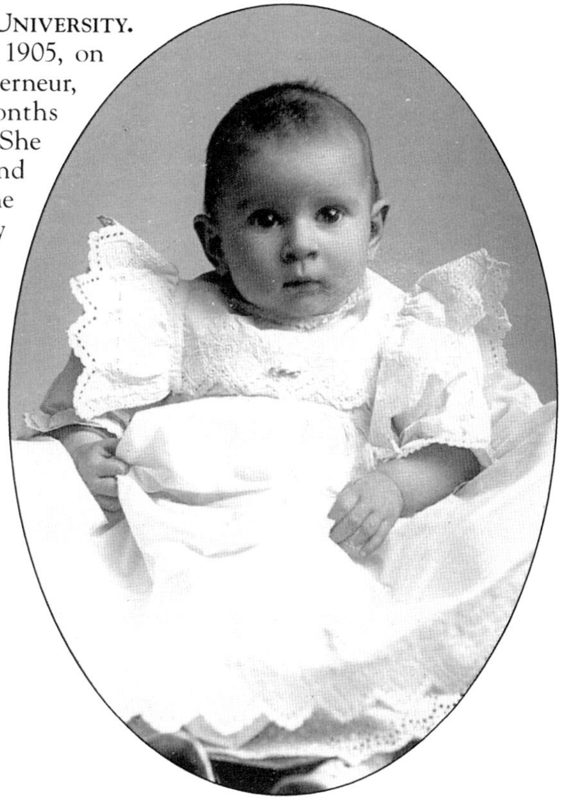

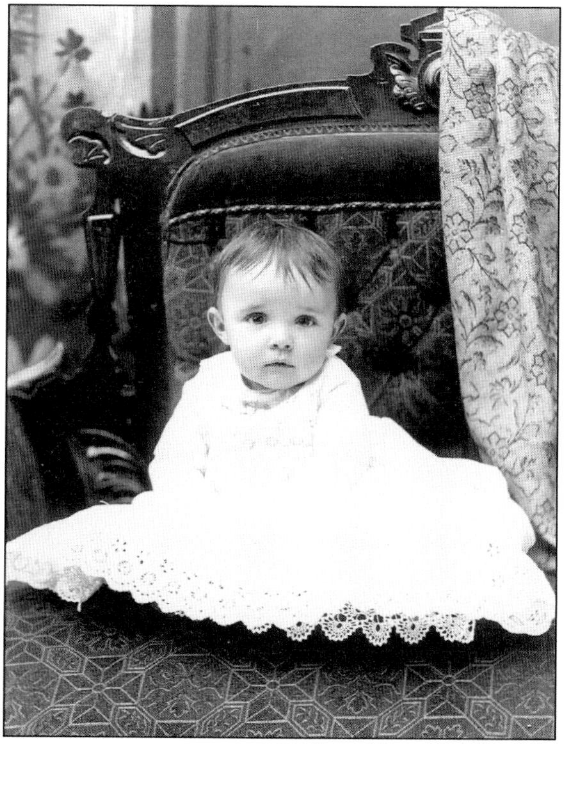

CANTON SON. This handsome baby boy is George R. Elmer, the son of Curilla Daley and Dickenson B. Elmer. Dickenson owned a dry-goods store in Canton. George was born in a house on the corner of Pleasant and Main Streets. He had a sister, Grace, and a brother, Hubert. They attended Canton schools. The large Elmer farm, located beyond Heaton Hill on Pierrepont Road, was their home for a time and still belongs to the family today. George worked for the New York Central Railroad. He married Edyth Marshall and had one son, John. (Courtesy of the Elmer family.)

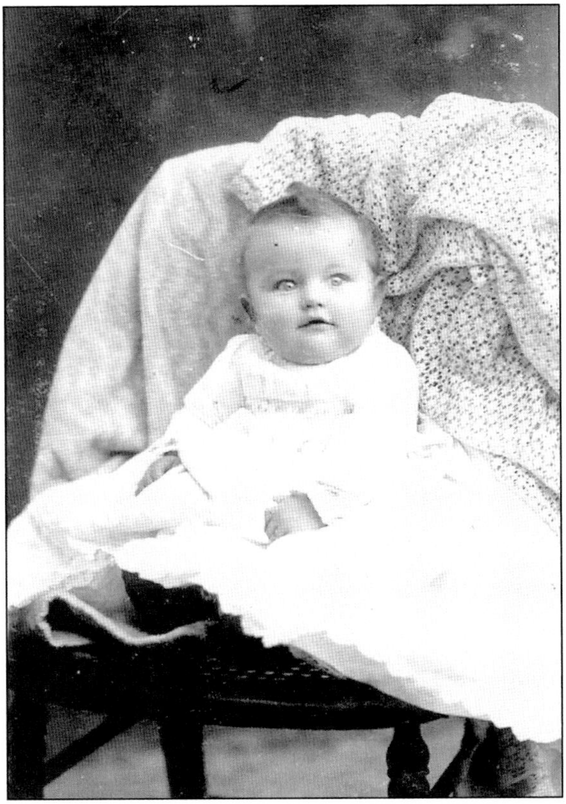

FUTURE FATHER OF SIX. William Henry Pharoah was born on April 15, 1901, in Waddington, New York. He married Rose Elizabeth Besio on June 14, 1933, in Potsdam. He worked at Alcoa in Massena and Montgomery Ward in Potsdam. He was buried in Madrid, New York on June 13, 1952. His children were Marlene Rose (born 1934), Walter James (1936), Elaine Joyce (1938), William Conway (1939), Harriet May (1941), and Barbara Jane (1952). (Courtesy of Ruth Pharoah.)

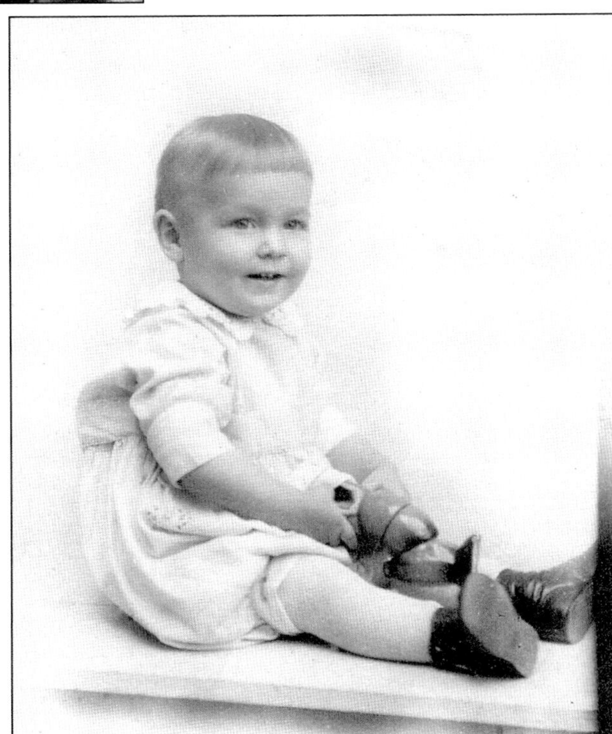

MEMBER OF THE MEDICAL CORPS. Lawrence was one of eight children born to Charles and Alice Tupper of Pierrepont. He was born on the family farm and went to Pierrepont schools for the first eight grades. He attended Canton High School before joining the army. He stayed in service throughout the war years. He was stationed in England and France as a medic. He later married, and he and his wife, Sally, had five children. He worked for 27 years as the highway superintendent of Pierrepont. (Courtesy of Sally Tupper.)

LITTLE LINDY. "Lindy," as she was often called, was Eula McKenney. She is dressed in a lovely hand-made pinafore, which was made of blue serge from her mother's wedding dress. The family's home was in Natural Dam. Her father, John W., worked at the paper mill, and her mother was a seamstress. (Courtesy of Malcolm McCormick.)

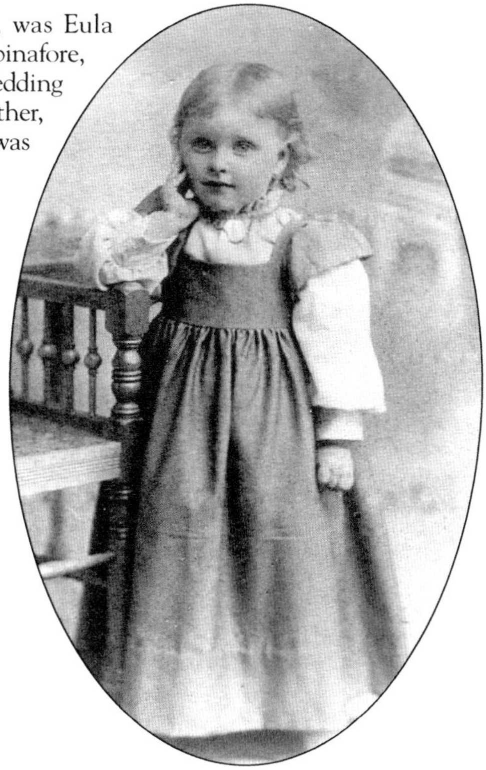

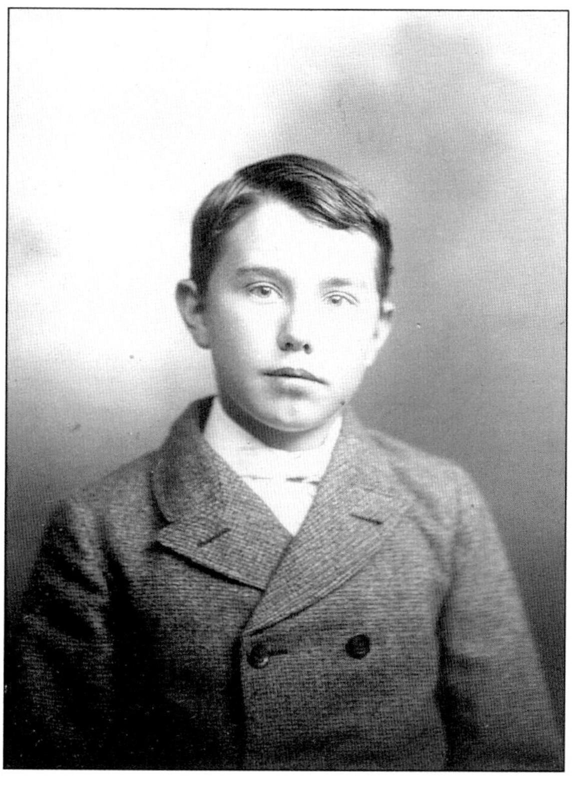

PIERREPONT VILLAGE JUSTICE. George Spencer Lobdell was born in February 1890 in Hannawa Falls. He was the son of Charles Willis and Edith Bancroft Lobdell. He married Harriet Transeau from Pennsylvania. They had two daughters, Betty and Mary, who grew up in Pierrepont. George graduated from Colton High School and Clarkson College. He later taught chemistry at Clarkson and did chemical research at General Cable Corporation in Rome, New York. He was a village justice in Pierrepont. He died on October 9, 1941, at the age of 57. (Courtesy of Mary Lobdell Harrington.)

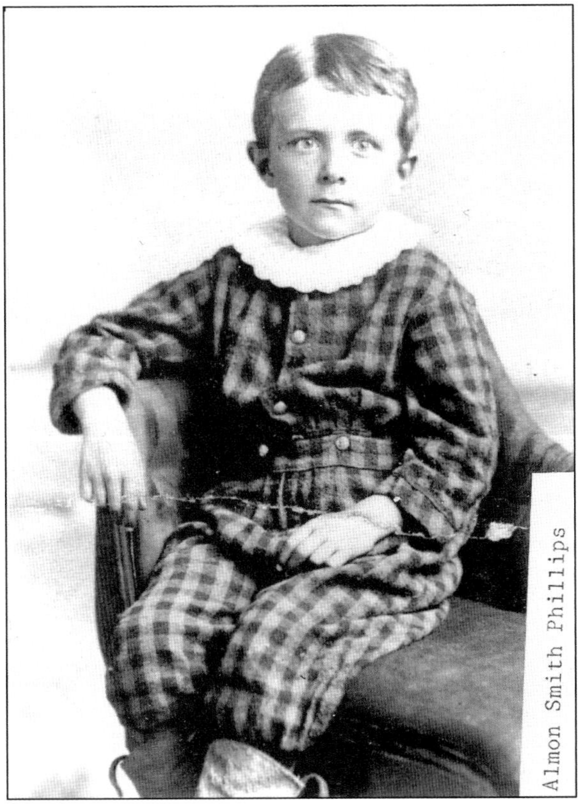

FAMILY ARRIVED ON THE *MAYFLOWER*. Almon Smith Phillips was born in September 1874 in West Parishville. He married Lucelia (Celia) Irish of South Colton in June 1904. Almon had a most interesting life. He was a farmer and a woodsman and served as a guide for the Grandshue Club and Killdare Park (two hunting clubs). Bertrand Snell from Potsdam was overseer. Almon was also a member of the High Falls Masons at Colton. In 1917, he purchased a farm on Potsdam/Colton Road, (formerly the Henry Day Farm). The Phillipses were parents of four daughters, Elva, Rena, Jessie, and Lillian. Almon's lineage goes back to the *Mayflower.* (Courtesy of Elva Billings.)

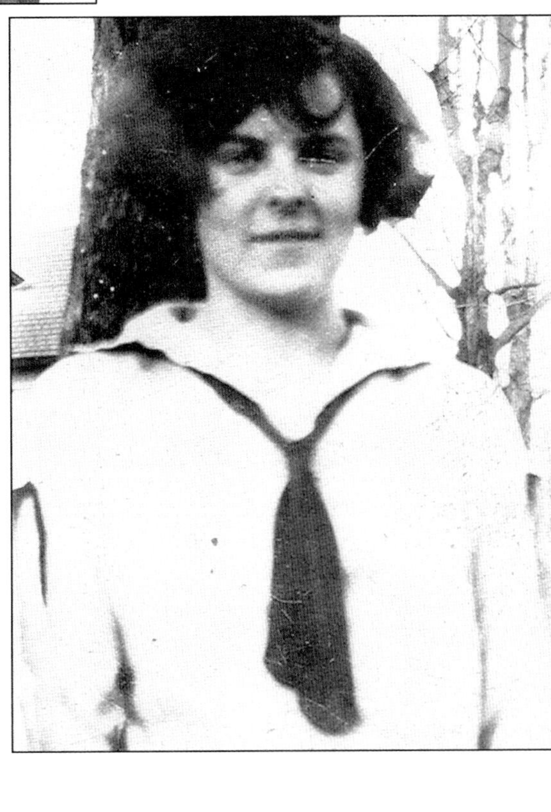

LOVELY LADY. Ethel Sanford, shown here, was the daughter of Dr. Frank B. and the first Mrs. Sanford. She was born in Canton and graduated from St. Lawrence University in 1925. Ethel married Joseph Ellsworth, son of Stanley and Alice Ellsworth, who owned the Ellsworth Shoe Store. Early in their marriage, they lived on Main Street in the lovely red brick family home where there were many Beta fraternity get-togethers. Joe graduated from St. Lawrence University in 1928 and was a Beta member. (Courtesy of Joan Ellsworth Place.)

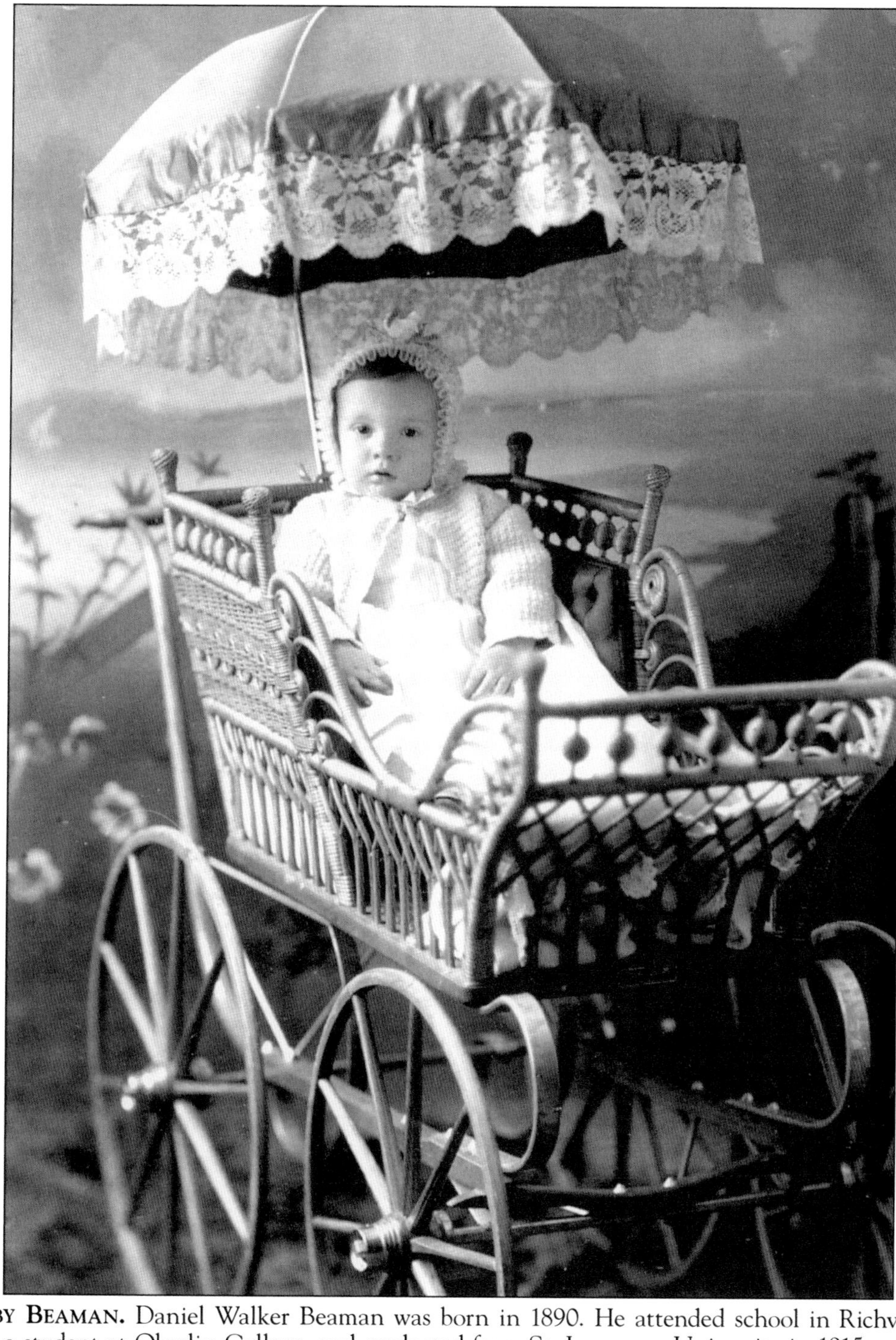

BABY BEAMAN. Daniel Walker Beaman was born in 1890. He attended school in Richville, was a student at Oberlin College, and graduated from St. Lawrence University in 1915, as did his wife Beatrice. He pursued various occupations over the years, ending his career in Richville as a high school principal and teacher. He was the father of five children: Donald, Frank, Lucille, Mary Ruth, and Paul. During his life, he also lived in Waddington, Ogdensburg, and Malone. (Courtesy of Mary Ruth Judd.)

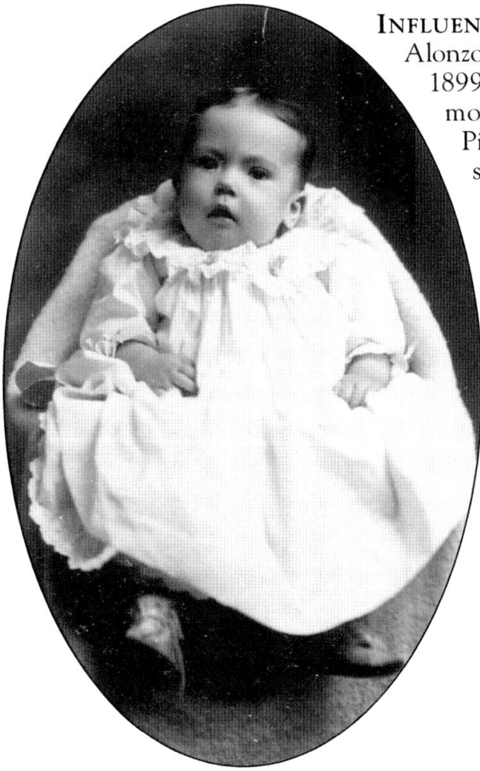

INFLUENZA EPIDEMIC SURVIVOR. Austin Todd, son of Alonzo and Sarah Briggs Todd, was born in Kendrew in 1899, the youngest of seven children. The family moved to Irving Bacheller's Paradise Valley in Pierrepont when Austin was about four. Influenza struck the family and two of his sisters died. Later in life, he and his wife raised eight kids on a dairy farm. He left farming years later and started a gas station and general store in Canton, eventually becoming a car and farm machinery dealer. He was artistically talented and had an affinity for math. (Courtesy of Jim Todd.)

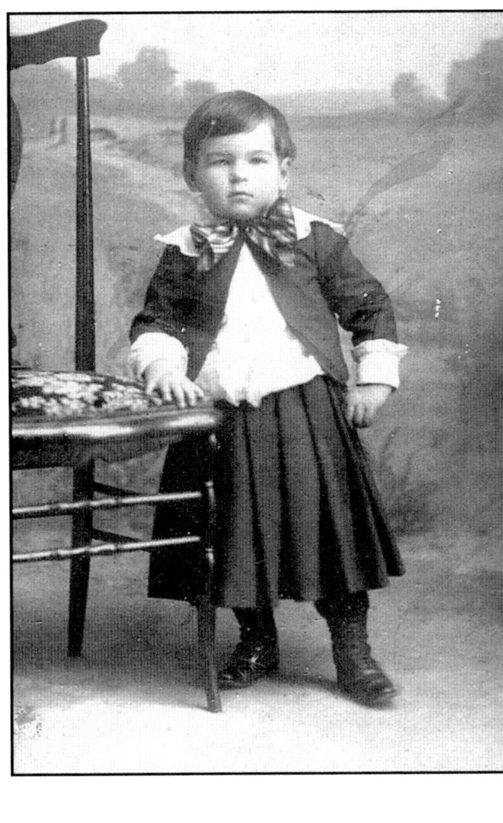

BORN IN PITCAIRN. Harvey L. Gleason was born on May 23, 1899. He attended country school until the family moved to Gouverneur, where he graduated from high school in 1919. He was a member of an award-winning football team. After a brief stint working for the New York Central Railroad, he went to work for the bank of Gouverneur, where he stayed for 44 years. He is the father of Bruce Gleason, from Gouverneur, and Mary G. Colton, from Canton. (Courtesy of Mary Colton.)

SITTING PRETTY IN A WHITE LACE DRESS. Maude Evelyn Wilcox was one year old in 1903 when this picture was taken. She was born in Russell, the daughter of Milton and Dora Cobb Wilcox, and the eldest of three girls. Her mother died very young and Dora's parents, Andrew and Ellen Cobb, brought up the girls. Maude attended Russell rural schools, including the Silver Hill School, and Knox Memorial High School. She married George Dodds Russell, at the home of Mr. and Mrs. Otis Fox in 1920. She was very active in local organizations and held offices in most of them. Maude passed away in 1994 and is buried in the South Russell Cemetery alongside her husband. (Courtesy of Jean Given.)

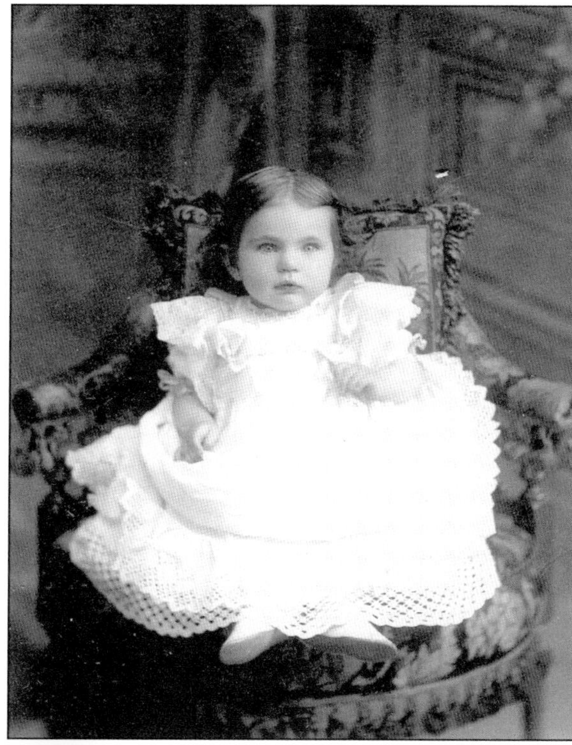

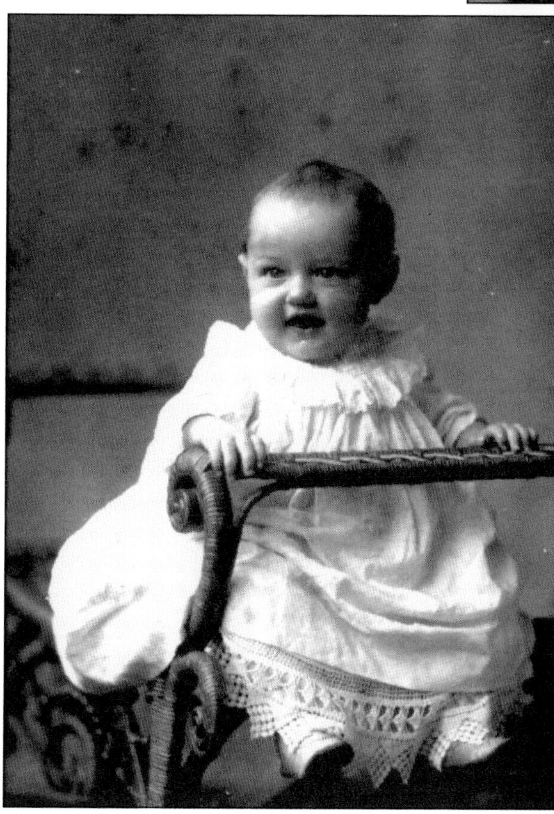

GIFTED SINGER. John "Darwin" Desmond was born in North Lawrence on October 20, 1905, to John and Ella Hill Desmond. Darwin was well known for his singing throughout St. Lawrence County and sang with the quartet, the Merry Monarchs. He also performed at the CBC studio in Prescott, Ontario, Canada. During this time he won a preliminary Major Bowes Amateur Hour Contest in Manhattan. Later he moved to Duchess County and broadcast from Newburgh, New York, and New Haven, Connecticut. (Courtesy of Teresa Desmond.)

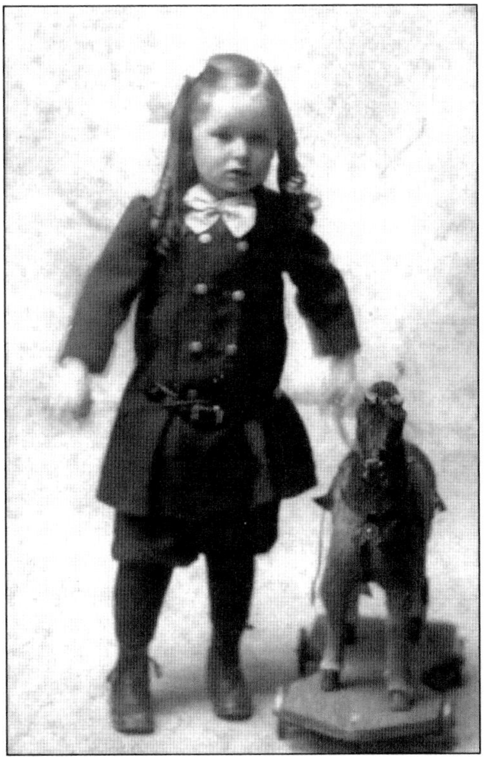

LITTLE BOY WITH A HORSE. Harold Goldie, pictured here with his toy horse, was born in 1902 in Madrid. He was the son of William L. and Rudy Thompson Goldie. He had a sister Emma and a brother Malcolm. Harold grew up in the Madrid area. In later years he owned and operated a dairy farm on the Norfolk-Madrid Road. (Courtesy of Marcia Ragan Thompson.)

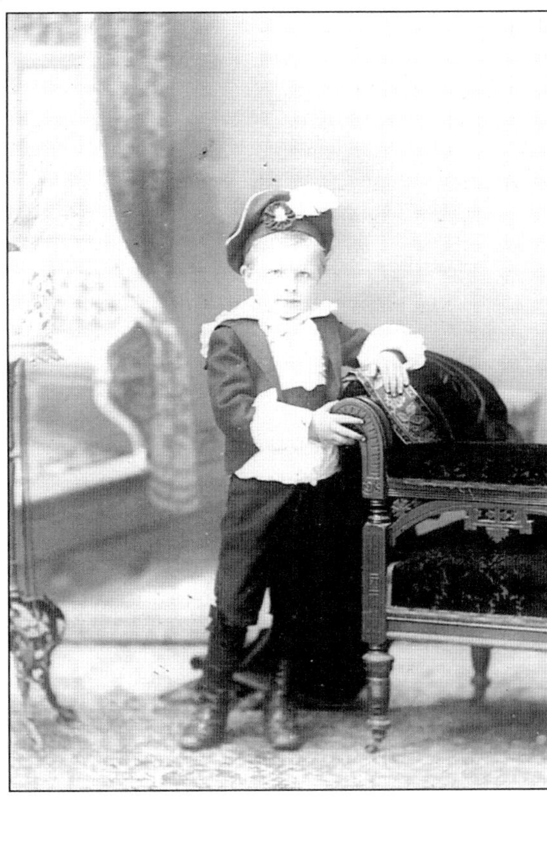

MOVED FROM LISBON TO NORFOLK. William "Willie" Kelly, born in 1889, was the third child of Owen Eugene Kelly and Henrietta (Hattie) Vallelley. Two months after William was born, his mother died from consumption and his aunt Sarah Egan raised him. He farmed all of his life, first in Lisbon on Tuck Road until 1940, and then in Norfolk. Bill married three times. He and his first wife Emma had one child, Dorothy. Emma died in 1916. His second wife was Josephine A Spooner and they had three children, Helen, Charles, and Patrick. Josephine died in 1949. William Kelly then married Effie Bell and retired from farming in the early 1960s. (Courtesy of Jim Kelly.)

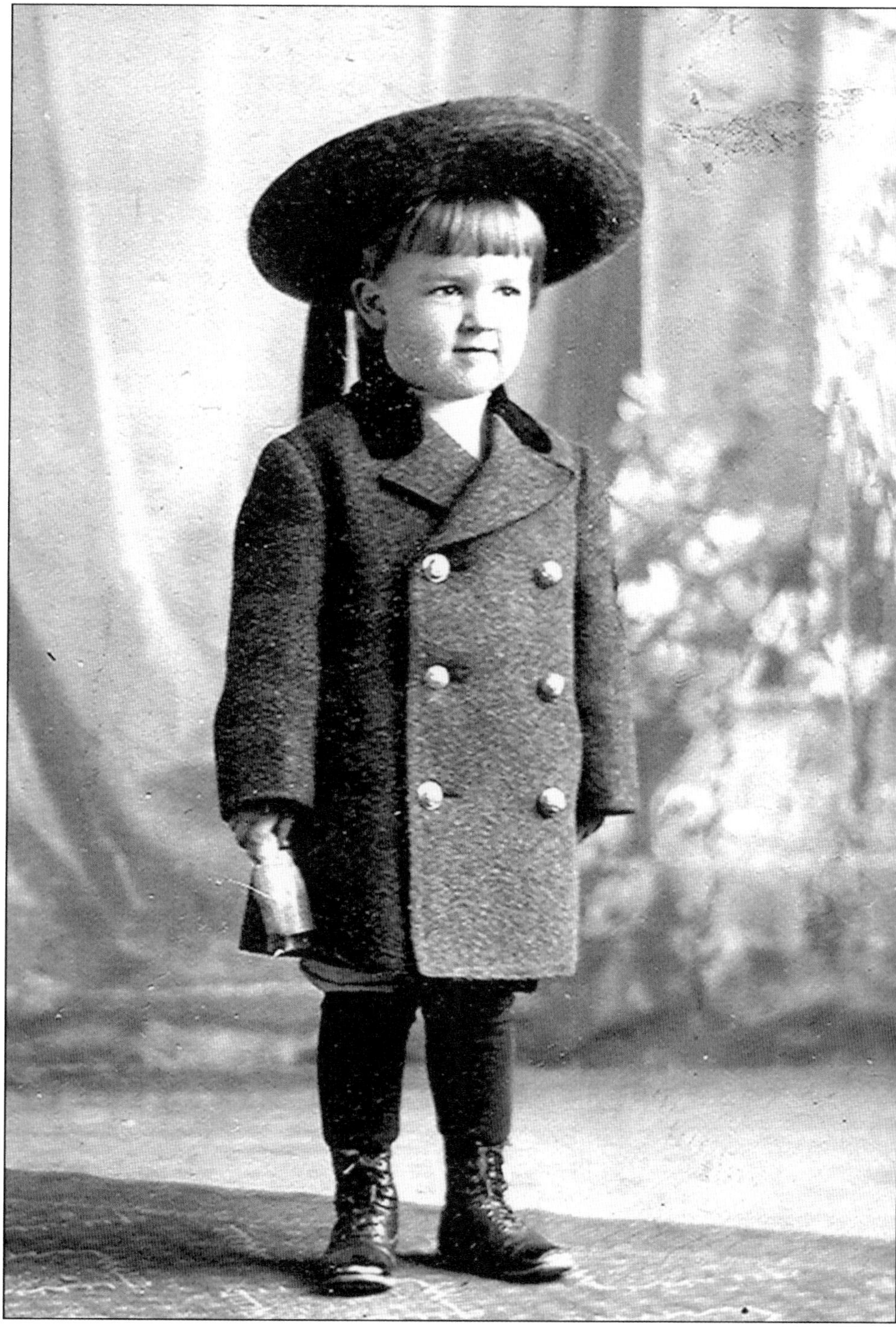

TO NEW YORK BY WAY OF QUEBEC. The Berniers first came to Quebec as farmers in 1653, and moved south in 1850 as jobs became more plentiful on the U.S. side of the border. Alvin Lee Bernier, pictured above, was born at the beginning of the 20th century. He moved to the Ogdensburg area from Canton to open a Ford dealership and later a retail liquor store. Alvin's son, Jim, is the founder of Bernier and Carr. (Courtesy of Joe McDonald.)

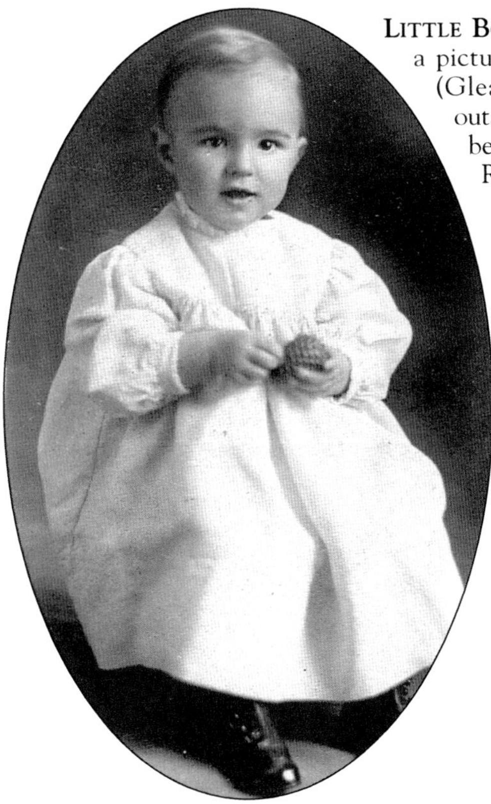

LITTLE BOY IN A LONG DRESS. This little boy posing for a picture is Miles Harrington, son of John and Verda (Gleason) Harrington They lived on a side road outside of Canton. Miles attended the country school before going to Canton High School. He married Ruth O'Brien and for a time ran the family farm. He later worked for Jones and Laughlin at Benson Mines. He did not have any children. (Courtesy of John Harrington.)

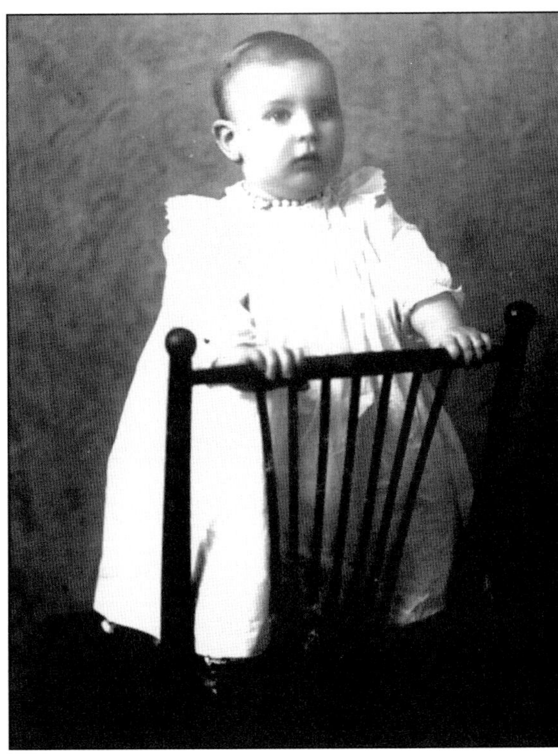

MECHANICALLY INCLINED. George Lyon Coughlin was born in 1900 in Watertown and moved to St. Lawrence County in 1936. He and his wife, Irene Arvilla Caswell, had two daughters, Rogene Coughlin Bessette (born 1930) and Naomi Coughlin Haven (1933). He worked as a mechanic in different garages and later ran the garage at the Evergreens in Canton. Later he worked at his own home on County Highway 25 doing mechanic work. After retirement, he delivered the *Watertown Daily Times.* (Courtesy of Nancy Bessette.)

GRADUATE OF CRANE SCHOOL OF MUSIC. Sara Clark was one of three daughters of Potsdam undertaker and furniture-store owner Horace N. Clark and popular vocalist Fanny Towne Clark. This picture was taken in 1912. Sara graduated from the Crane School of Music and taught vocal music in a number of school districts. She also was the church organist for the First Congregational Church of Hopkinton for over 55 years. (Courtesy of Varrick Chittenden.)

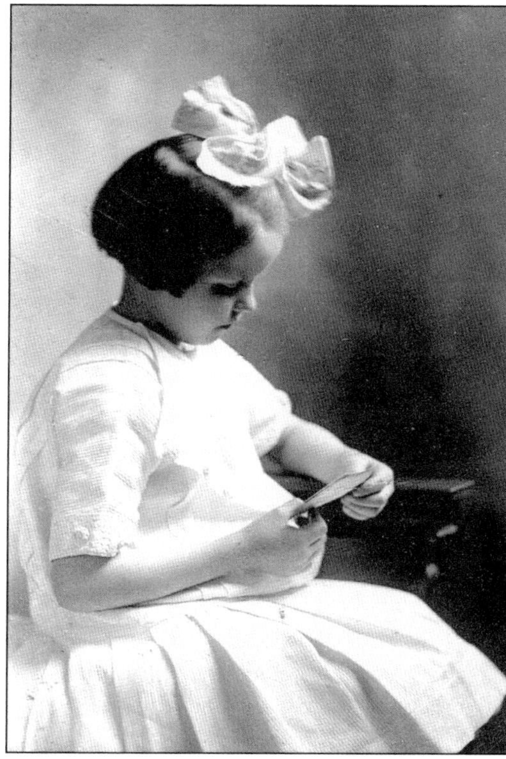

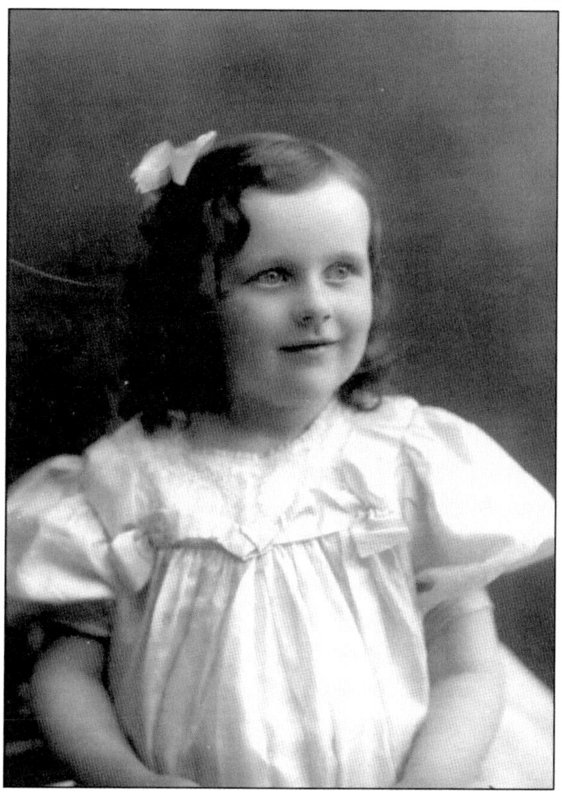

CONVENT EDUCATION. Irene Cunningham was born on a farm in DeKalb in 1900. Her father died shortly thereafter and her mother was forced to go to work. Irene was placed in a convent in Brasher Falls, where she received a good education and went on to receive degrees in occupational therapy and nursing. In 1930, she became director of occupational therapy at the Ogdensburg Psychiatric Center. (Courtesy of Joe McDonald.)

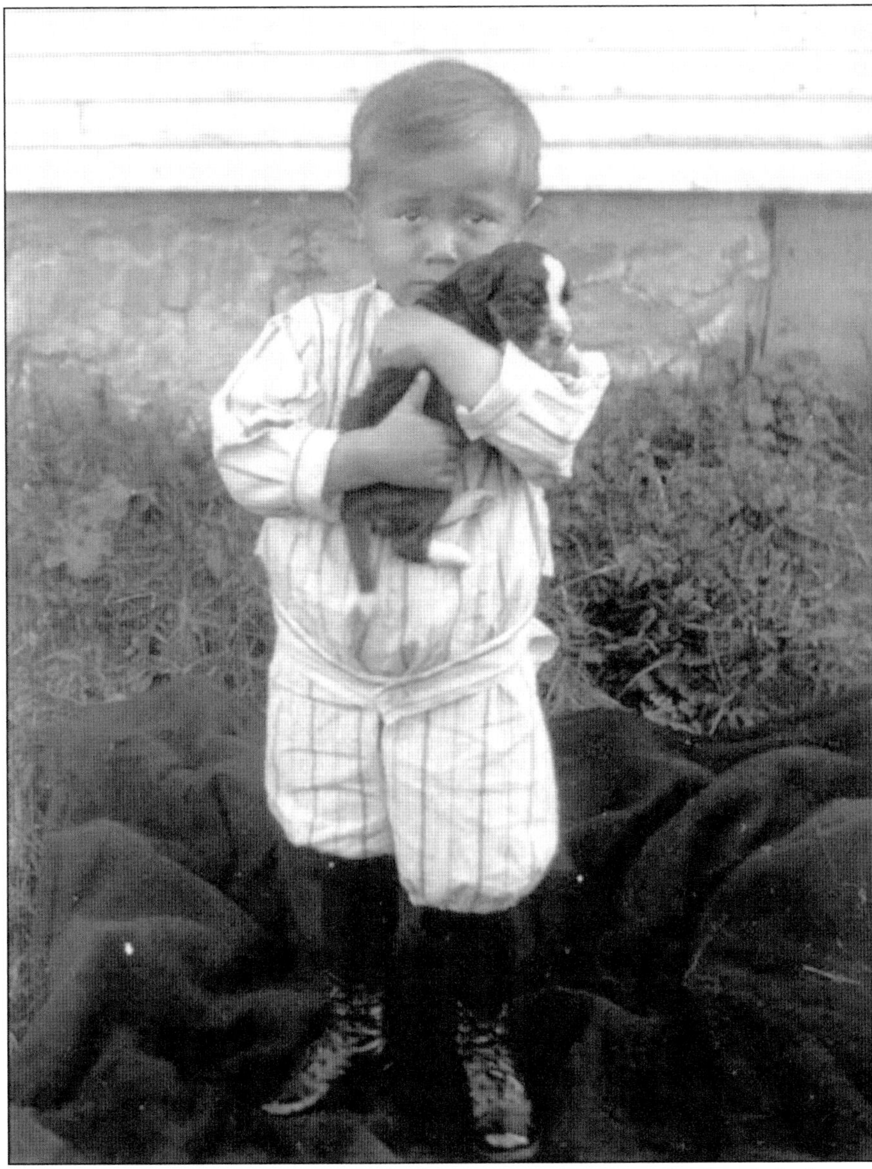

YOUNG BOY AND PUPPY. This photograph shows Peter Garrow, a Mohawk Indian, and his dog in the early 1900s. If history tells us anything, it is that such partnerships were as essential a part of life as food and water. The photographer was Francis San Jule—the postmaster in Hogansburg, a hamlet leased from the Mohawks by an Irish immigrant named William Hogan. The Mohawk name for Hogansburg is Tekaswen'karorens, which means, "where the logs are cut." This name came about because there was a lumber mill on the leased land. The Mohawk name for the entire community is Akwesasne, which means "land where the partridge drums." This name was given because the sound of the rapids on the St. Lawrence River was reminiscent of the partridge beating its wings. Development of the St. Lawrence Seaway extinguished the rapids, but the name remains. (Courtesy of the Akwesasne Museum at Hogansburg.)

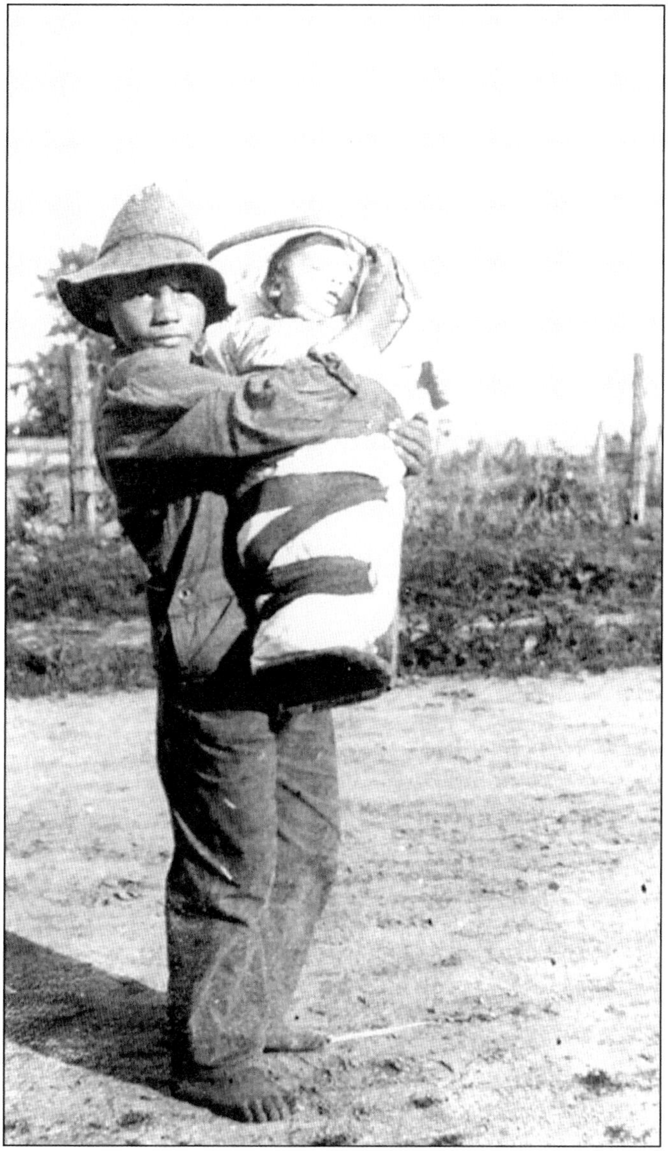

YOUNG BOY AND BABY. Cradleboards were common in past generations in Akwesasne, also known as the St. Regis Mohawk Reservation. Here a young boy is doing his best not to disturb the sleep of a slumbering baby. The line between St. Lawrence and Franklin counties once bisected the reservation. While the St. Lawrence County line now ends just before the western edge of Akwesasne, the Mohawk Indian Housing Corporation operates apartment complexes in Rooseveltown, New York, just inside the county line. Maps show the border of the United States and Canada bisecting Akwesasne, but it continues to be recognized as a sovereign nation—separate from both the United States and Canada—through the Grand Council of the Iroquois Confederacy, as the Mohawk Nation. The St. Regis Mohawk Tribe, recognized as Council of Akwesasne, is a self-governing entity recognized by the United States of America. The Mohawk Council of Akwesasne is a self-governing entity recognized by the Canadian government. While the polictics and jurisdictions of the area are complex, to Akwesasne Mohawks it is simply home. (Courtesy of the Akwesasne Museum.)

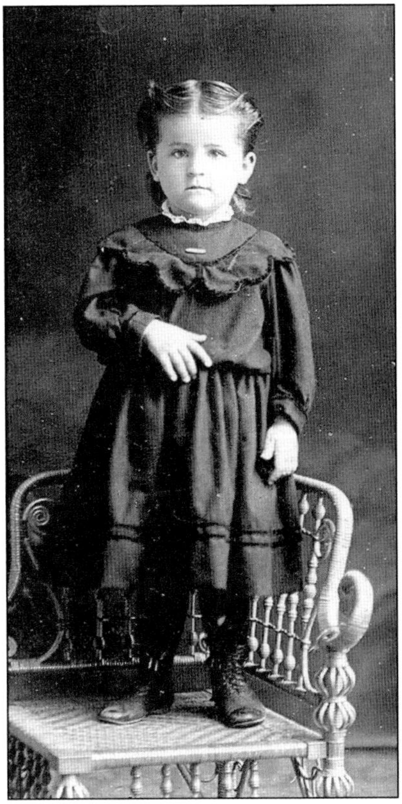

DAUGHTER OF A MILK MANAGER ON THE RUTLAND RAILROAD LINE. Dora V. Clark was three years old in 1905, when this photograph was taken. She was the sixth child of Fred Clark of Russell and Sara Robinson Clark of Lisbon. The family moved frequently because of her father's job as milk manager. His position required that they live along the railroad. While living in Madrid in 1919, she met Clark Stearns, who had returned from World War I, and they married in 1922. They are buried in the Fairview Cemetery in Canton. Their two children are Marjorie Hudson of Waverly and Donald Stearns of Brasher Falls. (Courtesy of Donald Stearns.)

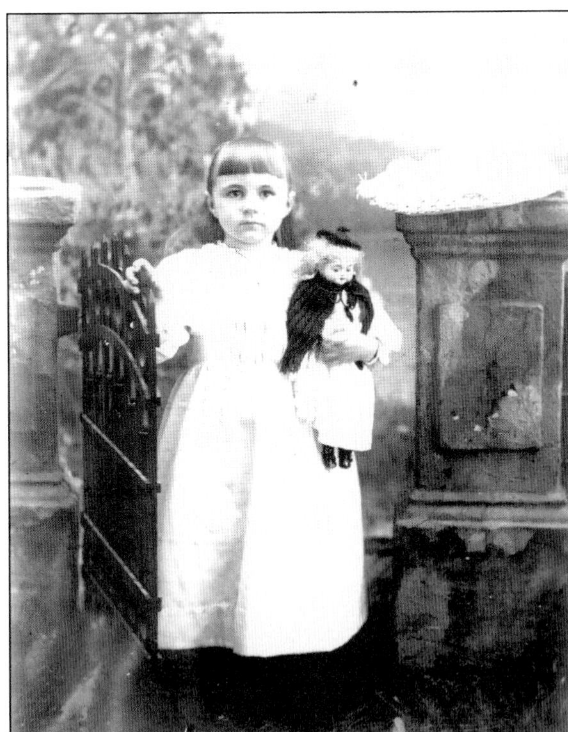

OAK POINT. Fleeta Arlina Powers was born in Oak Point in 1889. She attended elementary school in Hammond, high school in Antwerp, and teacher-training school in Antwerp. Her father was a buggy salesman and also worked in construction. He was killed on the job in Watertown. Her mother, Mahitable Nellie, was an excellent cook and seamstress. Fleeta taught school in Redwood, Spragueville, and Natural Dam. She married Charles Whalen in Gouverneur in 1923, and they made their home at 38 Park Street in Canton. (Courtesy of Mary Jo Whalen.)

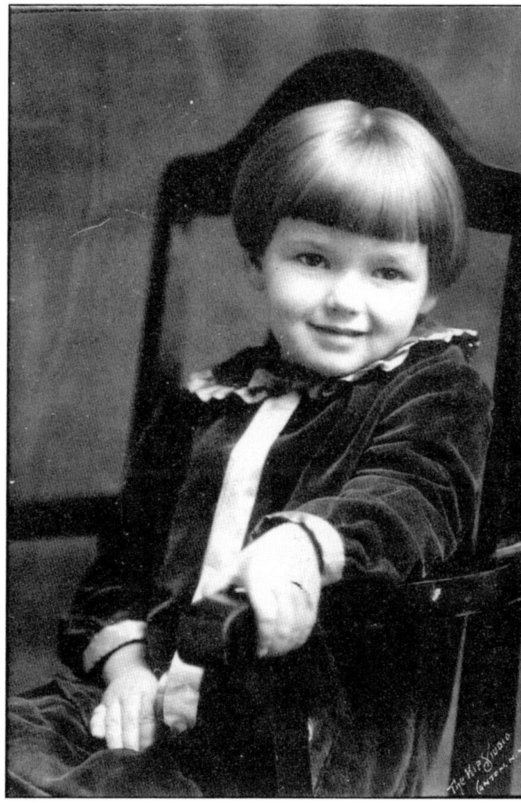

LATER OWNED A FLOWER SHOP. Beulah is the daughter of Fritz and Lillie Fordham Crossman of Canton. Beulah attended local schools and then business school. After finishing school, she married Frank White and together they developed a thriving flower business on Miner Street in the 1950s. After 30 years they sold their business to enjoy the life of retirement. Beulah's great-grandfather was a Civil War veteran along with his three brothers, Edgar, Edward, and Marcus. They lived in the Pierrepont area. (Courtesy of Beulah White.)

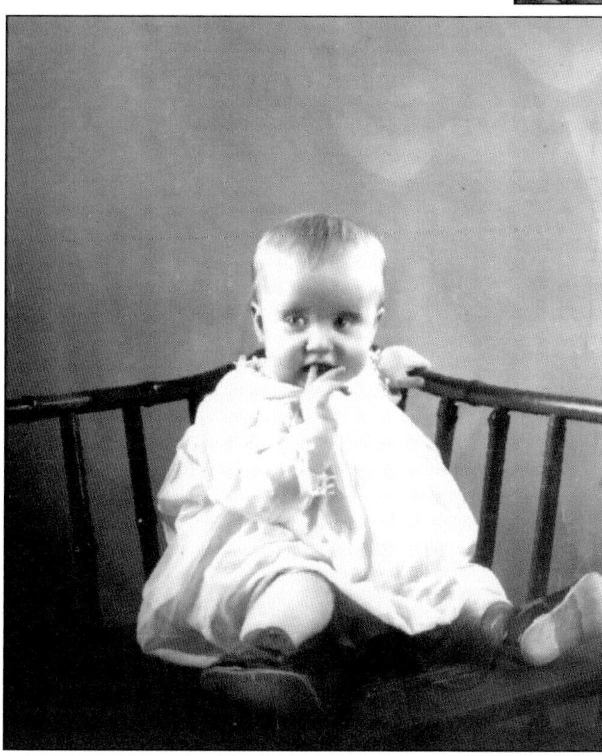

FIRST PICTURE. Nine-month-old Frances Helen, born March 7, 1927, looks pensive in her first photograph. Frances was the daughter of Ronald and Helen Potter McCormick. The family lived with Frances's maternal grandparents on the large Potter farm, located on the Pierrepont Road on Route 68. Her great- grandfather William faught in the Civil War. After his death, son Richard ran the farm and his brother Orin moved to Pierrepont Center where he lived in a large red brick house, now owned by the Tupper family. Sadly, Richard lost the farm during the Depression. (Courtesy of Frances Van Horne.)

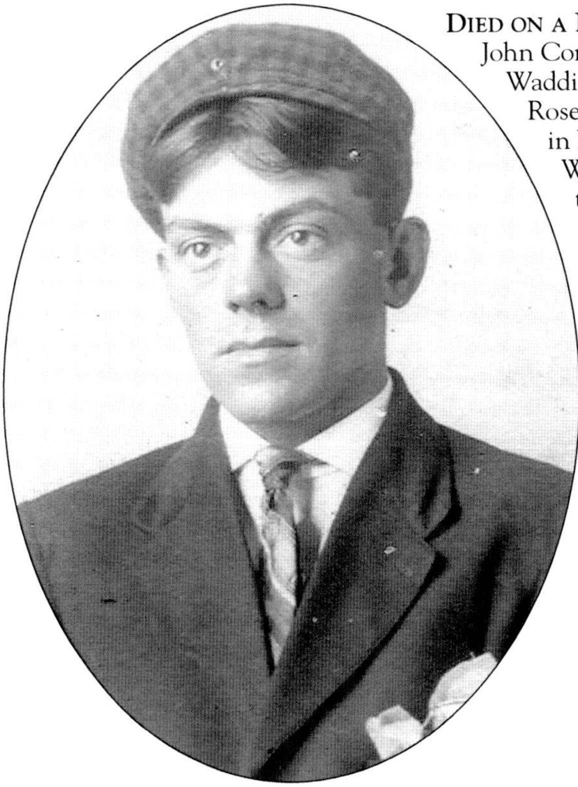

Died on a Hospital Ship, 1900. Albert John Conway was born in October 1874 in Waddington, New York, to Henry and Roseanne Trudell Conway. He was confirmed in November 1887 at St. Mary's Church in Waddington. This picture was most likely taken at that time. Albert Conway served at the Great Wall of China and in the Philippines in the early 1900s. He contracted dysentery and fell gravely ill. At the age of 26, he died aboard a hospital ship on the way home. (Courtesy of Ruth Pharoah.)

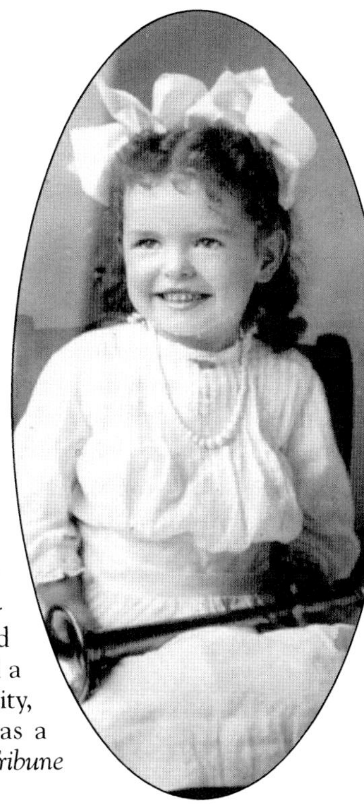

Little Girl with a Trumpet. Grace Witherell was born on December 18, 1906, in DePeyster. She was the daughter of Luda and Charles Witherell. She is seen here holding a trumpet, which was given to her to help her sit quietly while her picture was taken. She taught school in the one-room schoolhouse in DePeyster. When she was 25 she married Wilbert R. Parish, also of DePeyster. They owned and operated a farm and had seven children. Grace was active in the community, the Grange, the 4-H, and the Methodist Church. She was a correspondent for the *Ogdensburg Journal* and the *Gouverneur Tribune Press* for many years. (Courtesy of Sharon Murdock.)

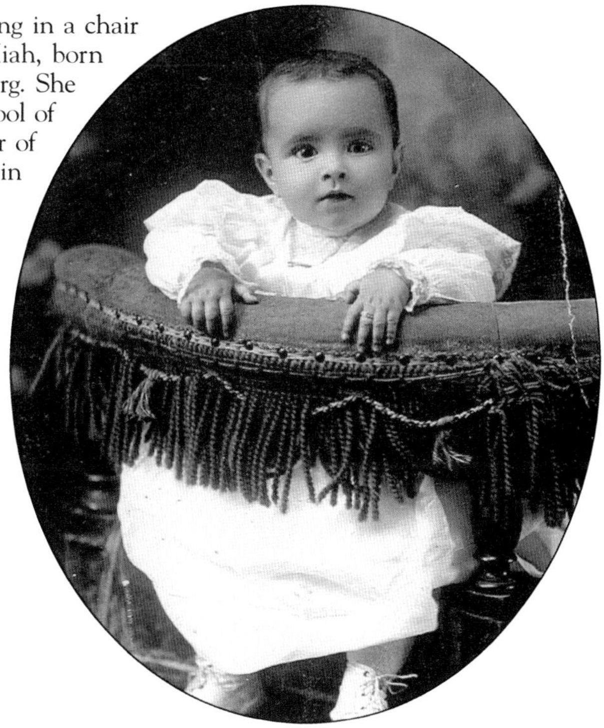

FANCY HIGHCHAIR. The little girl sitting in a chair adorned with fringe is Lillian Marie Kiah, born on Valentine's Day, 1904, in Ogdensburg. She graduated from A. Barton Hospital School of Nursing. Later she became an instructor of nursing at the same institution. She died in May 1974. (Courtesy of Monica LaRose.)

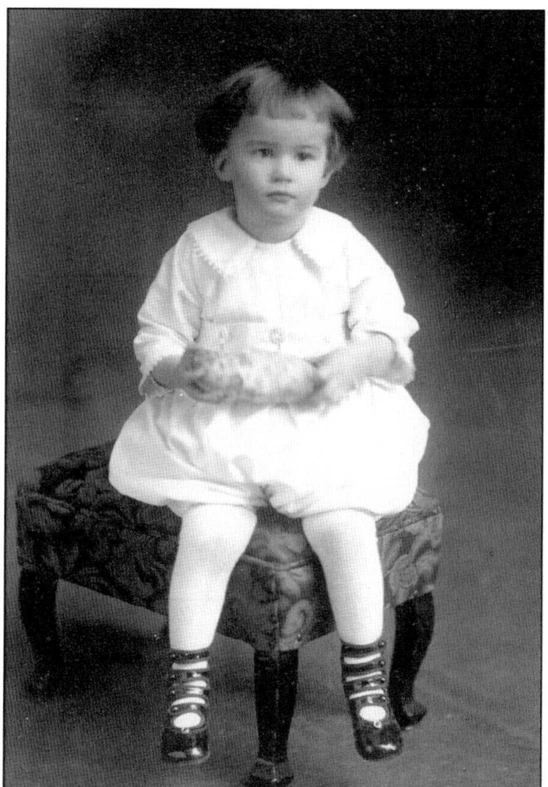

GROVER GARDNER. Grover was the son of Horace and Edith Hildrith Gardner. He married Axie Gillette and was the father of two children, Horace Gardner and Miriam Gardner June. He ran the dairy farm, previously owned by his parents, on Bilow Road in Richville, until his retirement. He then moved to Bigelow. He is buried at Maple Grove, Richville. (Courtesy of Helen Davis Reed Collection, SLCHA.)

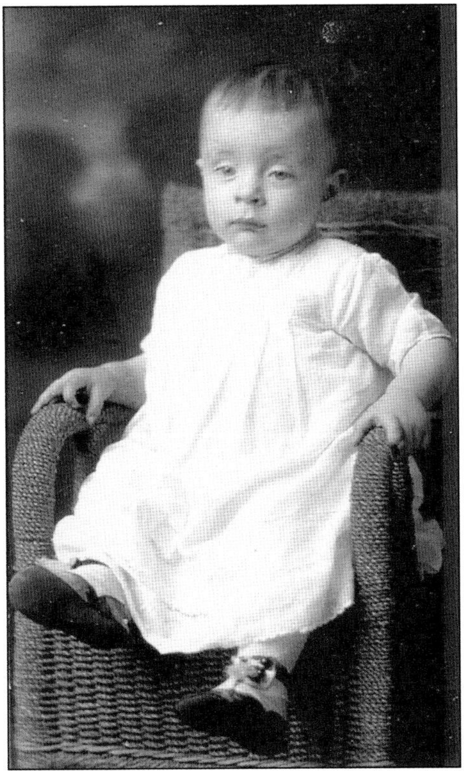

U.S. ARMY VETERAN. This baby boy with sleepy eyes is John Toomey. He was the only child of Michael and Alice Briggs Toomey. He was born in Pyrites in 1921. In Canton, he attended St. Mary's School and then Canton High School. John entered the army in 1942, serving in France, England, and Germany. Upon returning home he worked at Canton's Sunshine Store, Tisdell Electric, and St. Lawrence University in the electrical department. He died in 1973. (Courtesy of Pat Dominie.)

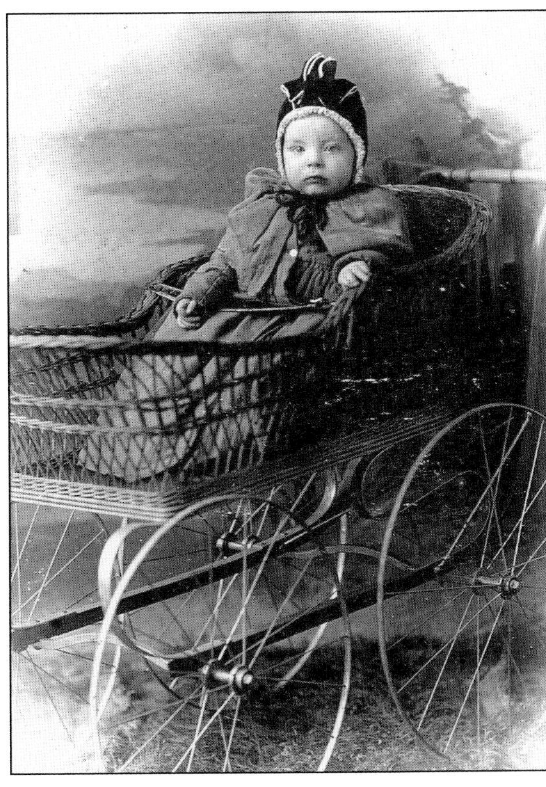

SON OF THE IRISH. The little boy in the wicker carriage is Michael Toomey, son of Irish immigrants Daniel and Katherine Hayes Toomey. The picture was taken about 1892. Michael married Alice Briggs, and they had one son, John. Michael, while still in his twenties, was killed in an accident at the Park Street Railroad Crossing in Canton. His only child, John, was still an infant at the time. (Courtesy of Pat Dominie.)

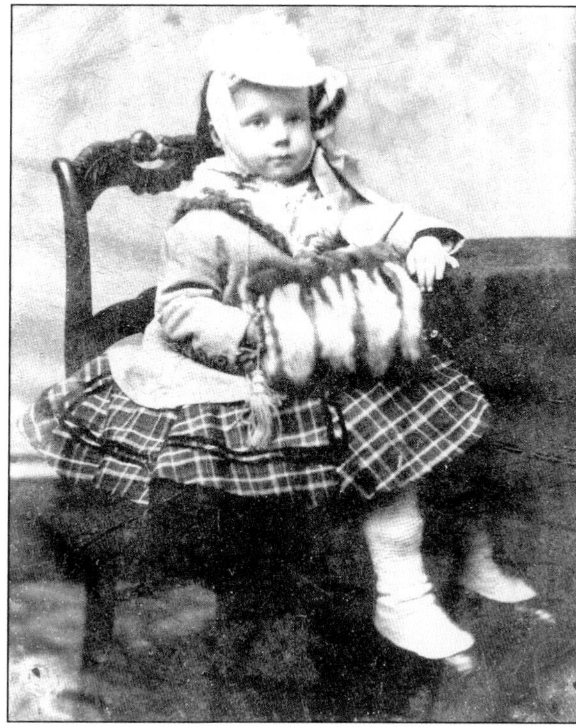

Little Girl with a Bonnet and Muff. Marion Paterson is all dressed up for her picture taking. She was born September 13, 1880. Her mother died when she was only four years old. Her 10-year-old sister fell heir to caring for the house and their two-year-old brother while Marion went to Ogdensburg to live with her mother's sister. This picture was made from an old tintype. (Courtesy of Fran Doyle.)

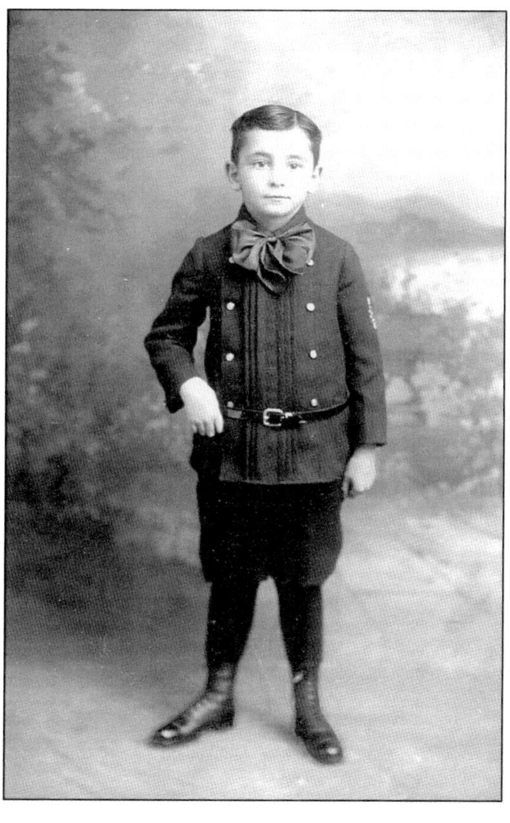

Related to Early Settlers. Richard Myers was born in 1901 in Canton. He attended the Olin School (named for his ancestors, who settled nearby in 1804). He married Margaret McKenna from Potsdam. In his adult life, he worked for Dr. Webb Speers, the veterinarian, doing tuberculosis testing on cattle. Richard later worked with Aubrey Todd disinfecting barns. With the advent of World War II, he worked at the defense plant in Massesa. (Courtesy of Joan Barrick.)

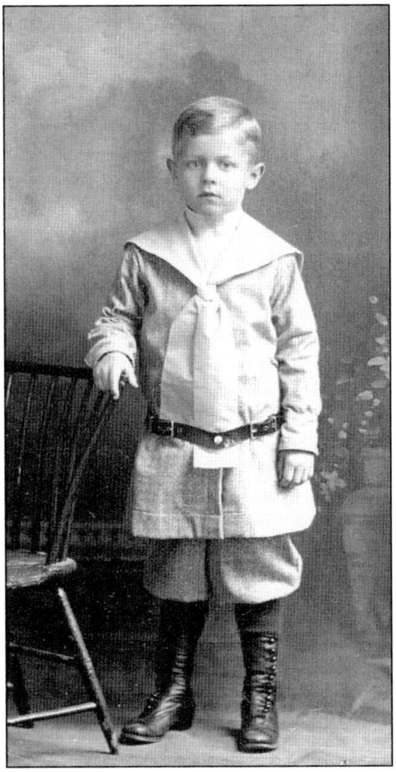

ATTENDED AVIATION SCHOOL. The fine boy pictured here is Eldred Billings, the adopted son of Charles and Catherine Billings. They lived on Park Street in Canton. Eldred attended local schools and went to aviation school in Cleveland, Ohio. During World War II, he was a mechanic in the Air Force and then worked for Bell Aircraft. After Pearl Harbor, he reentered the Air Force and later, upon discharge, returned to Canton. He worked for Railway Express, Gray's Garage, and then the New York State School of Agriculture at Canton for 25 years. He married the young girl pictured below, Elva Phillips. (Courtesy of Elva Billings.)

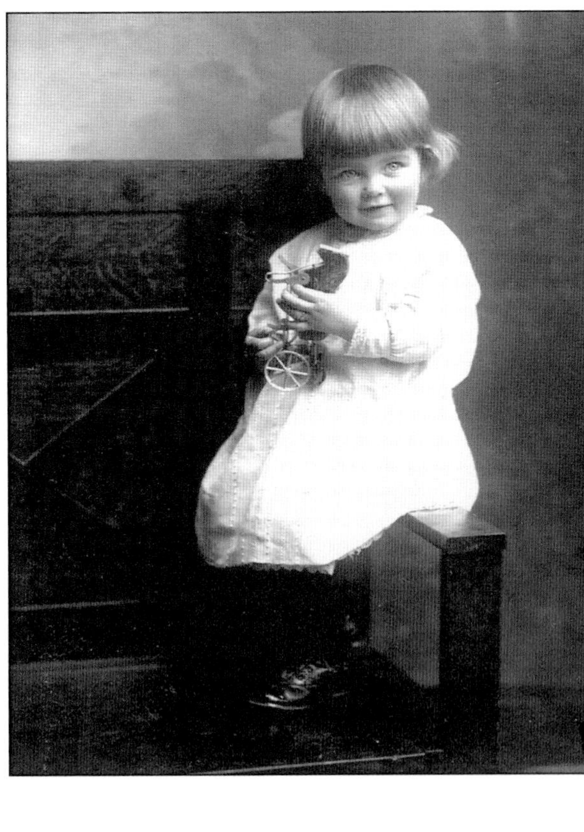

EARLY LOVE OF HORSES. In this picture is Elva Mae Phillips, who was born in August 1914 in Pierrepont. She was the first child of Almon and Celia Phillips. Three more sisters, Rena, Jessie, and Lillian, followed her. From her earliest years, Elva loved horses. Her little toy horse seems to be a sign of her early love that lasted throughout her life. Her father, knowing how much she longed for a horse of her own, sold one of his cows to buy a small horse, which she named Pedro. Later on she purchased a registered Morgan mare named Lassie's Gay Lady. Elva worked in admissions at the New York State School of Agriculture at Canton, retiring in 1973. In 1940, she married the young man, Eldred Billings, pictured above. (Courtesy of Elva Mae Billings.)

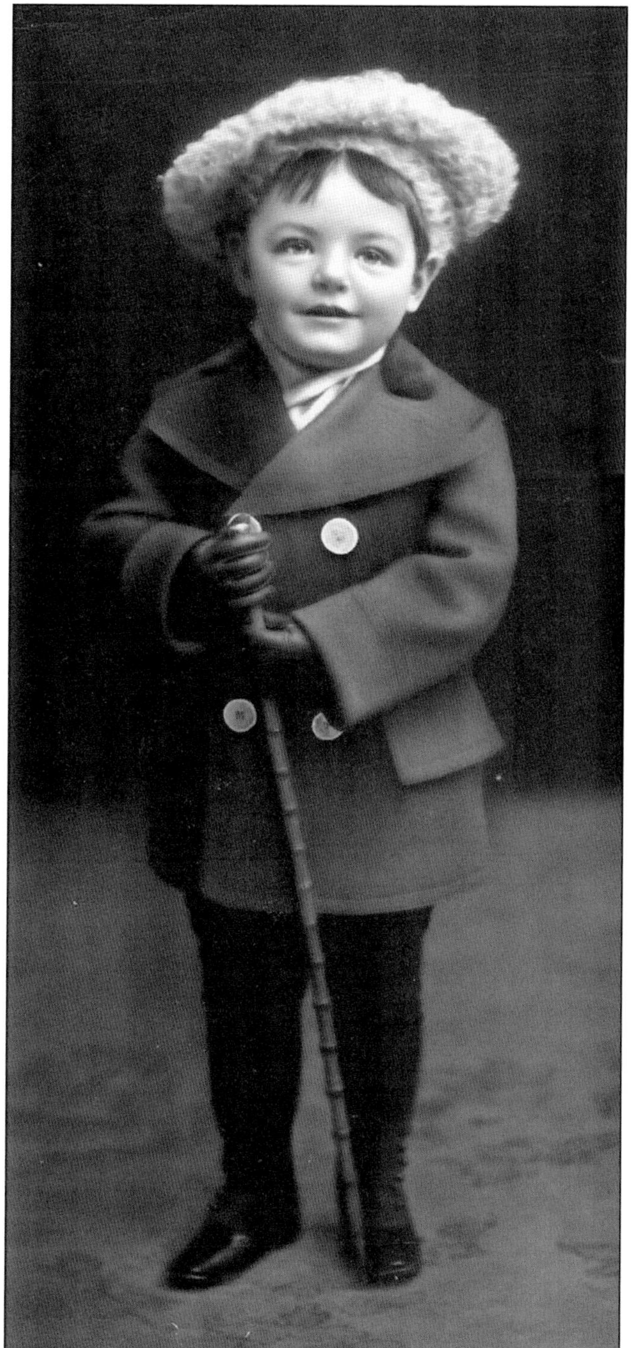

BUSTER BROWN. Leonard Nelson Beylea was born in 1898. He was the son of a professional photographer, who took this picture when Leonard was three or four years old. By the time he was five, he was the model for Buster Brown shoes. Later in life he became an optometrist with an office in Massena. There was a jewelry store in the same building where his wife-to-be, Ruth Balch, worked. Ruth was born in Massena Springs in 1897. They had two children, Robert James and Ann Louise. (Courtesy of Shirley Beylea.)

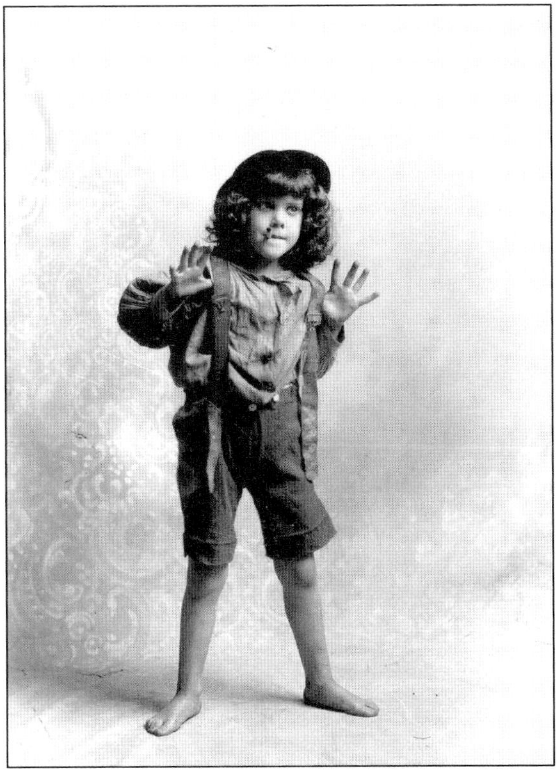

There's No Business Like Show Business. This little girl was a member of one of the troupes that traveled the area performing in the various theaters and opera houses throughout St. Lawrence County. It was an era when much of people's social lives revolved around the silent movies as well as vaudeville shows and local plays. We assume that the cigarette is a prop. (Courtesy of SLCHA.)

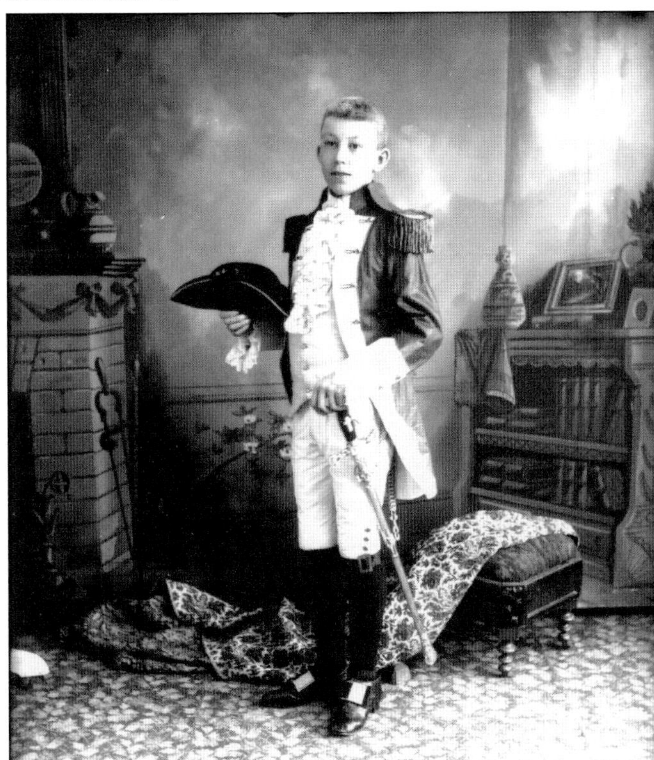

Child Actor. This child actor strutted the stage in many of the town halls and opera houses in the area. Each of the towns was proud to claim its own hall or theater where live performances were held. Theater played a large part in the social life of everyday people. This photograph was taken in Benjamin Kipp's studio, recognizable by the carpeting and furnishings. For over half a century, Benjamin Kipp photographed local residents from all walks of life. The elegance of his studio added charm to his portraits. (Courtesy of SLCHA.)

EDWARD JOHN NOBLE. Born in Gouverneur in 1882 to a family with limited means, Noble worked his way through Yale University. He founded the Life Savers Company in 1913. Later he served as undersecretary of commerce and owner of the American Broadcasting Company (ABC). He formed his namesake foundation in 1940, the E. J. Noble Foundation, which was crucial in setting up hospitals in Gouverneur, Canton, and Alexandria Bay. Present-day organizations still benefit from his largesse. He was on the board of trustees of St. Lawrence University for 25 years and served as president of the board for a decade. Noble spent much of his life living on the St. Lawrence River. He died in 1958. (Submitted by St. Lawrence University Archives.)

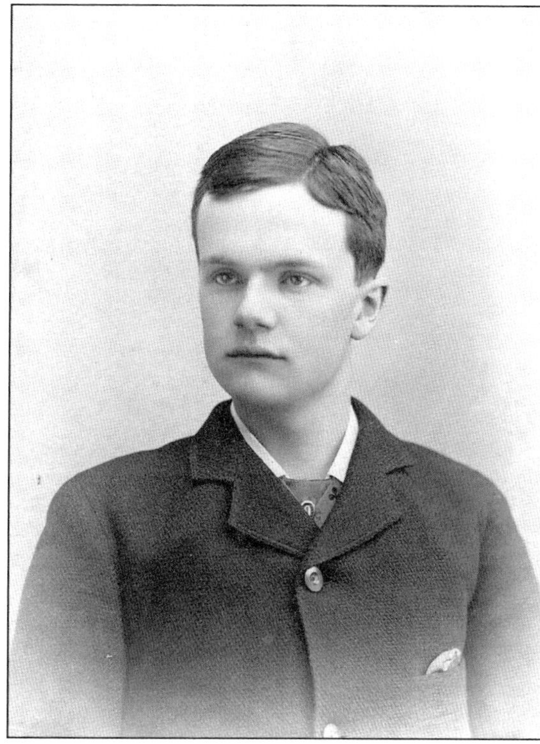

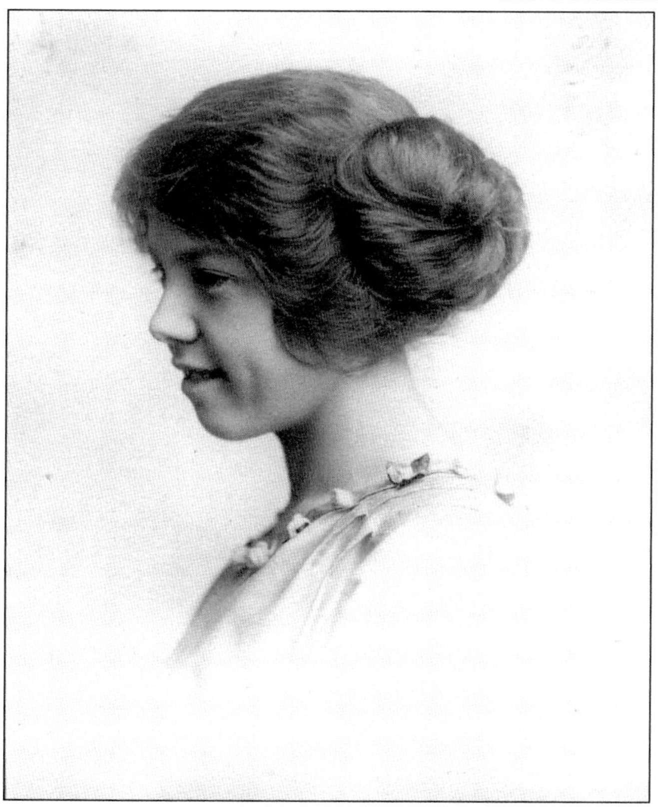

EMILY OLIVIA SEALY. Emily was born on April 14, 1889, in Potsdam, the daughter of Walter and Lorena Sealy. Emily and her sister Burnetta lived with their family on Cottage Street in Potsdam. At age 25, Emily married Roy Baker who owned and operated pharmacies in northern New York. She was later employed by Elliot Hardware Company for many years. Emily died on October 20, 1962, and is buried in Bayside Cemetery in Potsdam. (Courtesy of David Baker.)

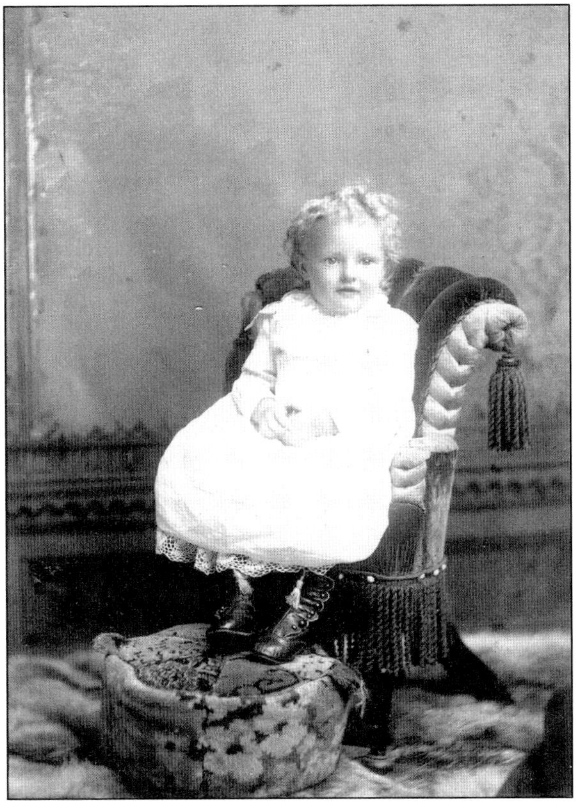

Born in Parishville. Gladys Mary Hayden was born on October 31, 1888, in Parishville. She lived with her family on a small farm. After graduating from high school in 1906, she left the farm to find employment. She took a job as a chambermaid at the Sylvan Falls Hotel. Sometimes the lady of the hotel would ask the girls who worked there to go pick blueberries. She would give them gum to chew, so they would not eat the berries. Gladys met her future husband, Earl Copeland, at the hotel. The couple married on December 16, 1914. (Courtesy of Serena McDonald-Carr.)

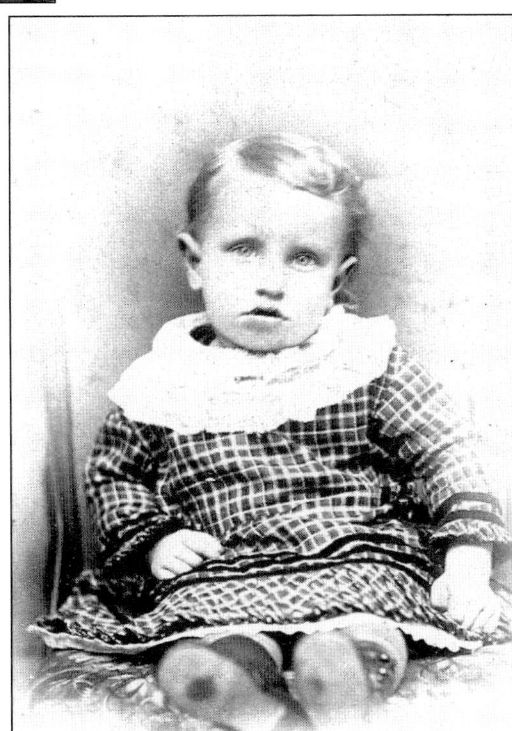

Born in Hopkinton. Earl Harper Copeland was born on October 5, 1881. He went to work for his uncle, Absalom Harper, at the Sylvan Falls Hotel. There he met his wife, Gladys Mary Hayden. Later he began to drive the stagecoach to the Potsdam railroad depot to pick up visitors from cities, especially Rochester. (Courtesy of Serena McDonald.)

HOW GRAND AM I? Pictured here is two-year-old Dart Weed Everett, second of the six Everett children who grew up in Potsdam. He is posed in a professional studio with an ornate balcony as a background. Dart was named for his father's former law partner, William A Dart. After graduating from Potsdam High School, he attended and graduated from Clarkson College of Technology. During World War I, Dart served as lieutenant of the 308th Motor Battalion AEF. In 1936, he married Ruth Schook of Utica. (Courtesy of Virginia McLaughlin.)

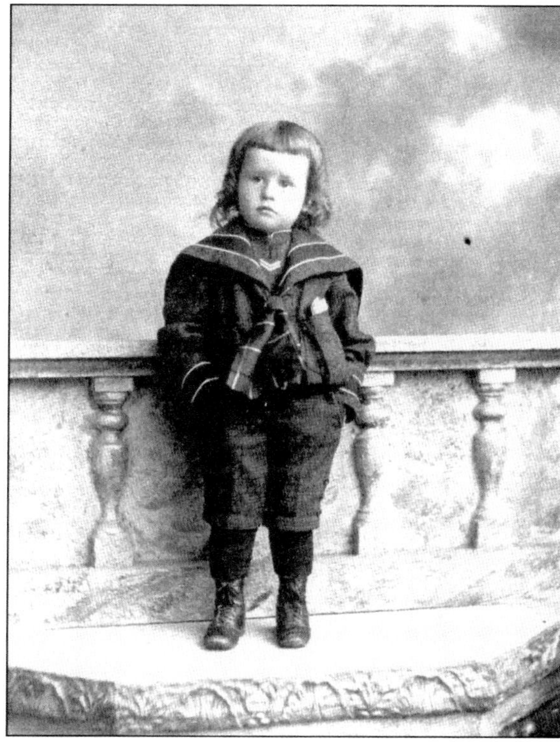

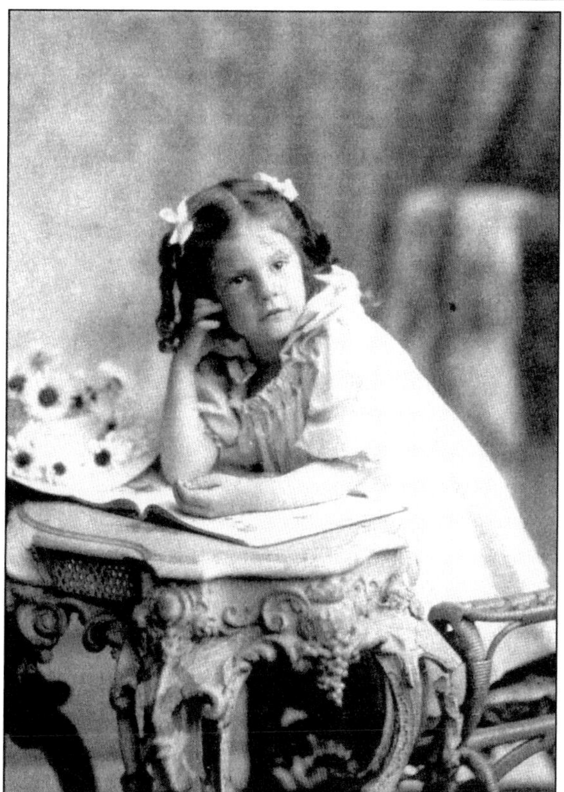

THE AGE OF INNOCENCE. This girl, so beautifully attired in the ornate setting of a professional studio, is Annar Everett from Potsdam. Annar was one of six children. Her father Edward A. Everett was a lawyer, businessman, and political figure who served as state assemblyman from 1914 to 1922. Named for her grandmother, Annar Weed, Everett was educated at Potsdam Normal and the Crane Institute of Music. She later married Courtland Huling and had two children. (Courtesy of Virginia McLaughlin.)

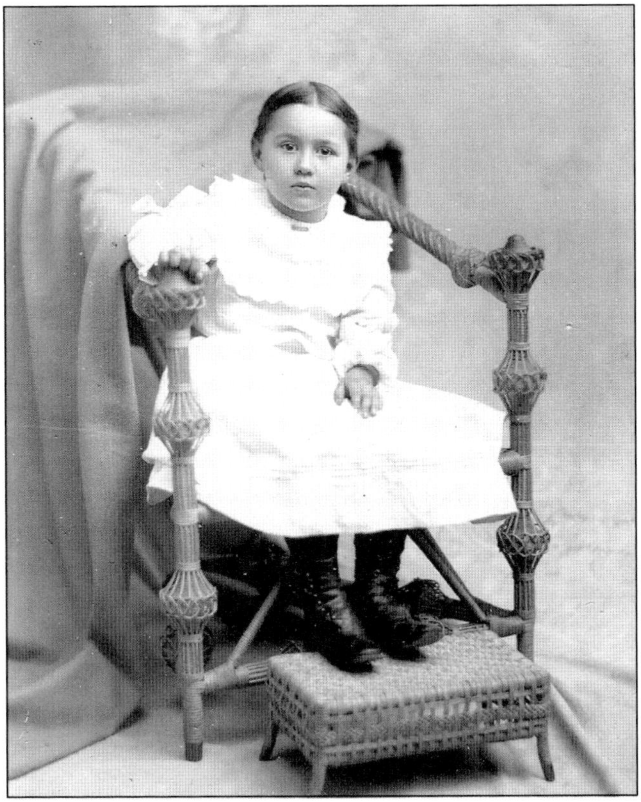

SITTING PRETTY. This is Polly McLellan, the daughter of John and Emma Vaughn McLellan. Born in Canton in 1892, she married Almeran Judd in 1914. Polly and Almeran owned and operated a farm on Farnes Road in Canton. Polly was active in the Crary Mills Church and the Grange. She was known for her pumpkin pie and raised donuts. (Courtesy of Mary Ruth Judd.)

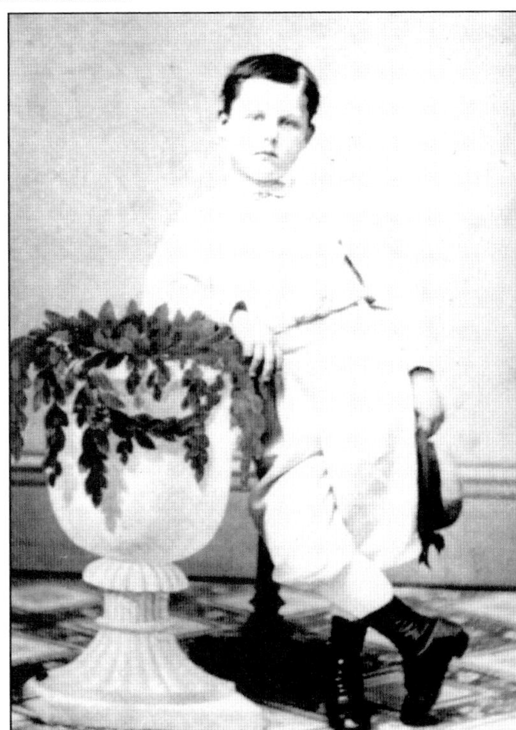

FREDERIC REMINGTON. In 1861, a baby was born in Canton who later became a world-renowned painter and sculptor. Frederic Remington's grandfather, Seth Williston, had accepted a call to Canton's Universalist Church in 1854. Frederic's father, Seth Pierre, was a printer by trade and joined with a local lawyer in publishing a weekly newspaper called the *St. Lawrence Plaindealer.* Seth married Clara Sackrider, and Frederic was their only child. In 1872, the family moved to Ogdensburg. Later Frederic relocated to the West, where he created the bronzes that are much valued today. The Frederic Remington Art Museum on Washington Street in Ogdensburg is dedicated to his work. (Courtesy of Frederic Remington Art Museum.)

BETTER TAKE MY PICTURE FAST. Looking like she is ready to take off at any moment is Katherine Benton, the daughter of Jay W. and Isabel Dumphy Benton of Canton. Katherine was a St. Lawrence graduate in 1937. Her parents, as well as her younger sister Joan, were also St. Lawrence University alumni. Jay Benton acted for many years as the university treasurer. He also owned a boys' and men's clothing store with his partner, John Fitzgerald. (Courtesy of SLCHA.)

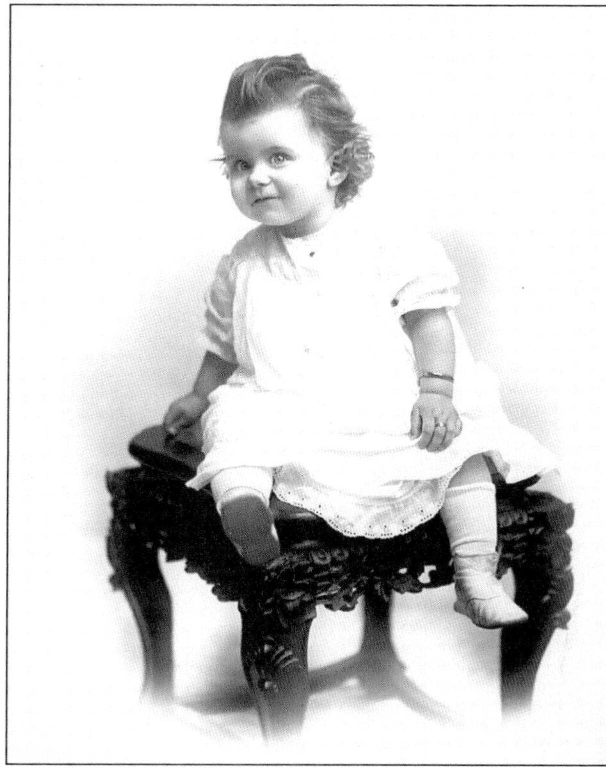

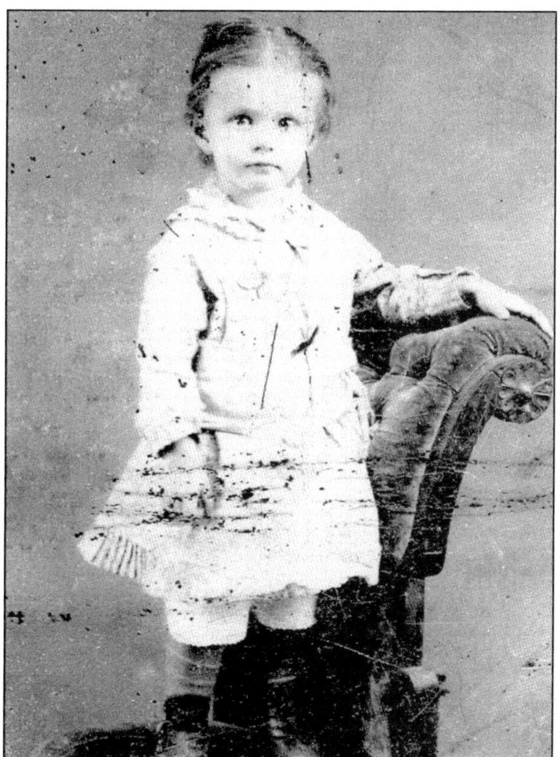

OSBORNVILLE, TOWN OF DEKALB. Adeline Hurlbut was born on January 8, 1881. She was the daughter of Emina Minerva Poor and David Giffin Hurlbut. She had two brothers and three sisters. Adeline attended the DeKalb District School No. 15 in Osbornville. She married Herbert P. Thompson on January 6, 1906. The Thompsons were farmers, living a short distance from where she was born 25 years earlier. Adeline died on April 22, 1974, leaving behind three sons, Donald D., Leo L. and Clinton S. (Courtesy of Sally A. Thompson.)

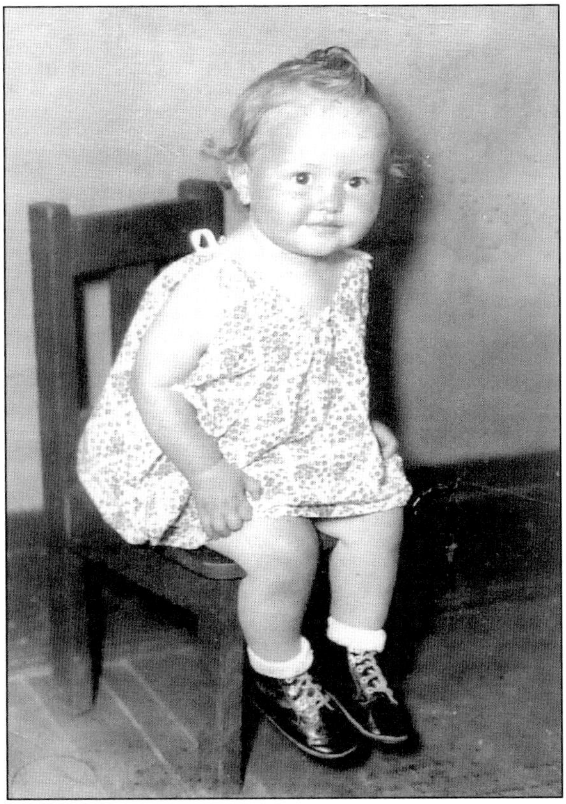

LITTLE GIRL KEWPIE DOLL. Marlene Rose Pharoah was born on Ames Road in Potsdam, next door to Giffins' schoolhouse. The family later moved to Massena to be with Marlene's grandparents, where her father worked for Alcoa. They later moved back to Canton and helped the other grandparents run their farm. The Kewpie doll has been manufactured by J. D. Kestner and other German firms since 1913. (Courtesy of Ruth Pharoah.)

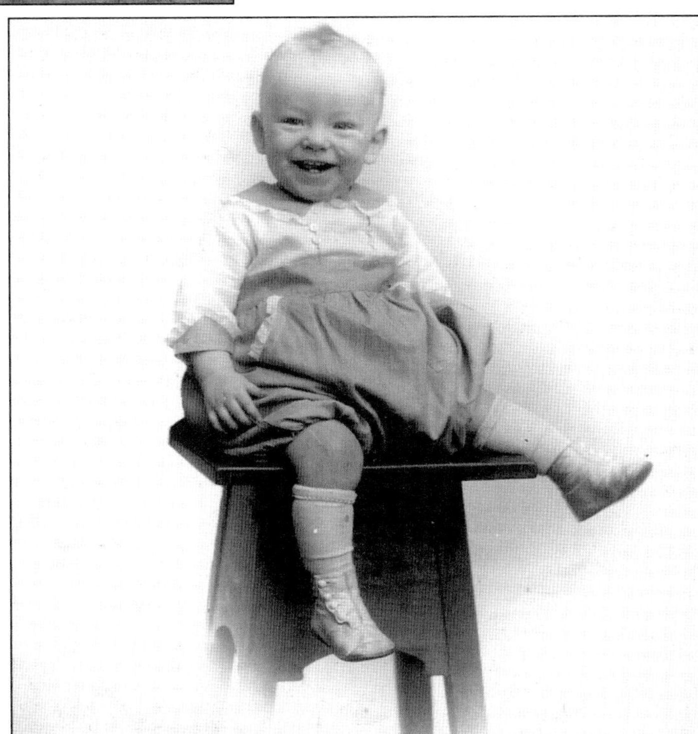

LITTLE BOY KEWPIE DOLL. The boy pictured here is Robert O'Leary. He was the son of John and Gertrude Ridge O'Leary. He was born and raised on Butternut Ridge Road in Potsdam. Born in 1924, he died in 1940 while fighting in Italy in World War II. He left behind a wife, Anna Noonan O'Leary. (Courtesy of Karen O'Brien.)

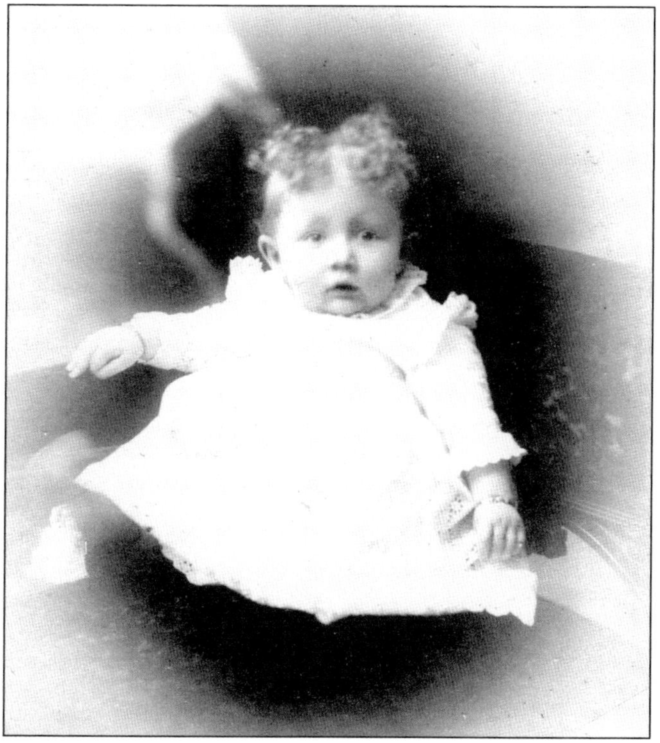

Social Activist. Ada Louise Nelson was born in Ogdensburg in 1885. She was the daughter of a Norwegian ship captain, Nicholas Nelson, and his wife, Bertha Christenson. Ada married the city engineer, Charles H. Lord, when she was 31 years of age. She spent her life raising four children and participating in all the activities of St. John's Episcopal Church, the Girl Scouts, the Alpha Reading Club, and any group where her help was needed. She died on January 22, 1967. (Courtesy of Dorine Lord.)

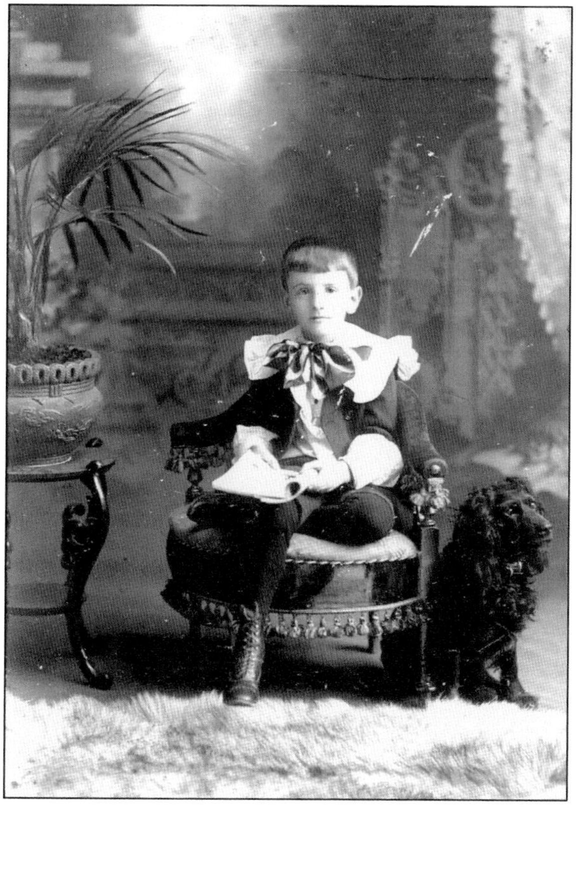

Child Model. This photograph is from around 1900. Charles Lord, son of Ogdensburg's water commissioner Harry Alexander Lord and Harriet Gary Lord, was an only child. He was photogenic as a child and posed often for children's clothing stores. He was a graduate in engineering from Cornell University and, after the death of his father, was appointed city engineer. He held this position until his own death. (Courtesy of Dorine Lord.)

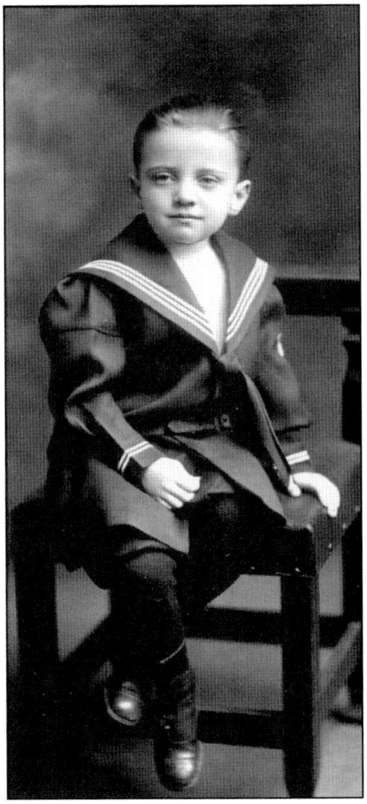

FASHIONABLE FIVE YEAR OLD. This is Joseph T. Barnett, all dressed up to go to the Potsdam Opera House where his father, Michael, and mother, Rose Taney Barnett, were to perform. The pair sang, danced, and played parts in various productions. The Potsdam opera house was a beautiful building with Potsdam sandstone-trim, located between today's fire station and museum. It featured both local and traveling events during the time period from 1875 to 1934. Joseph graduated from Notre Dame in 1929. (Courtesy of Kate Newell.)

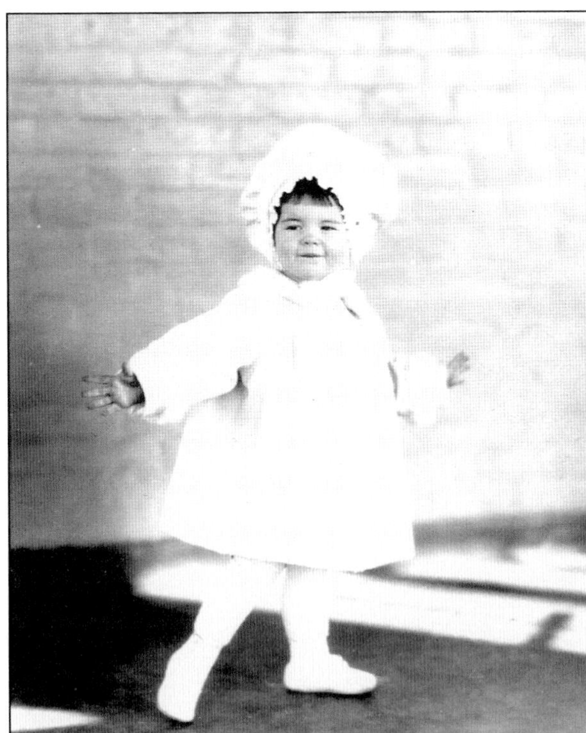

BEST BIB AND TUCKER. This is Jean, the first-born daughter of Michael and Mable Harrington, owners of the Harrington Hotel in Canton. She is dressed in a coat and bonnet, handmade by her maternal grandmother, Harriet Hall. Jean is standing on the veranda, which was on the Grasse River side of the hotel. The Harringtons purchased the hotel shortly after the end of World War I. The porch was added the following year. It had glass-paned windows for the colder months, alternating with green and white striped awnings for summer. (Courtesy of Patricia Harrington Carson.)

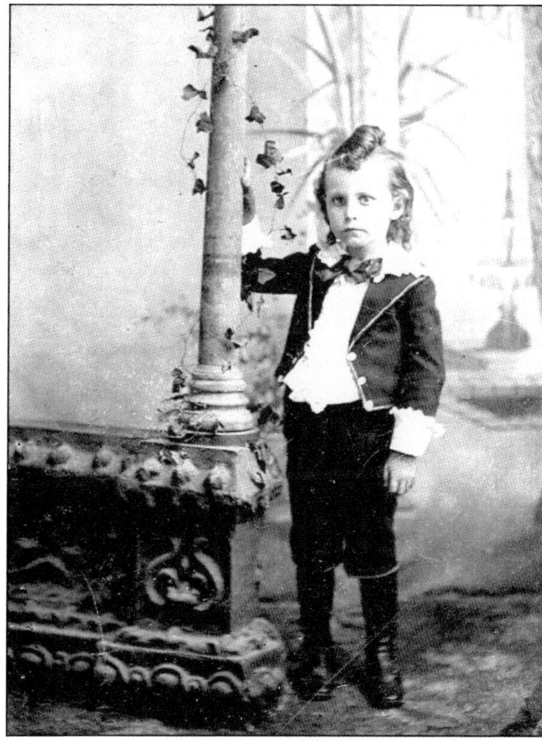

Stockholm Youth. This is the professional photograph of Roy Graves, son of Auborn Graves of Stockholm. Roy was born in Stockholm on January 25, 1888. This charming portrait with such an ornately decorated background was taken in the studio of Clow and Son in Potsdam, which is a fine example of the photographer's unique style. To the great sorrow of his family, Roy died of appendicitis at the age of 18. (Courtesy of Otis Van Horne.)

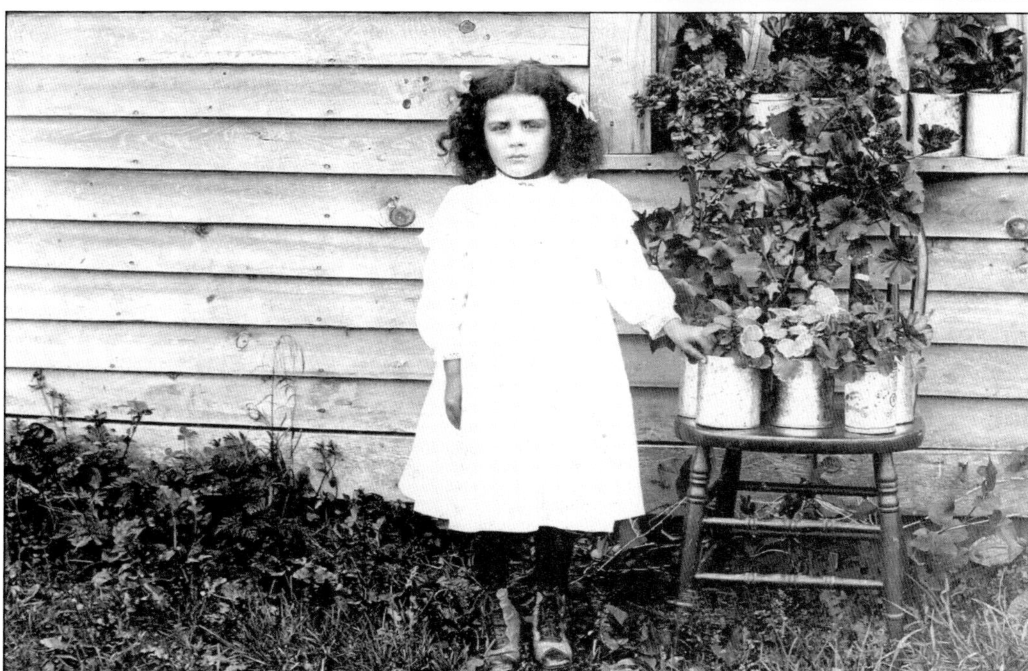

How Does Your Garden Grow? This little girl is Maud Kennedy, the daughter of Warren and Clara Merkley Kennedy. She was born in 1900. Her mother, Clara, was a relative of the Van Horne family of Canton. Maud is dressed in a pretty white dress while displaying her flowers. (Courtesy of Otis Van Horne.)

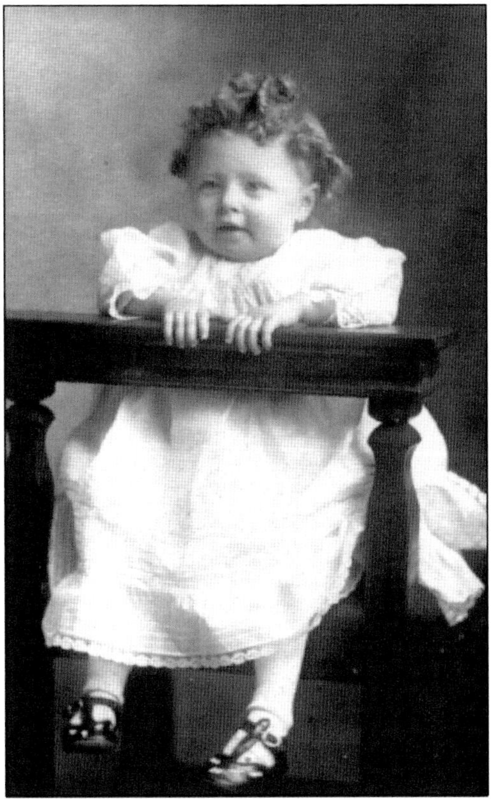

RAISED IN MADRID. Marjorie Loretta Bradley is pictured at 15 months of age. She was the daughter of Leland and Margaret Cox Bradley. Dressed in her lovely white dress, with snappy shoes and curly hair, she makes a very pretty picture. She and her sister, Eunice, were raised on a farm in the Madrid area. She married Charles Cryderman in Norwood. (Courtesy of Marsha Regan Thompson.)

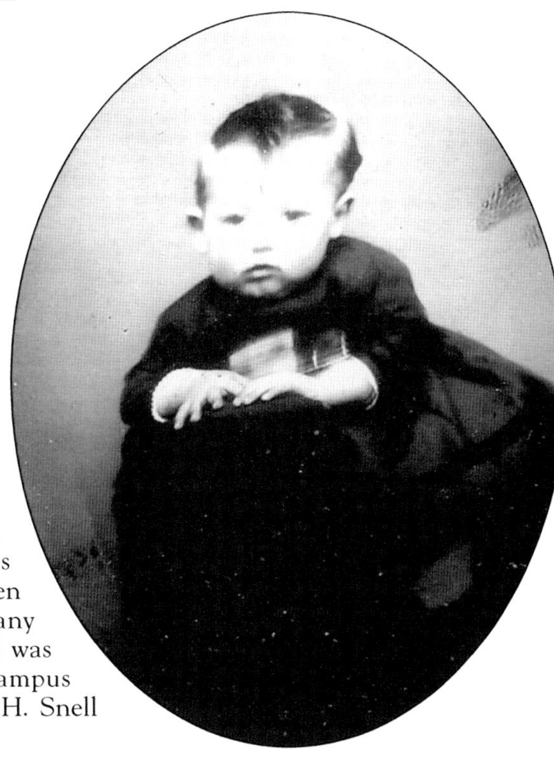

CONGRESSMAN. Bertrand Snell was a congressman and, along with his wife, Sara Merrick Snell, contributed greatly to the Potsdam community. In 1908, the Snells and their daughter, settled into their lovely Queen Anne–style home on the corner of Market and Garden Streets. Their house guests included Presidents Taft, Harding, and Hoover, as well as other congressmen. The Snells have been benefactors of Clarkson College for many years. Their daughter, Helen Snell Cheel was the main contributor to the Cheel Campus Center, the Cheel Arena, and Bertrand H. Snell Hall. (Courtesy of SLCHA Archives.)

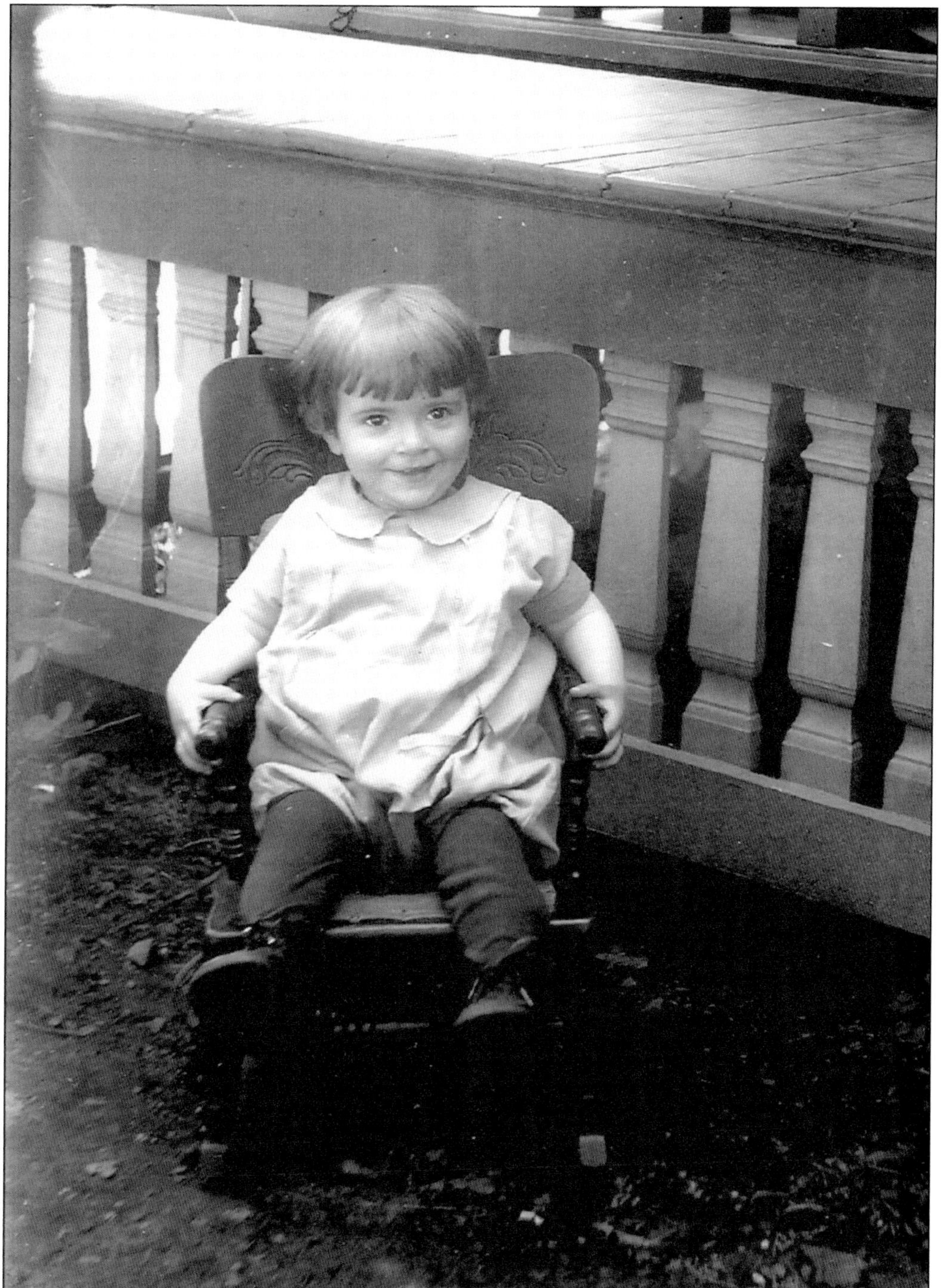

JUST A LITTLE ANGEL. This little boy sitting so contentedly in his rocking chair is Gerald Heffernon, the youngest child of Richard and Clara Heffernon of Canton. He had two older brothers and two older sisters. In 1929, baby Gerald contracted scarlet fever and died shortly thereafter, leaving a heartbroken family. This picture was taken before he became ill. (Courtesy of Rita Heffernon Foote.)

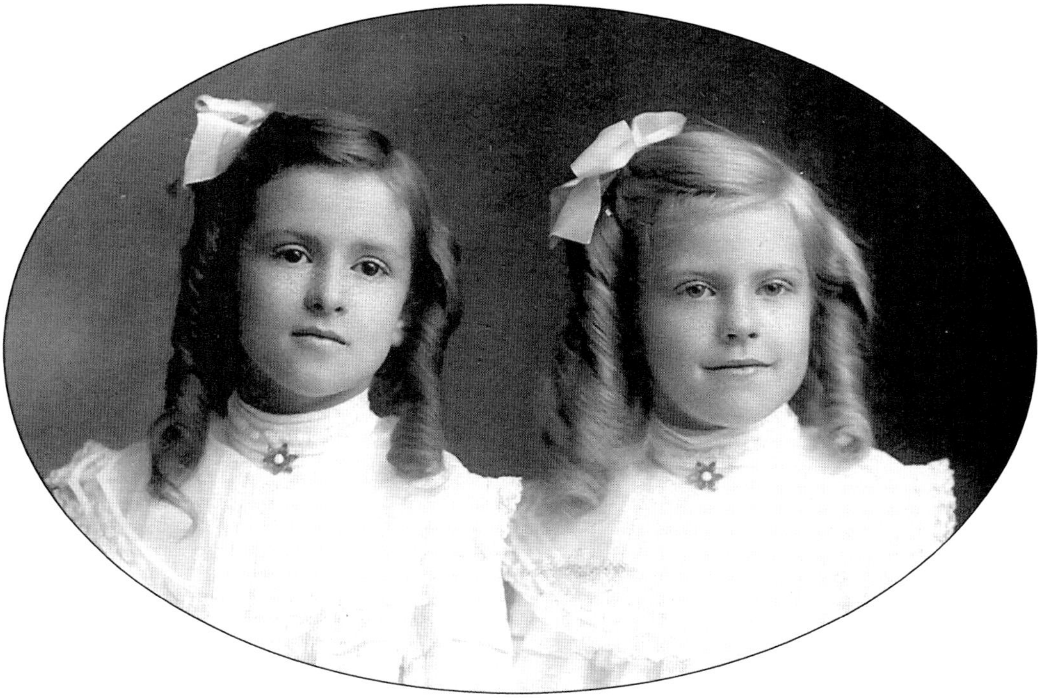

SISTERS FROM RICHVILLE. Carrie (born 1893) and Irene (1895) White were the daughters of Chapman and Anna Shippee White. Carrie married Clark Dodds and moved to Bayshore in Long Island, New York, where they had three children, but moved back home after retirement. Irene married Ivan Coats and owned a farm on Welsh Road in Richville. Both are buried in the Wayside Cemetery. (Courtesy of Helen Davis Reed Collection SLCHA.)

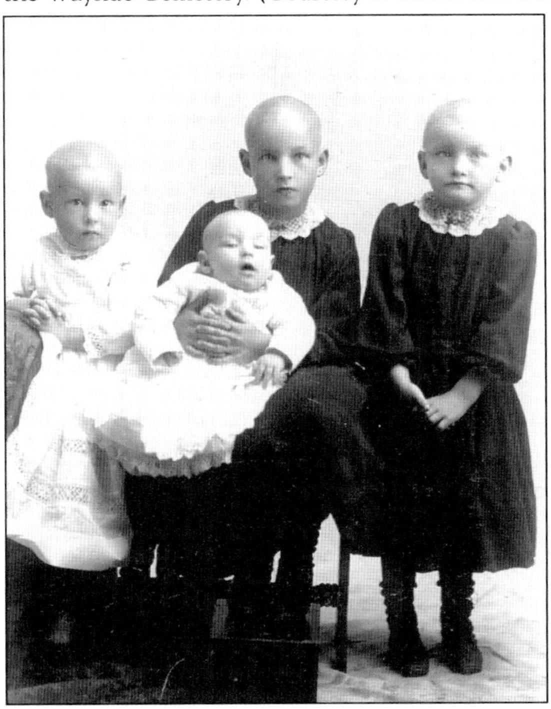

A MYSTERY. These four children are members of the Lacombe family. The unusual thing about the picture is that the children, dressed so beautifully, are bald. The person who offered it for inclusion in the book did not know the reason for their condition. It was conjectured that perhaps they had been ill with typhoid or scarlet fever or perhaps they had come through Ellis Island where their heads had been shaved in order to prevent the spread of lice. (Courtesy of Rebecca Ferankle.)

Two

SIBLINGS

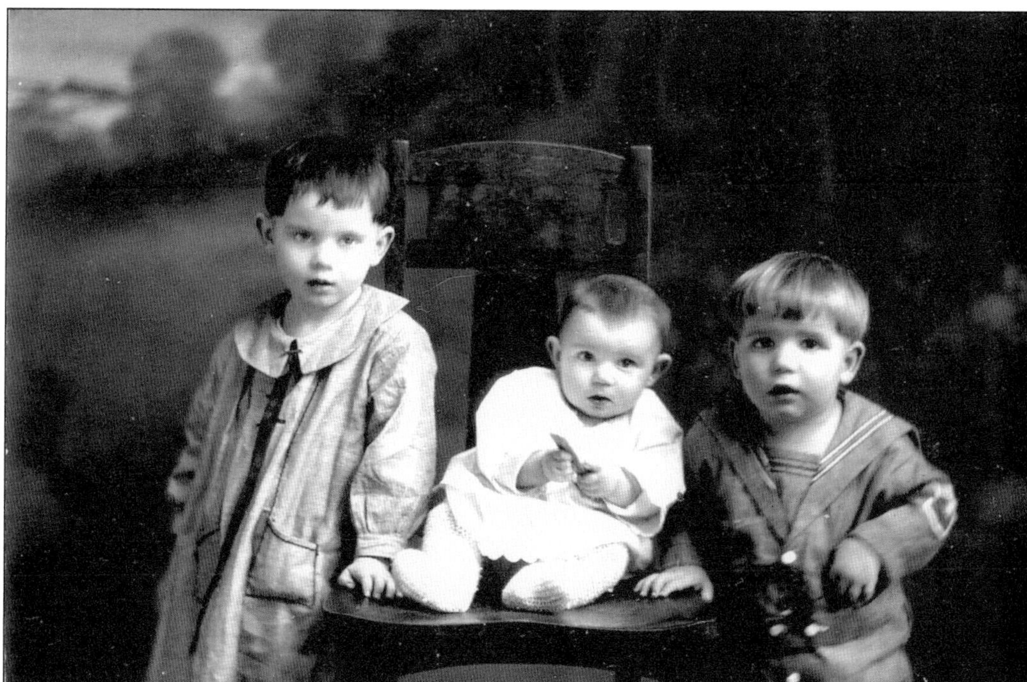

OPERATED LARGE SUGARBUSH IN PIERREPONT. Thelma, Eleanor, and Francis Todd are the first three of eight children of Austin and Flossie Robinson Todd. They were born and grew up on a farm in Irving Bacheller's Paradise Valley in Pierrepont. The farm had one of the area's largest sugar bushes. They raised sheep, horses, and chickens, and had a donkey for riding. The mother, father, and all eight children attended Howard School District No. 6, which was just across the road from their home. (Courtesy of Jim Todd.)

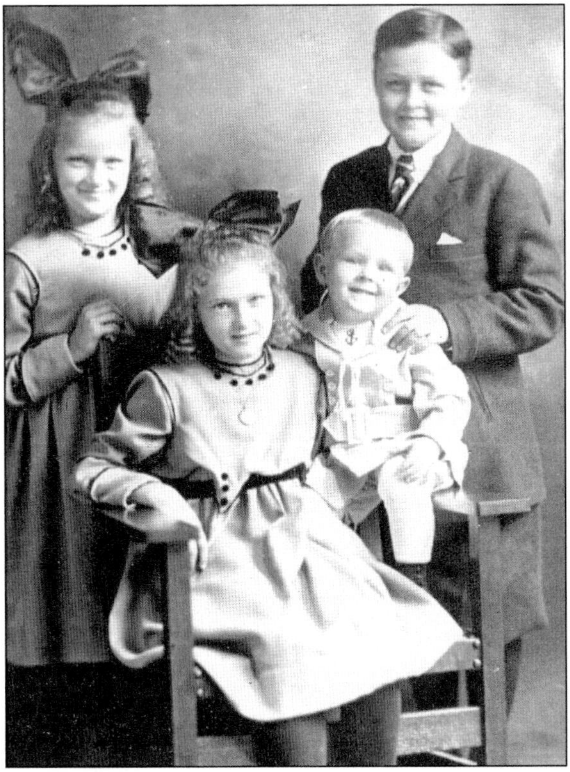

THE BARBOURS. In the photograph above are the four children of Elmer and Maude Brooks Barbour. Elmer and Maude were married in 1906 and began their married life on a farm on Ogdensburg Road. Later Elmer owned a harness-making business on Hodskin Street in Canton. Shown, from left to right, are Cora (standing), Bessie, little Donald, and, the oldest of the family, Myron. A third son, Frederick, was to join the family later. (Courtesy of Bessie Barbour.)

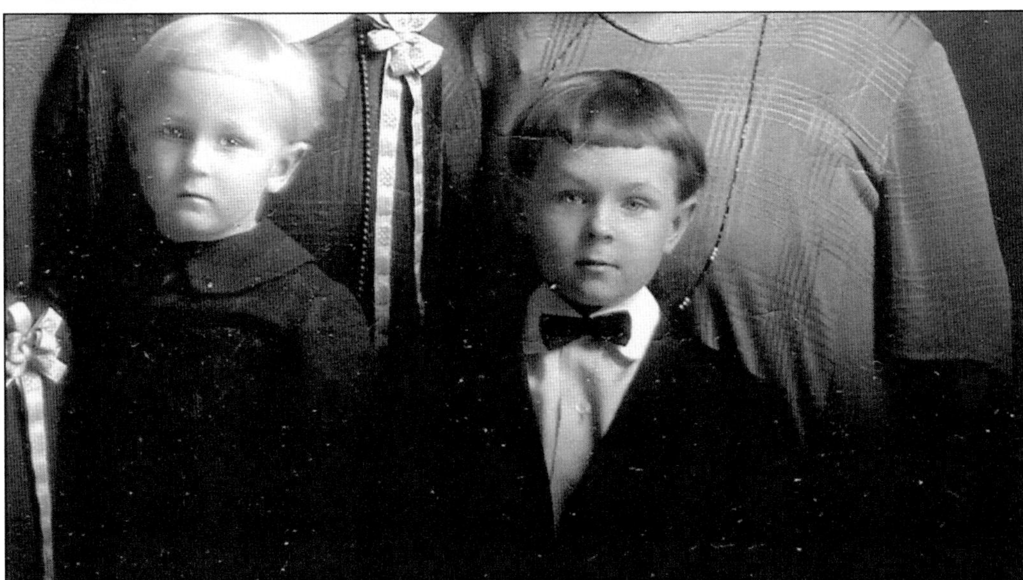

BROTHERS AND FRIENDS. Frederick and Donald Barbour were sons of Elmer and Maude Brooks Barbour. They lived in a large, red-brick house located on Goodrich Street in Canton, with their older sisters, Cora and Bessie, and brother, Myron. Donald and Frederick were both in the service during World War II. Upon returning home, Fred, along with his father, turned his father's harness shop into a successful men's clothing store, later adding women's clothing. (Courtesy of Bessie Barbour.)

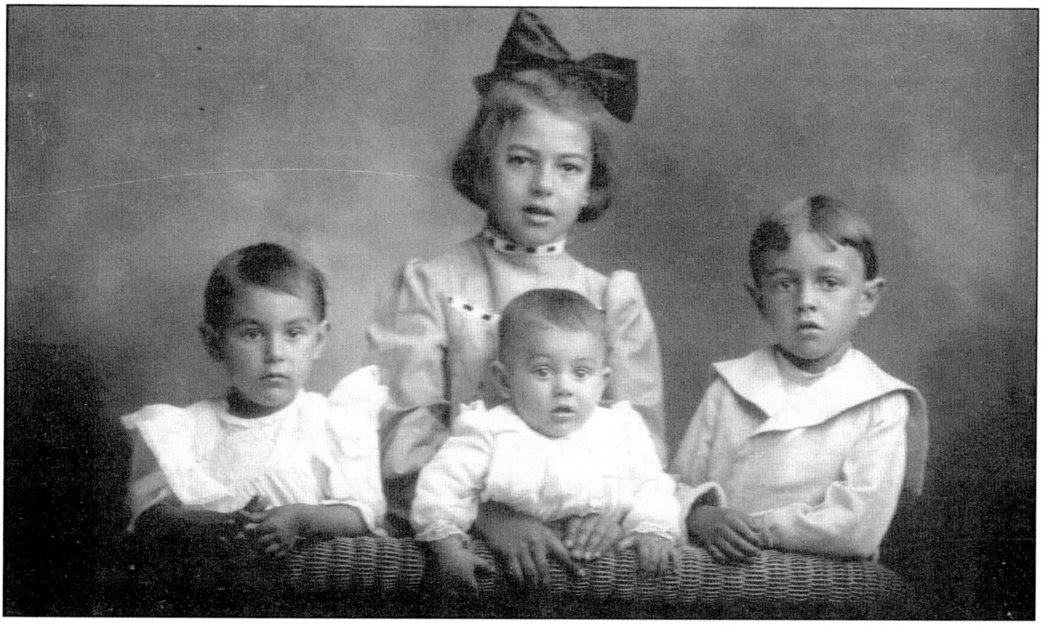

PHOTOGENIC SIBLINGS. These are the children of Frederick and Harriet LaFay of Potsdam. Taken in 1910, Mabel, the oldest, is holding baby Harvey, with sister Doris and brother Leon close by. Sadly, Harvey died the following year of diphtheria and Leon died in World War I at the age of 19. Leon was shot in the neck while in France and died at a hospital in England. To help with the family finances, their mother worked in various resorts. She was working at Big Moose on Loon Lake when Grace Brown was drowned. Chester Gillette was put to death in the electric chair for her murder. Grace's murder was the basis of Theodore Dreiser's *An American Tragedy*. (Courtesy of Patricia H. Carson.)

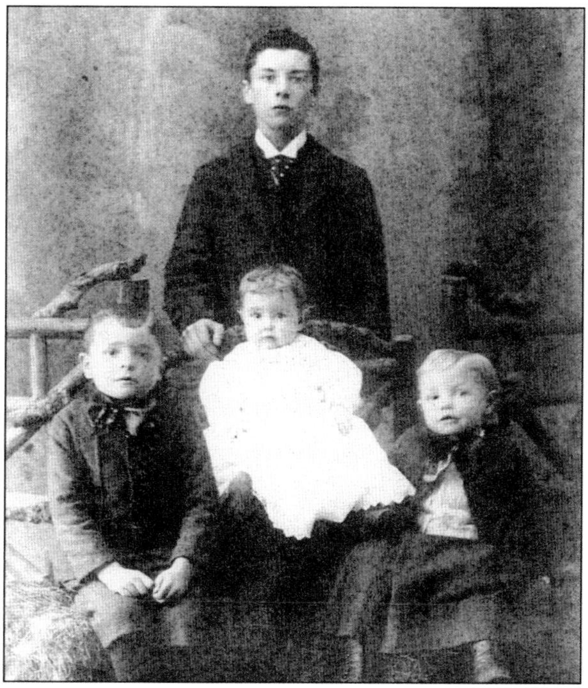

LITTLE SISTER DIES IN INFLUENZA EPIDEMIC. Arthur Floyd Griffiths, the oldest child in the family, was born in 1878. Eben, on the left, was born in 1886 and David, on the right, was born in 1888. Little Esther was born in 1891. She became ill with influenza and died at four years of age. Arthur became president of Punahou College in Honolulu. Eben was an executive with Mobil Oil and a trustee of St. Lawrence University. Griffiths Art Center was named for him. David was a shipping clerk at Alcoa. The photograph was taken at the Mann Studio in Gouverneur in 1893. (Courtesy of Barbara Klemens.)

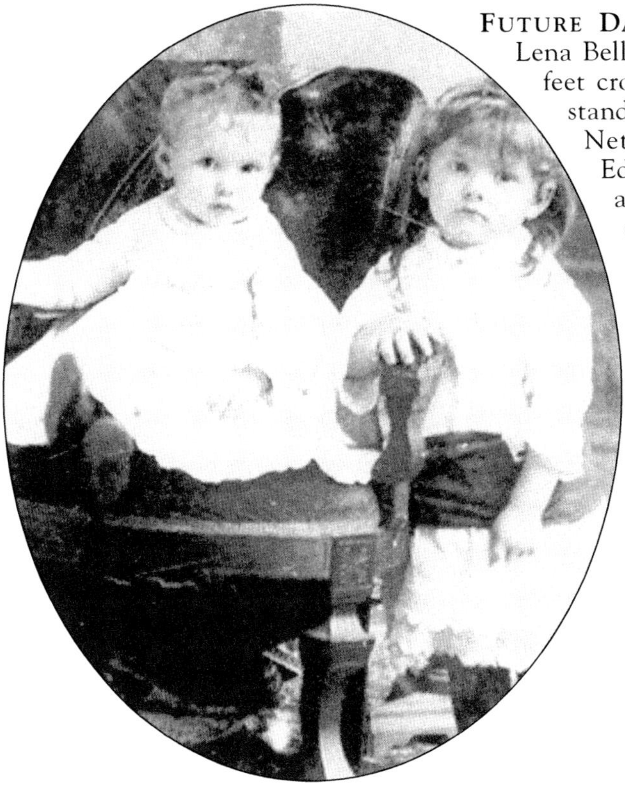

FUTURE DAIRY FARMERS FROM EDWARDS. Lena Belle (1887–1938), sitting with her tiny feet crossed, and Stella May (1885–1960), standing, are the daughters of Fred and Nettie Jane Washburn LaMonda of Edwards. Lena married Harry Parker and had three children, Freddy, Ina, and Harriet. Stella May married Charles Tiel and had two children, Wiltz and Carl. The two families operated dairy farms in St. Lawrence County. (Courtesy of Dick Tiel.)

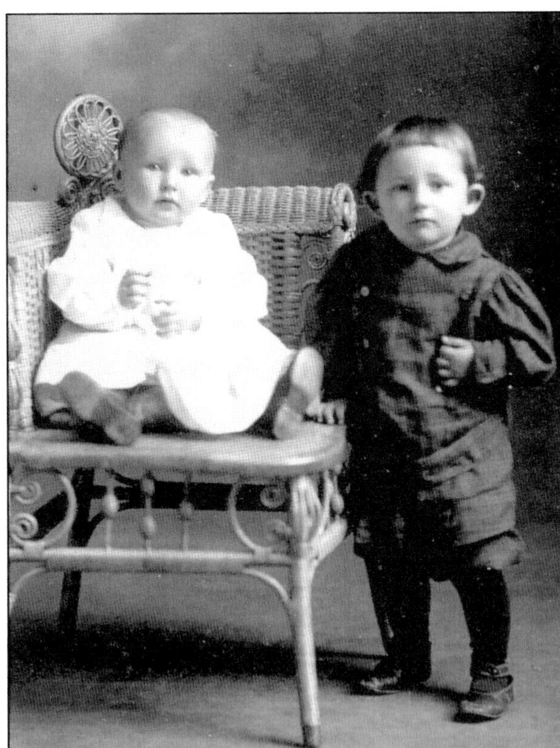

TIEL BROTHERS BOAT LIVERY. In this picture, Carl F. Tiel (1908–1976) is sitting while Wiltz J. Tiel (1907–1978) is standing. They are lifelong residents of St. Lawrence County and the only children of Charles and Stella May Tiel of Russell. Carl was a North Russell dairy farmer and part owner of the Tiel Brothers Boat Livery (grocery and gas station business) at Little River Bridge in Canton. Wiltz graduated from St. Lawrence University in 1930. He operated a dairy farm for several years and taught social studies at Knox Memorial High School from 1931 to 1962. (Courtesy of Dick Tiel.)

The Gunnisons. Shown here, from left to right, are Herbert, Foster, Walter, and Almon Gunnison. Their mother, Blanche Eaton Gunnison, moved to Canton following the death of her husband, Rev. Nathaniel Gunnison. Almon attended theological school at St. Lawrence University and graduated in 1868. He left the area for some years but returned to Canton in 1899 as president of St. Lawrence University, where he had been a trustee for many years. Walter and Herbert also graduated from St. Lawrence University, while Foster received his higher education at Westbrook Seminary. The beautiful Gunnison Memorial Chapel on the St. Lawrence University campus was named in the family's honor. (Courtesy of Patricia Gunnison.)

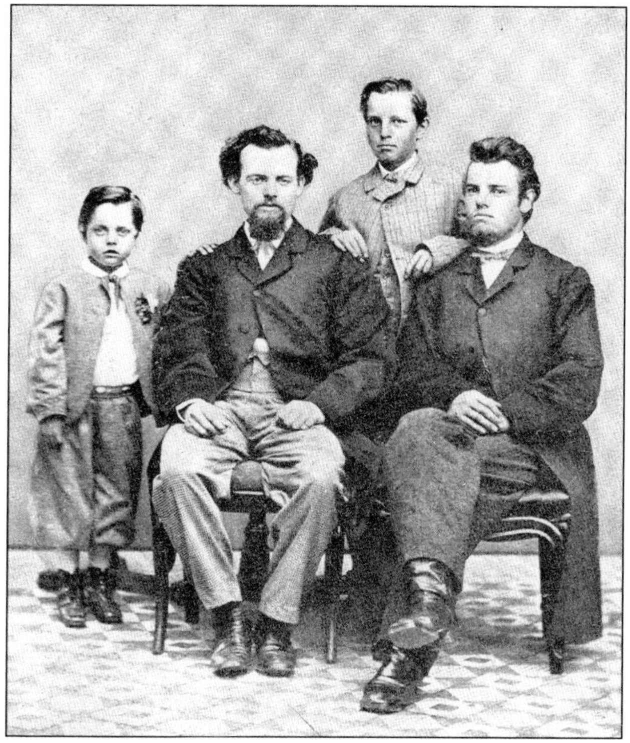

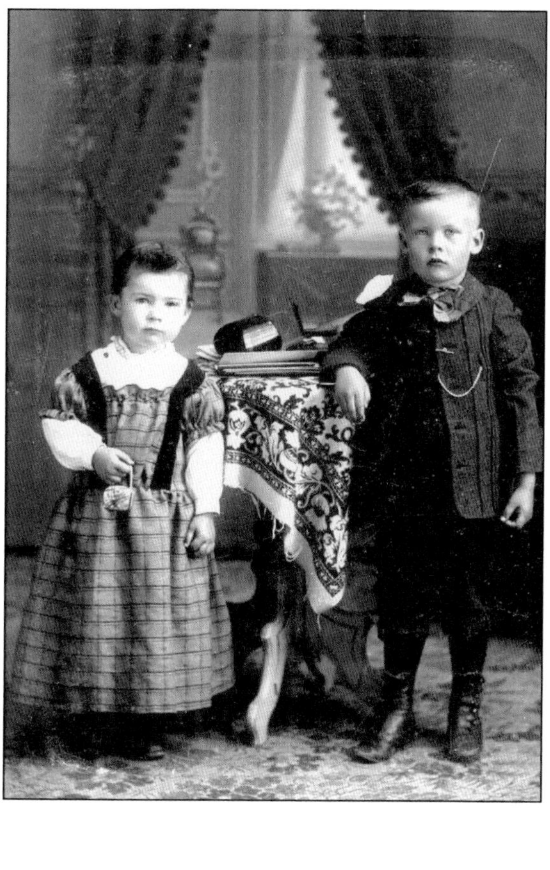

Victorian Era. Looking like miniature adults, Dwight and Florence Payne stand grandly in the parlor of their home. The background evokes the warm feelings of the Victorian era, with the heavy draperies and the ornate table cover. (Courtesy of SLCHA.)

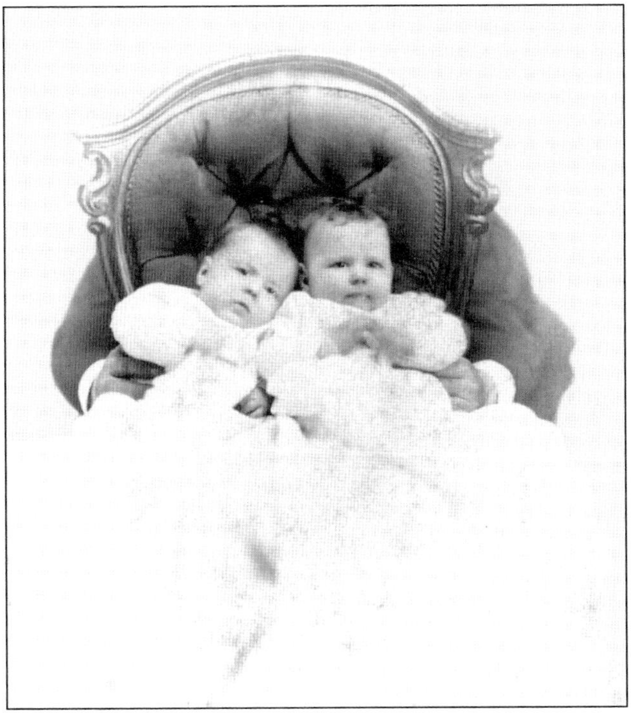

The Pickins Twins. The Pickins twins, Bessie and Jessie, were born in 1878 in Heuvelton. The girls began their musical careers in vaudeville houses. The two sang at Windsor Castle for King Edward VII and Queen Alexandra. They later changed their last name to Abbott. Bessie was encouraged to pursue grand opera and made her debut in 1901 at the Paris Opera House. In 1906, she joined the Metropolitan Opera as Mimi in *La Boheme*. After Bessie married sculptor T. Waldo Story, she retired from the stage. (Courtesy of Linda Marshall, town of Oswegatchie historian.)

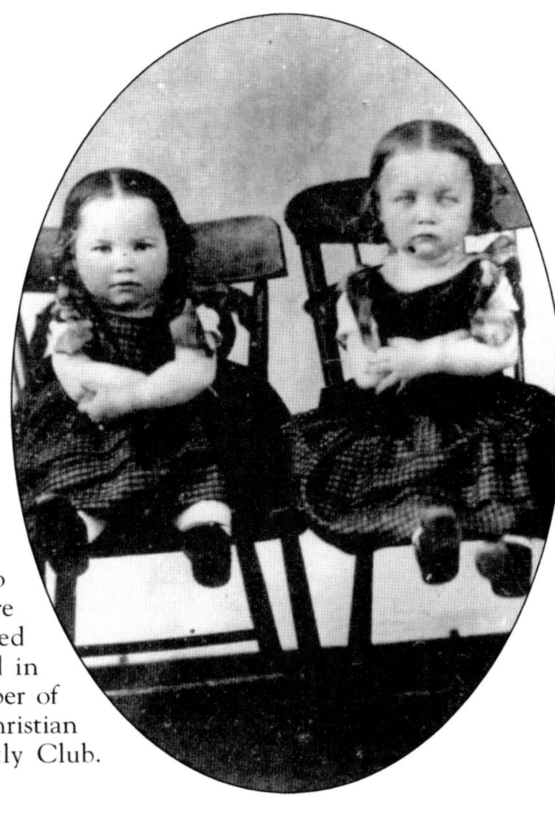

Fraternal Twins from Lawrence. Emma Cornelia and Ella Cordelia were born in 1861 on the family farm, which was built in 1853 and still stands today. They were two of six children. Emma married James Bacon in 1886 and went to Nebraska to live, but she returned to St. Lawrence County after his death where she gave painting lessons. Ella married Dr. Daniel Finnimore in 1891 and lived in Potsdam, where she was a staunch member of the Presbyterian Church, the Women's Christian Temperance Union and the Fortnightly Club. (Courtesy of Virginia McLaughlin.)

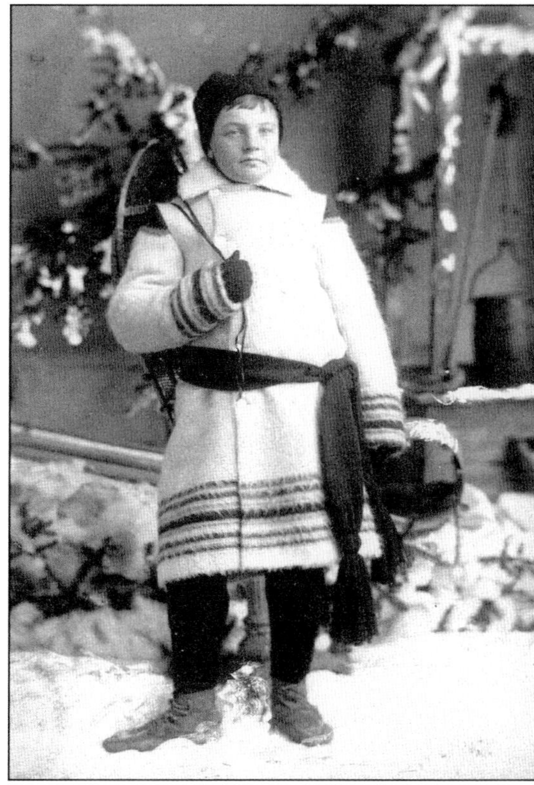

DAPPER SONS OF LOCAL BUSINESSMAN. These are the children of Edmund Kingsland of Morristown. He was the manager of Dr. Morris's Indian Root Pills. This was the largest employer in Morristown in the 19th century. Dr. William Comstock of Brockville, Ontario, Canada, owned the company. Morristown's location on the St. Lawrence River made it an excellent location to have a branch of the company on the U.S. side. The Kingslands originally moved from Massachusetts to work with the company. The photographer was A. C. McEntyre of Brockville, Ontario, Canada. (Courtesy of Joe McDonald.)

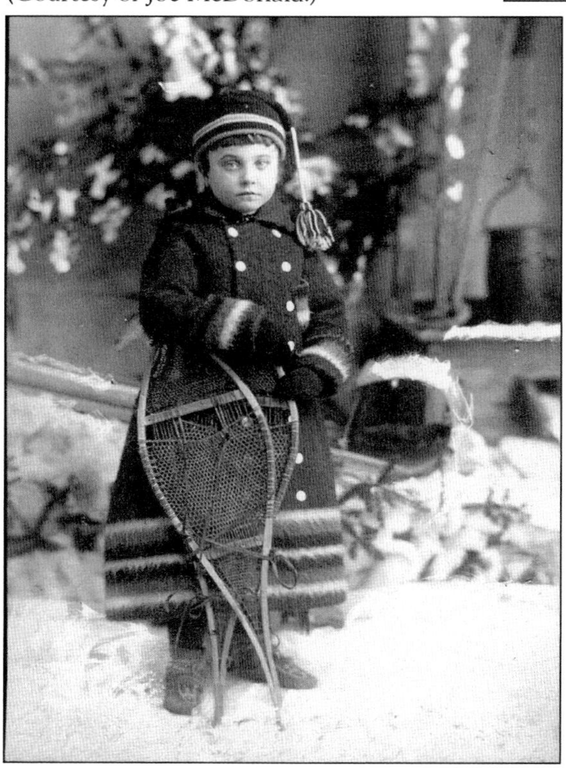

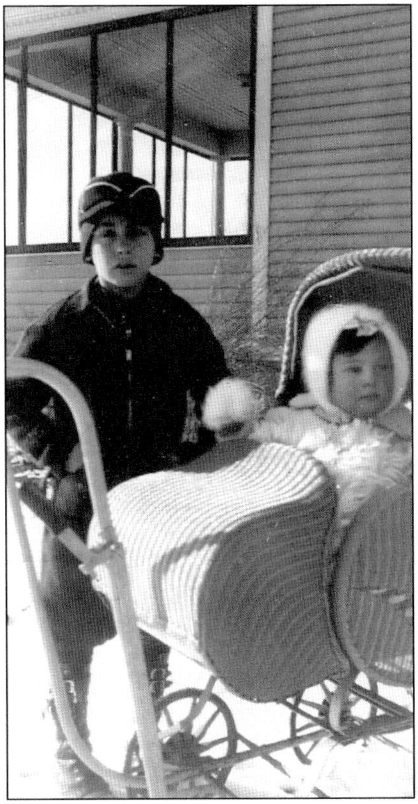

Fun in the Snow. Shown here are brother and sister, Bernard (Bun) and Rena Sperling, enjoying an outing on a winter's day in Ogdensburg. They were the children of Mayer and Anna Sperling of Proctor Avenue. Both children attended local schools. Bun graduated from St. Lawrence University and married a St. Lawrence University classmate, Peg Henshaw. They made their home in Ogdensburg, where he operated the family business—the upscale Sperling's Furniture Store. Rena attended Harcum College in Pennsylvania. She married Milton Goldberg. (Courtesy of Peg Sperling.)

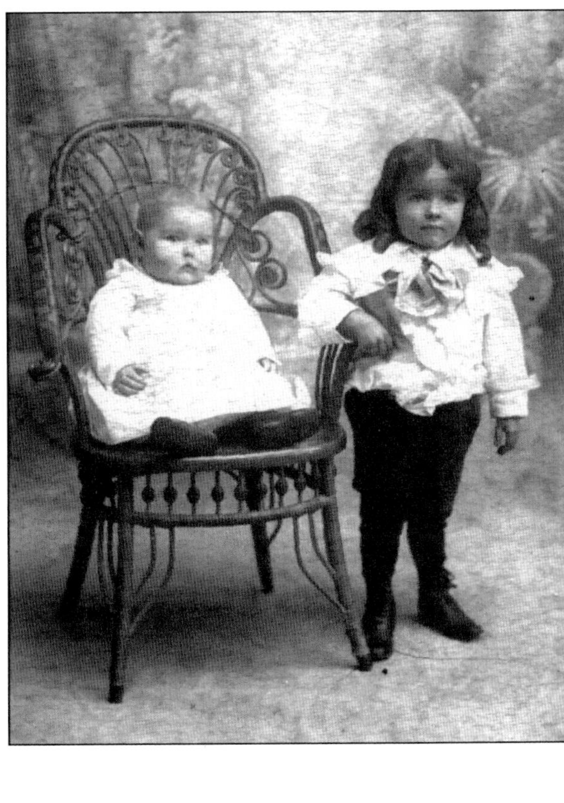

Father Trained Light Horses. Helen and Everett Bradley were the children of Arthur and Gertrude P. Bradley of Madrid. Their father was a trainer and driver of light-harness horses. He was well known for his stallion, Lorenzo Hamlin. (Courtesy of Marcia Ragan Thompson.)

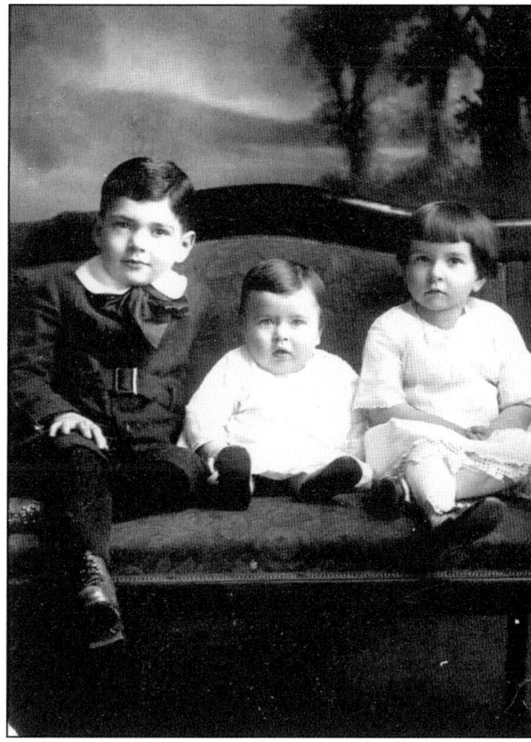

THREE ST. LAWRENCE UNIVERSITY GRADUATES. The three Heffernan children are dressed for their photograph in very fine attire. Robert is on the left, Walter is in the middle, and Mary is on the right. All three graduated from St. Lawrence University as their father had before them. Two other siblings joined the family, Rita in 1921 and Gerald in 1926. (Courtesy of Rita Heffernan Foote.)

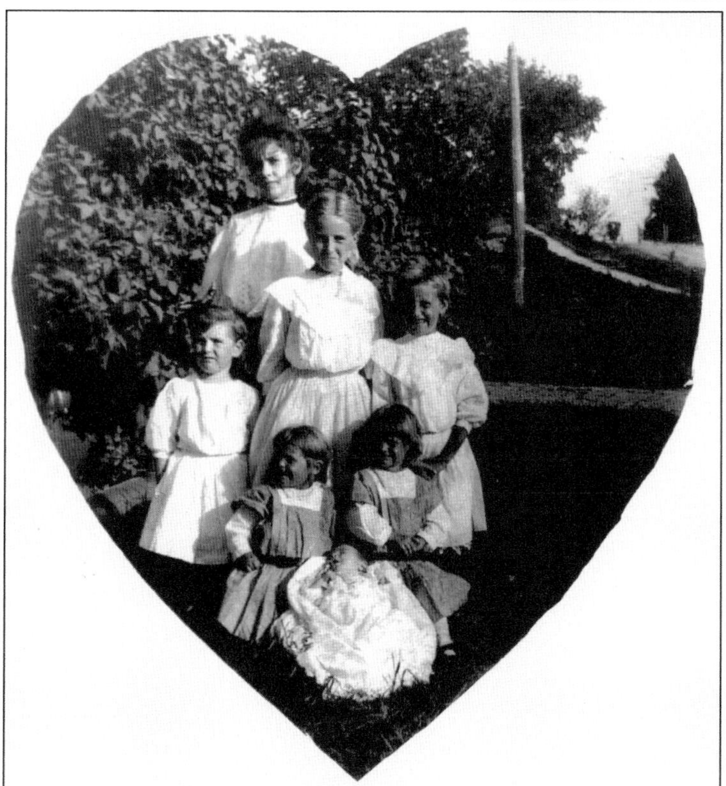

HOME IS WHERE THE HEART IS. Photographed within a heart are the MacTurk daughters of Hailesboro. Pictured (oldest to youngest) are Jesse, Ellen, Bessie, Belle, and twins Martha and Mary. Grace, sitting with her sisters, was a "blue baby." She died at six months, not long after this photograph was taken. Thomas, the patriarch of the family, came from Dundee, Scotland, in the 1800s and married Jessie Stewart in 1890. Thomas was a foreman at the Gouverneur Talc Mines. (Courtesy of Ellen Burns.)

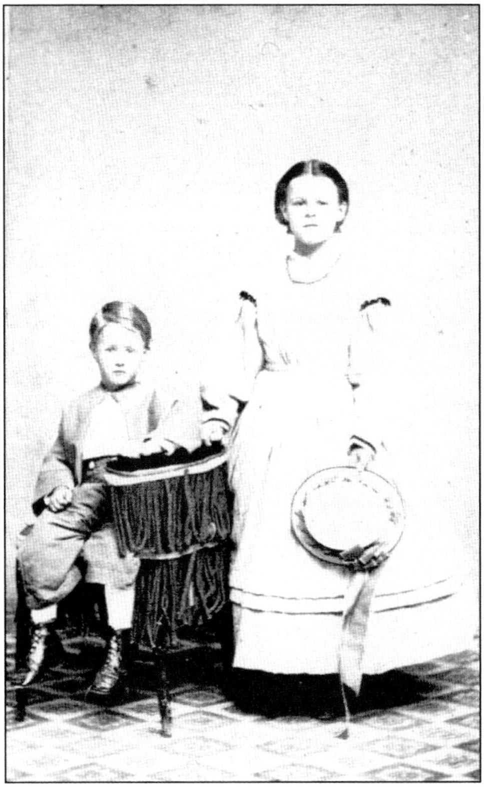

QUARANTINED IN RICHVILLE. Alfred Henry and Elizabeth "Lizzie" Ann Bradford were the only children of William and Sarah Malt Bradford from Cambridgeshire, England. The parents immigrated separately in the early 1850s to Niagara County, New York. Lizzie married Milton Mills Brooks of DeKalb in 1878. They moved to Richville in 1886. Lizzie found the northern climate harsh and Milton found employment a challenge. In March 1888, an outbreak of smallpox and diphtheria caused them to be quarantined in Richville and the only work they could find was digging graves. Lizzie never recovered after the birth of her youngest child, and the family decided to move to Chicago. Later that year she was diagnosed with consumption, and died on June 12, 1890. (Courtesy of Bill Hull.)

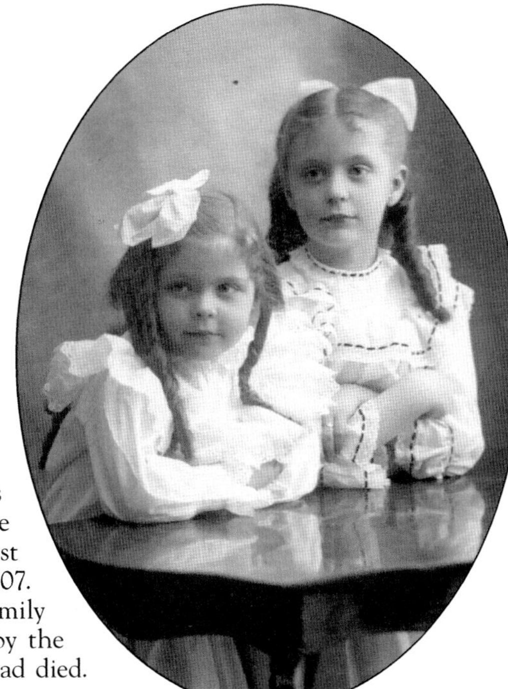

EARLY DEMISE. Genevieve and Muriel were the daughters of Pliny and Vinnie Maine of Hermon and DeKalb Junction. Genevieve Elizabeth Maine was born in Hermon on June 11, 1895. She died March 21, 1910. She and her sister, Doris, and her grandfather, Milton Rundell, all passed away within one week. An article in the *Watertown Daily Times* said it was from diphtheria, but the death records dispute this. Muriel Kennen Maine was born on August 17, 1898, and passed away on January 22, 1907. She probably died of acute appendicitis. The family had to go to Hermon to find a doctor, and by the time they got back with the doctor, Muriel had died. (Courtesy of Stan Maine.)

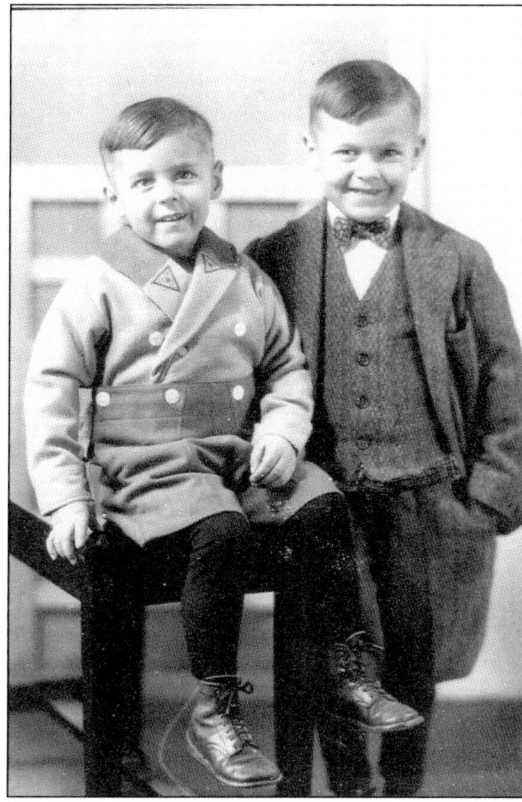

BROTHERS ALL DRESSED UP. The boys shown here are Max and Lawrence Tupper. They grew up in Pierrepont on the family farm. They both attended grade school in Pierrepont and high school in Canton. Lawrence went into the army in 1942 and later worked for the village of Pierrepont, while Max stayed and ran the farm. (Courtesy of Sally Tupper.)

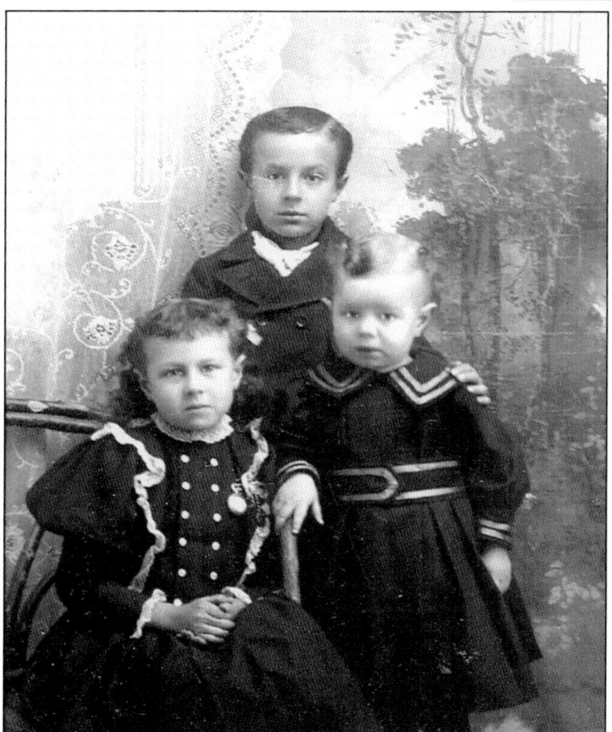

THE FOUNTAIN CHILDREN. The young man in the background is Bert Fountain (1888–1970). The girl in front is Matie Fountain (Decker), who was born in 1891 and died in 1969, and the boy in front is D. Lyle Fountain, who was born in 1898 and died in 1967. D. Lyle Fountain was father to Emma Fountain Remington, Parishville town historian. (Courtesy of Emma Remington.)

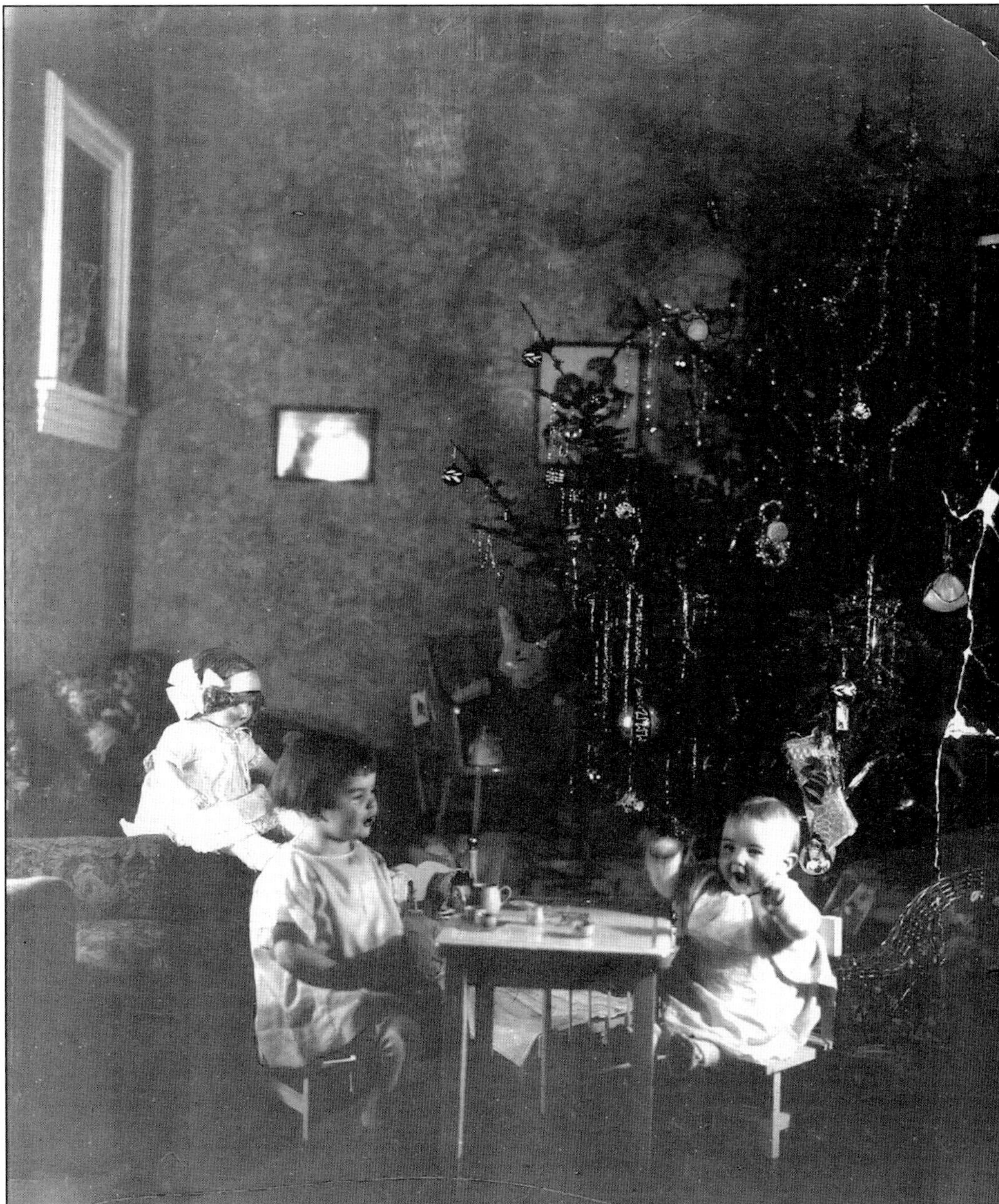

CHRISTMAS AT THE HARRINGTON HOTEL. This is three-year-old Jean Harrington and her one-year-old brother, Jack, on Christmas Eve, 1925. They are sitting in the glow of the Christmas tree, awaiting the arrival of Santa Claus in their suite in the Hotel Harrington. Probably one of the first of its kind, Jean's doll, which is seen sitting on the couch, was able to talk thanks to a cylinder in her back. Interestingly, these dolls were given free with a subscription to the *Watertown Daily Times* newspaper. (Courtesy of Patricia Harrington Carson.)

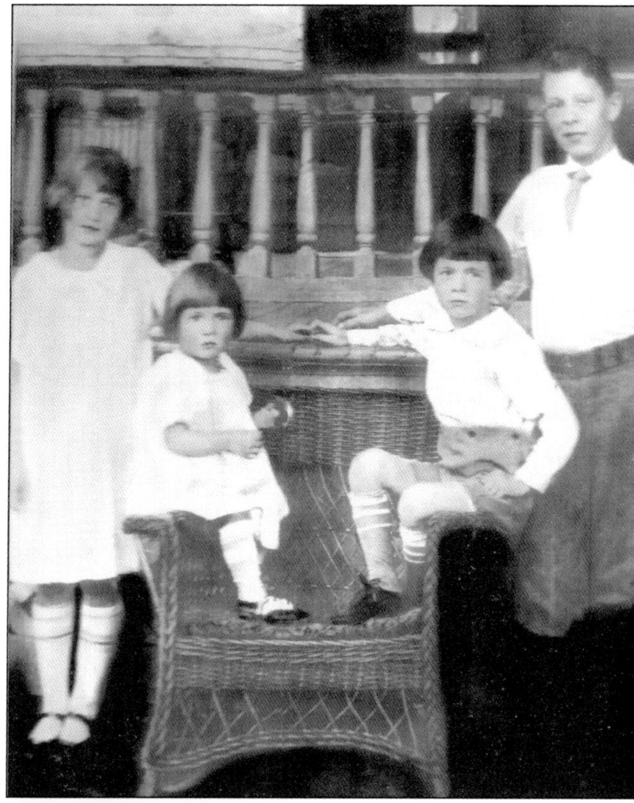

A FINE FOURSOME. These are the four children of Fana and Stanley Cornell, photographed in 1924. From left to right are Dorine, Alma, Stanley Jr. and William. Two children were yet to be born, Jack and Betty Jane. Stanley had a motorcycle business. He was a promoter of motorcycle races, and he was a fine rider. Fana was born in the village of Gouverneur and was a "joiner;" she was very active in many organizations in Canton. Sadness overwhelmed the family when Stanley Jr. was killed in World War II. The other three children became educators and were highly regarded in their profession. (Courtesy of Clare Grant Allen.)

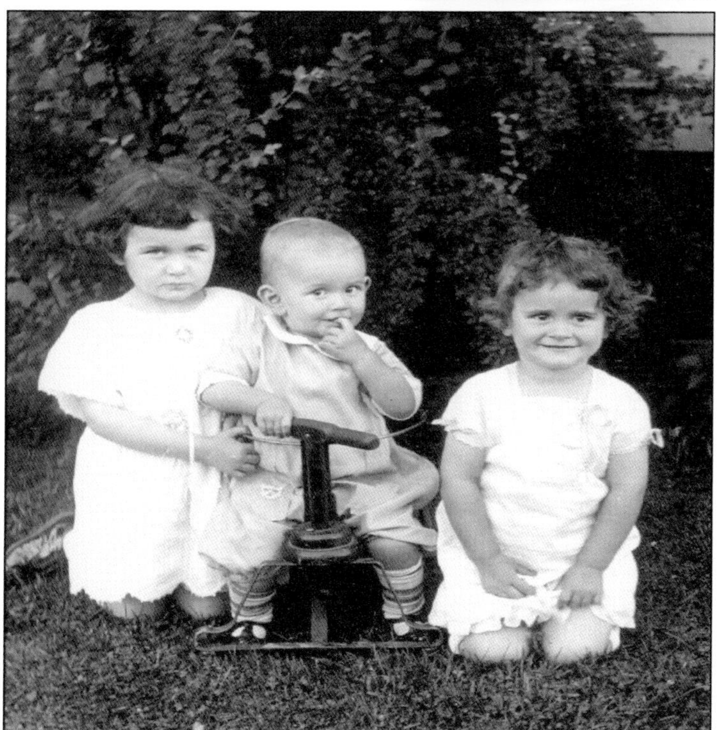

FUN IN THE SUN. From left to right, the Carl Clark children, Mary, baby Langdon, and Lillian play in the yard of their Chapel Street home. They were soon to be joined by two more sisters, Ruth and Lura. The Clarks' large home was for many years a gathering place for all the neighborhood children. With a backyard that sometimes held an army tent, a big barn filled with bikes and scooters, and an attic with trunks of dress-up clothes, the home attracted many visitors and all were warmly welcomed. (Courtesy of Helen Clark.)

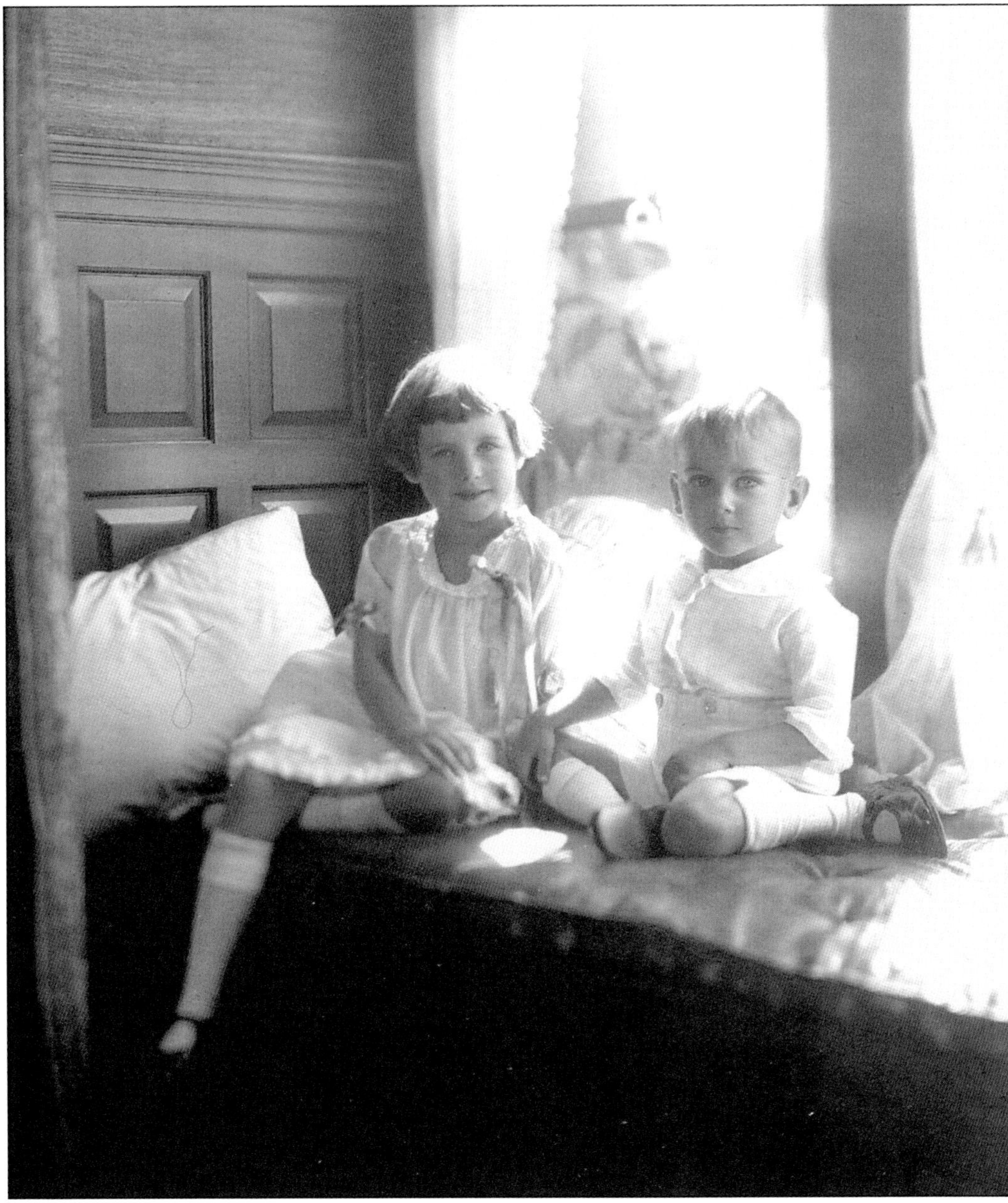

POSED IN THE SUNSHINE. Sitting in a window seat in their home's formal dining room are Claire Delano and brother George Judson Newell. They were the children of assemblyman and Newell Company board chairman William Allan and Edith Judson Newell. This photograph was taken in 1923 by the renowned New York City Bachrach Studio. The photographer traveled to the family home at 414 Caroline Street in Ogdensburg for the photo session. (Courtesy of Allan Newell.)

THE INFANTINE FAMILY. Thomas and Mary Infantine owned a fruit and vegetable market on Lower Main Street in Canton, opposite the Hotel Harrington, in the 1920s. They played a large part in the life of the town. Thomas and Mary met on a boat coming from Sicily to New York and were married shortly thereafter. Later they became the owners of the silent picture theater. Blanche Browe, a young local girl, was the pianist for the silent films. The Infantines had three sons, Bill, Dominic, and Joe; all became local businessmen. The photograph features Bill's children: Baby Harlan, Bill Jr., and Helene. (Courtesy of Marilyn Mintener.)

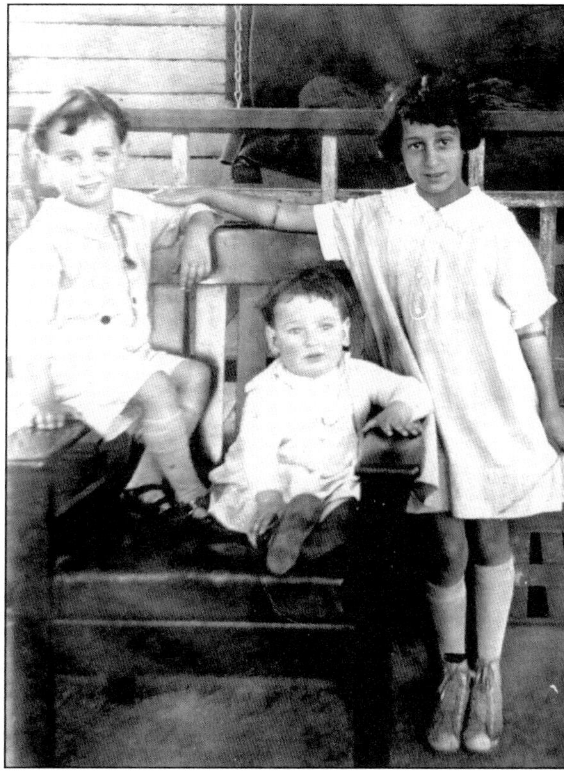

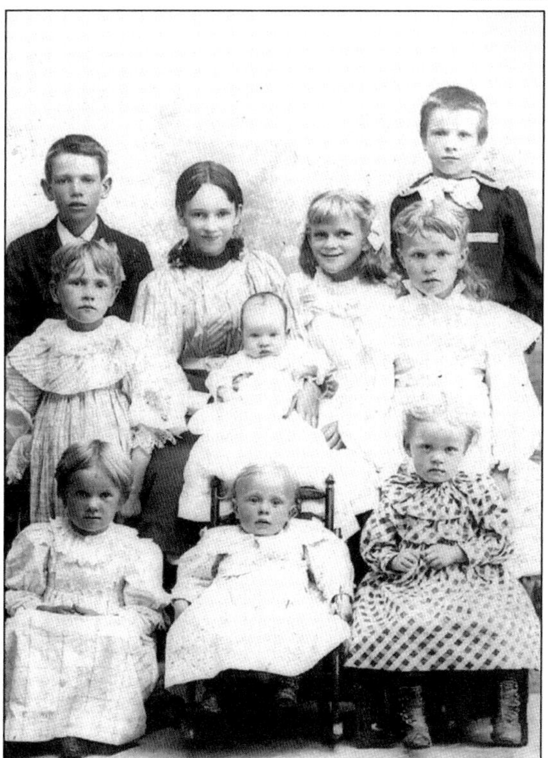

THE CORNELL CHILDREN. These are the children of Alfred and Carrie Petersen Cornell of Cowan Mansion Road in Canton. Pictured here, from left to right, are as follows: (first row) Marion Wade (1895–1985), Herbert (1897–1983), and Amy Mitchell (1894–1918); (second row) Charlotte Pierce (1891–1977) and Dewey (1898–1984, being held by Jenny); (third row) Charles (1884–1973), Jenny Quigley (1862–1945), Bertha Strobel (1887–1959), Inez Purvee (1889–1937), and Lewis (1890–1962). Two more children were born later; Alfred (1901–1974) and Harriet Cornell Grant (1900–1937). (Courtesy of Clare Grant Allen.)

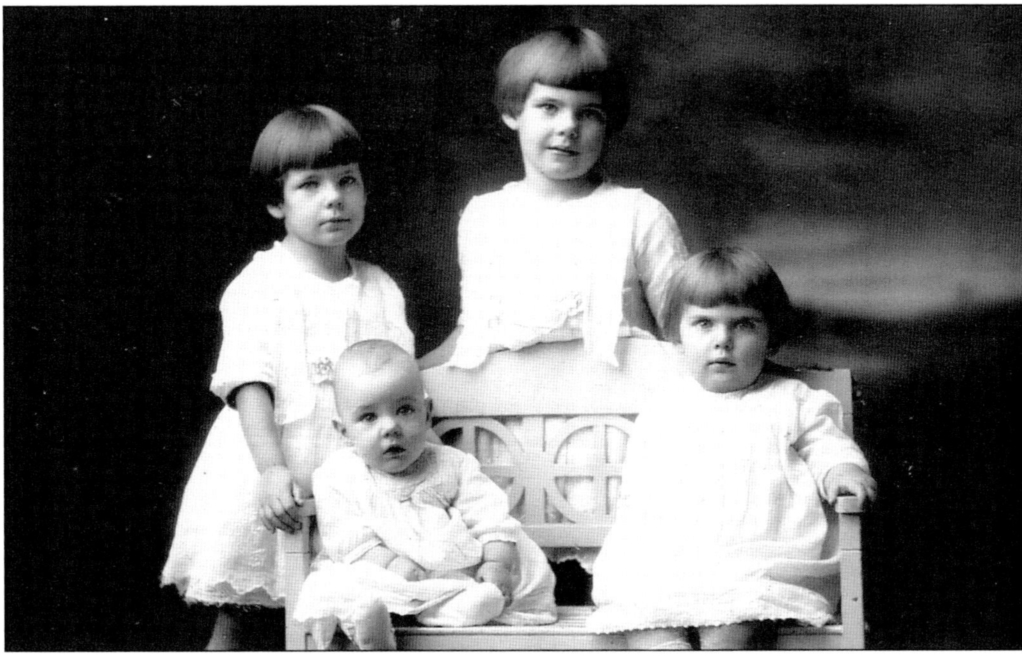

FOUR CHILDREN ON A BENCH. This picture, taken in the 1920s, shows the children of Roy and Myrtle Rosenbarker Crossman of Potsdam. Roy was a grandson of Julius Crossman, a Civil War veteran from Pierrepont. Roy worked for many years in the Sunshine Store in Potsdam and his children went to Potsdam schools. The children are, from left to right, (standing) Claudia, born in 1916; and Eileen, born in 1915; (sitting) Mark, born in 1920; and Thelma, born in 1918. (Courtesy of Beulah White.)

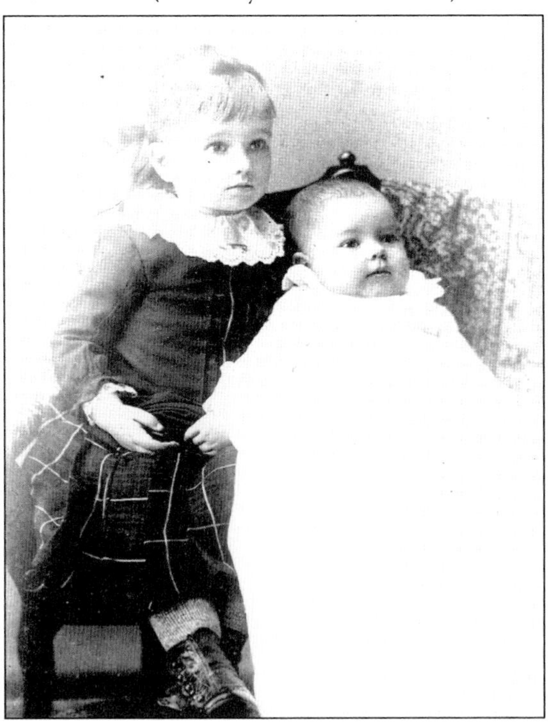

RUSSELL FAMILY FROM WINFARTHING, ENGLAND. Lillie (born 1886) and Lelia (1888) Fordham were from Russell. They were the daughters of Robert and Ella Fordham, who were farmers. Robert came to the United States in 1866 with his mother, four sisters, and his uncle from Winfarthing, England. Along with the Fordham family, 15 to 20 other people came from the same town on the same ship. They settled in the Russell, Hermon, DeKalb, and Crary Mills area. Lillie and Lelia and two of their siblings became teachers and taught in rural schools in the North Country. (Courtesy of Beulah White.)

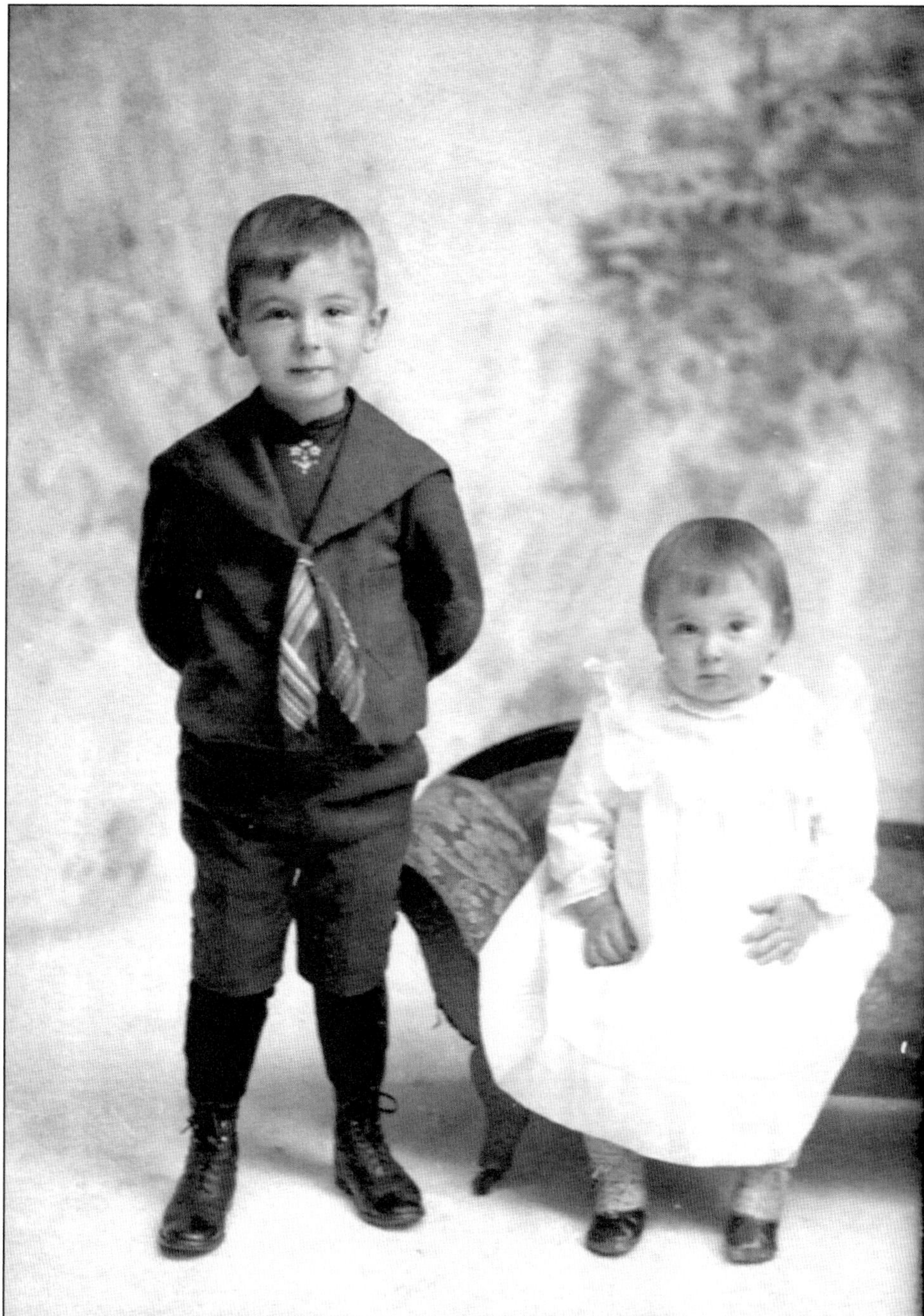

EGGLESON FAMILY. Brother and sister Herbert and Doris Eggleson were born on the family homestead on State Street in Canton. The house is still in the Eggleson family and was the first two-story house built in that area. Herb and Doris attended the Olin School, the eight-grade one-room schoolhouse for area children. It was located on the corner of Morley Potsdam /Sykes Roads. After finishing Canton High School, Doris graduated from St. Lawrence University and Herb ran the family farm. They both raised their families in Canton. (Courtesy of Peggy Eggleson.)

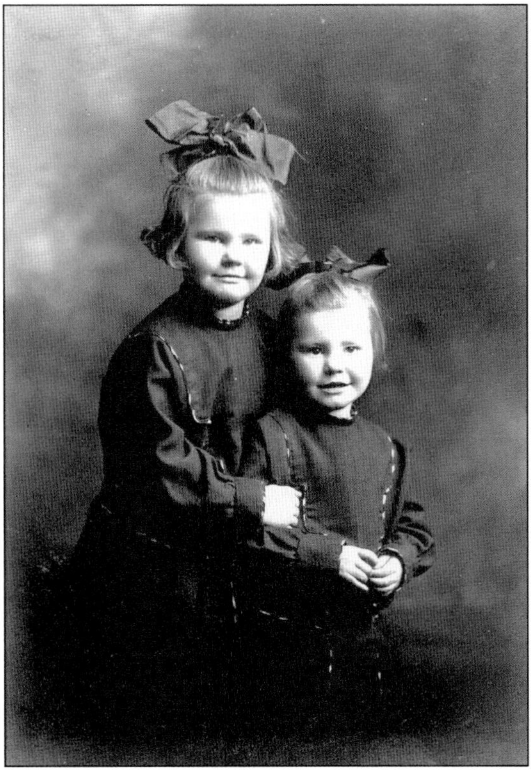

SISTERS IN THE EARLY 1900S. Sisters Grace (left) and Gladys were the only children of Mahlon and Edith Hunkins Bancroft. They pose attractively for the camera in their black outfits and black hair ribbons. Grace married Chester Frederick and Gladys married Lawrence Dow. Gladys died at 28 years of age, leaving behind one daughter, Janice, who went on to graduate from Potsdam Normal School. Grace, a housewife, had five children, twins Lois and Louise, Marilyn, Richard, and David. (Courtesy of Mary Lobdell Harrington.)

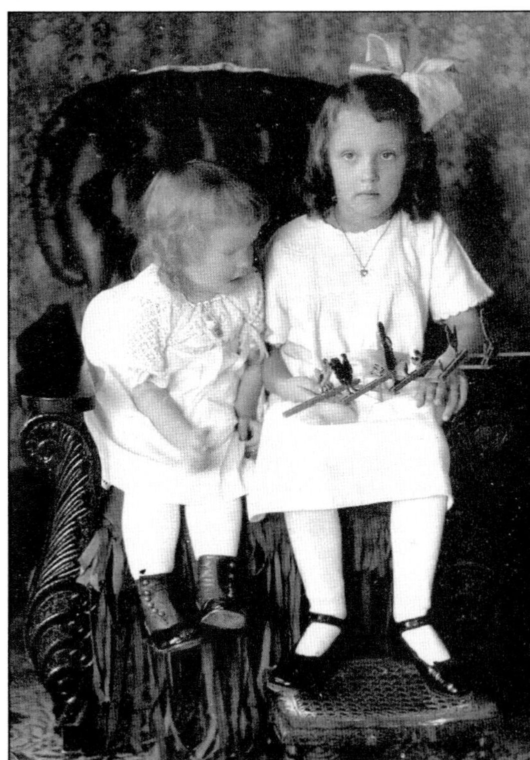

STRESSFUL DAY FOR SERENA. Shirley Olive Copeland (left), born in 1917, is trying very hard to amuse her younger sister, Serena (1922). This picture was taken after many trips to the photographer, where Serena would cry, making her hair and clothes messy. Both girls were born in Parishville to Earl Harper Copeland and his wife, Gladys Mary Hayden Copeland. Serena loves the outdoors and still lives in St. Lawrence County (Massena). She spends her winters in Florida. (Courtesy of Serena McDonald-Carr.)

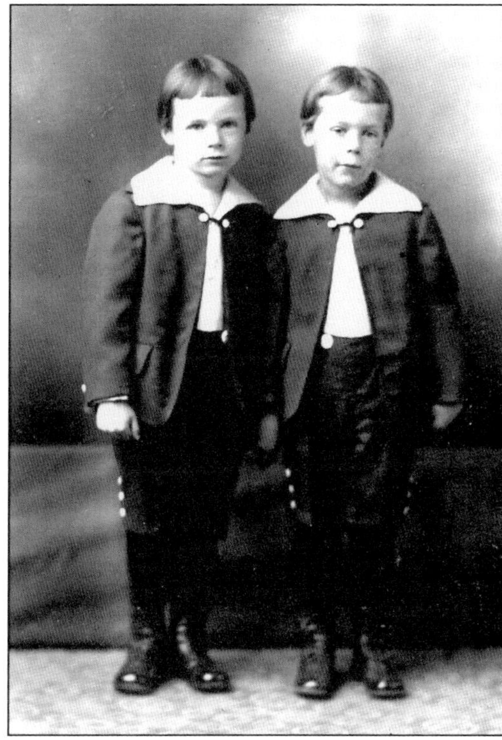

TWO FUTURE LAWYERS. On the left is Giles Elihu Chase, born in 1909 in Massena. He graduated from Middlebury College and Albany Law School in 1936. He practiced law with his father, Giles Aquila Chase, in Massena for 50 years. He was a Captain in the U.S. Army during World War II. He married Shirley A. Furgison in 1953 and had three children. Lester Hall Chase (right) was born in 1910 and attended St. Lawrence University and Cornell Law School. He enlisted in the navy in 1942 and served in the Pacific under Admiral Nimitz as Lieutenant Commander. He married Marguerite Alice Tobin in 1944 and had three children. (Courtesy of the Chase family.)

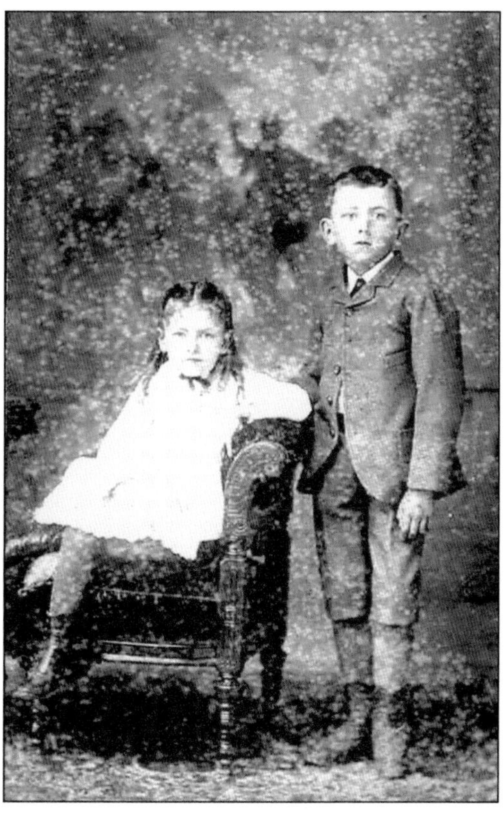

LUDA AND WILLIAM BADGER. Luda and her brother William, standing by her side, were the children of William J. and Mary A. Badger of DePeyster. Luda was born in 1881 and William in 1878, and both were raised in DePeyster. Sadly, William died at 14 due to an attack of appendicitis. Luda married Charles Witherell in 1905. They operated a farm and were the parents of three daughters, Grace, Alice, and Betty. Luda was very active in the DePeyster Methodist Church and in later years took up painting as a hobby. She especially enjoyed painting winter scenes. Luda lived to be 93 years old. (Courtesy of Sharon Murdock.)

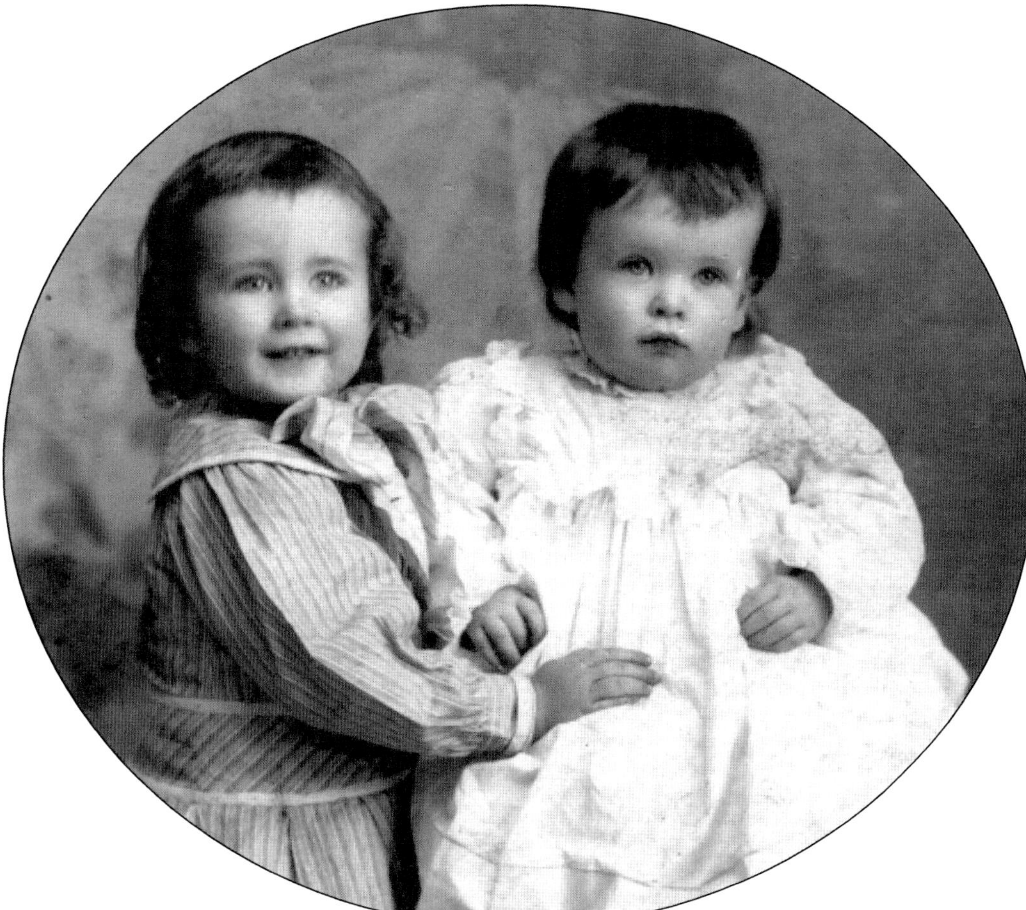

HARVARD GRADUATES. This is a picture of Adrian (left) and Albert McDonald taken in 1899. Both boys attended schools in Ogdensburg before graduating from Harvard University. Albert became deaf as the result of a high school accident. He spent a year at the Massachusetts Eye and Ear Infirmary and learned to communicate by lip-reading and signing. After graduation from Harvard, Adrian served in World War I in France and Belgium. He became engaged to Yvonne Casse of Luxemburg and returned to the United States to start a business career. He died at age 26 from peritonitis following surgery for appendicitis before he and Yvonne could be married. Albert went on to graduate from Harvard and the Columbia School of Mines as a chemical engineer, and then as an assayer of metallurgy. He became successful as a starter of a copper mine named Kamiscotia near Timmins, Ontario, Canada in 1926. He lived most of his life in Ogdensburg and Morristown. (Courtesy of Joe McDonald.)

SOUTH RUSSELL SIBLINGS. Nellie Clintsman was born in South Russell in 1906. Nearby, her brother Joe is sitting contentedly in his wicker carriage. They were the children of Stanley and Elizabeth Raycraft Clintsman. Joe grew up to obtain an engineering degree from Clarkson College in 1931 and worked for the New York State Highway Department in Watertown, while Nellie worked with her sister, Marjorie, running a beauty parlor and dress shop in Carthage. (Courtesy of Gary Bushaw.)

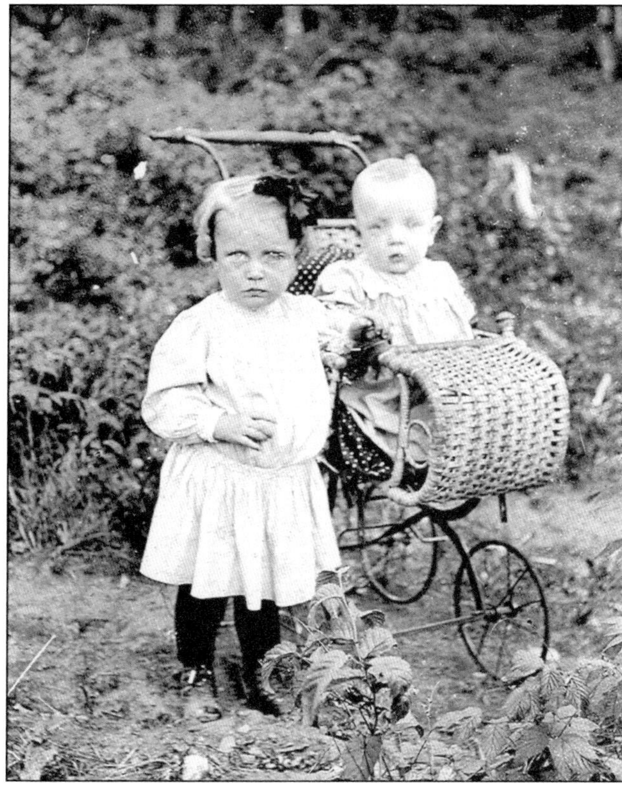

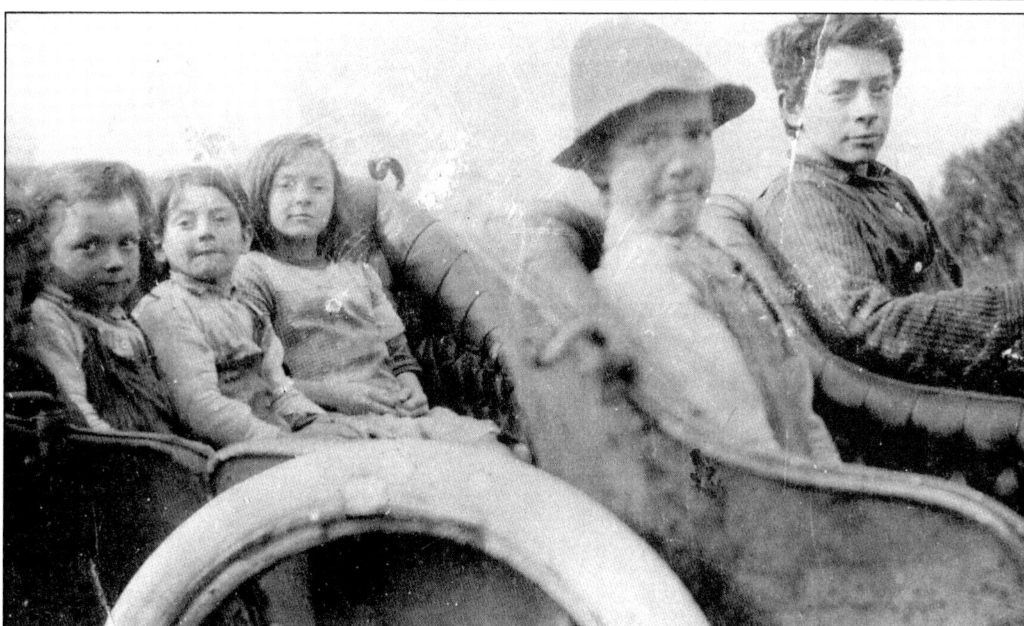

A 1915 NASH RAMBLER. This was the first automobile in the Frank and Katie Young family. Their oldest son Frank owned the car and his younger siblings, from left to right, Kenneth (born 1910), Leland (1908), Myrtle (1906), Forrest (1904), and Seymour (1901) are seated in it. (Courtesy of Norman Young.)

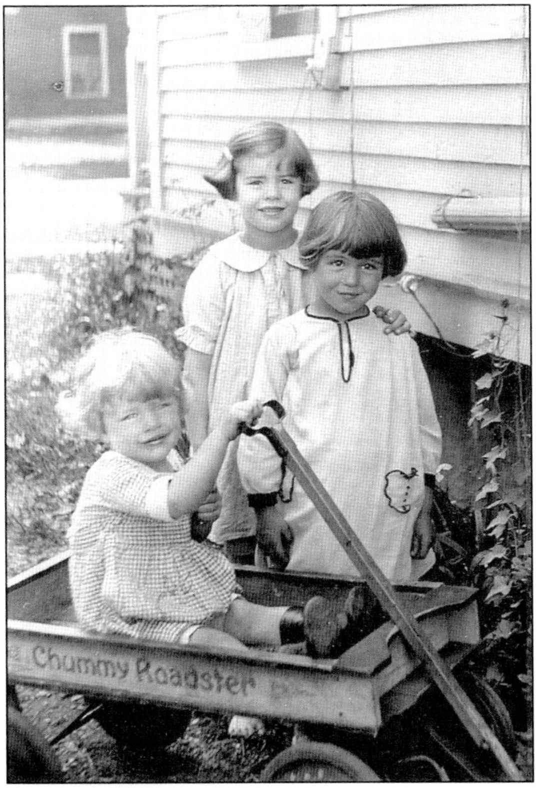

CHUMMY ROADSTER. This picture of the McMasters children was taken in the summer of 1924. Rouette (in back), Helen (front), and Phil (in the wagon) lived in the house that the Infantine family later owned. Their parents were Norman and Zona McMasters. It is believed that Zona made the dresses that the girls are wearing. Phil is looking quite comfortable in Chummy Roadster, wearing Helen's favorite boots, which she had recently outgrown. (Courtesy of Helen McMasters Wallace.)

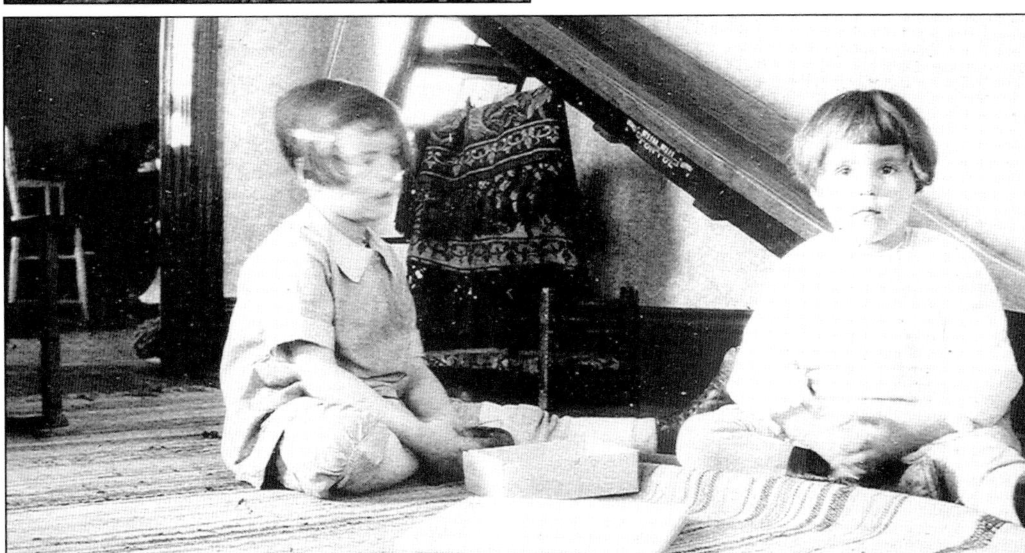

THE EVERGREENS. Sisters Rouette and Helen McMasters are sitting on a rug handwoven by their maternal grandmother. The girls were the children of Noman and Zona Sprouse McMasters of Canton. The family built the Evergreens in 1926, located across from the Evergreen Cemetery. Here Norman opened a gas station and a tire and battery shop, while Zona hosted a tea room. She made sandwiches and served coffee and tea to hungry travelers. St. Lawrence University functions were oftentimes held there. (Courtesy of Helen McMasters Wallace.)

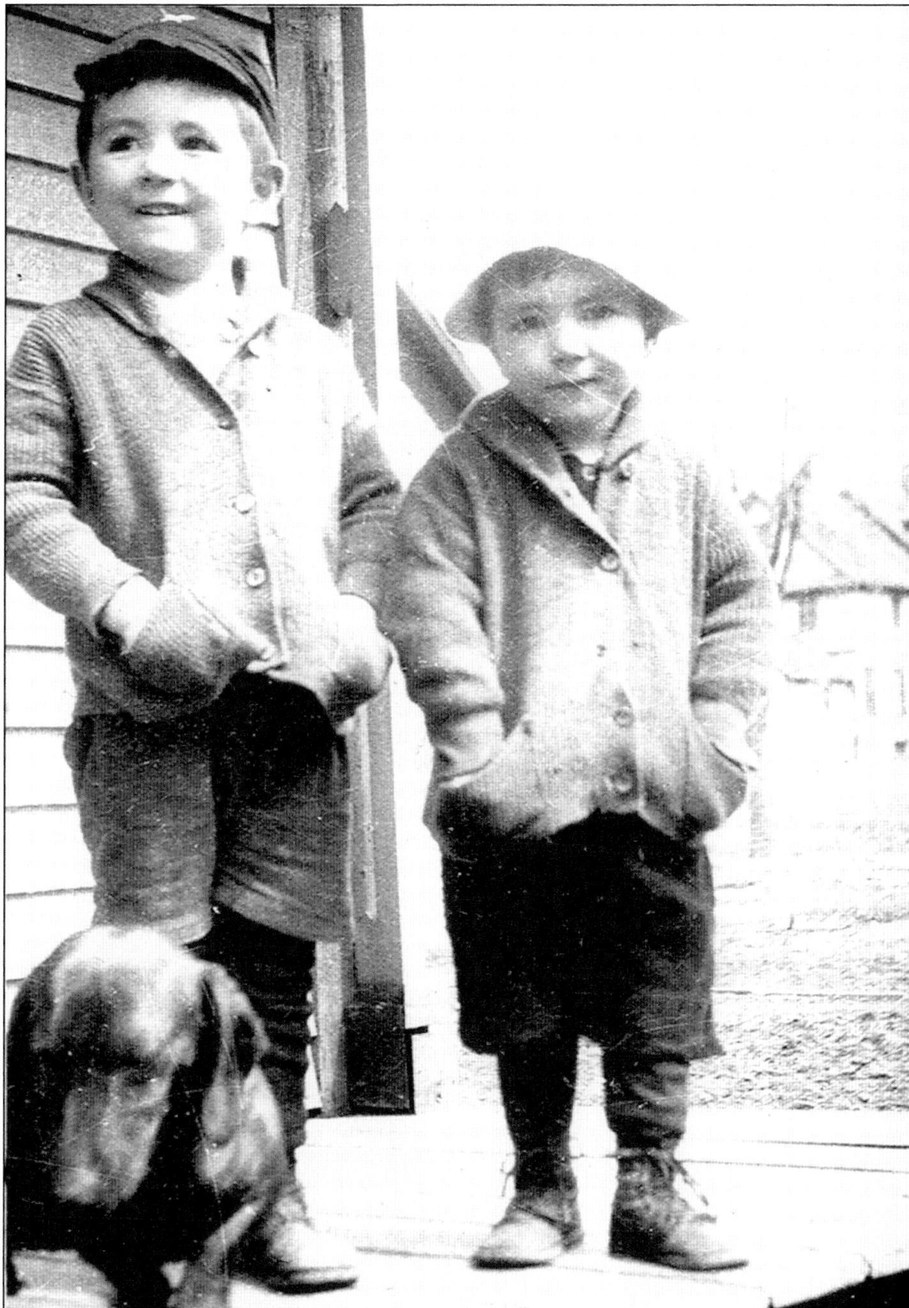

BROTHERS JOINED THE NAVY AND THE COAST GUARD. Ledyard Park Hale (left) was born in 1921 and his brother, John, was born one year later. Their home was at 4 Elm Street in Canton. Both boys attended local schools and enrolled at St. Lawrence University in 1939 and 1940 respectively. In the summer of 1941, Ledyard enlisted in the Coast Guard and served in the Pacific. John joined the navy and was appointed to the naval academy. This picture of the two boys and their dog was taken in 1925 at the farm on Hale Road. Ledyard has his father's Exeter cap on. (Courtesy of Ledyard Park Hale.)

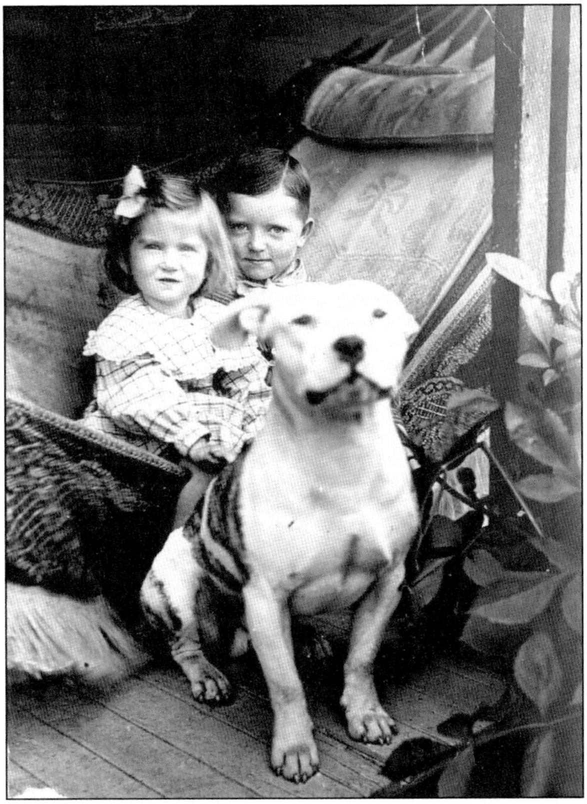

Speer Children. Webster E. (born in 1905), his sister Leola Speer, and their dog Max make an interesting grouping. A postcard that was made from the photograph and mailed to their grandmother states that the picture was originally supposed to be of Webster only, but at the last moment Leola and the dog jumped in and the photographer took them all. Webster went on to graduate from Cornell University in 1933 as a doctor of veterinary medicine. He had his own practice in Canton until his death in 1965. His son, David Speer, also became a veterinarian and practices in Canton. (Courtesy of Pat Speer.)

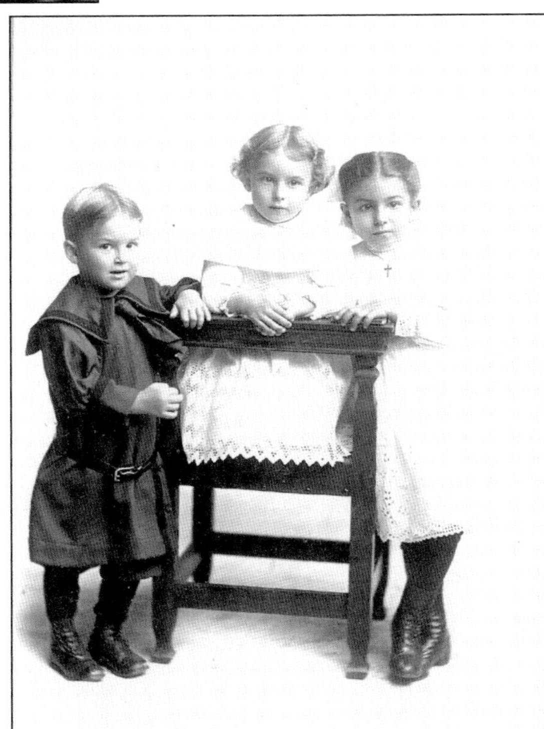

Three Little Charmers. These charming children, photographed in 1912, are members of the Magnan family. Their parents are Alex and Adelaide Dame Magnan of 8 Clinton Street in Potsdam. Shown, from left to right, are George, born in 1909; Lillian (on chair), born in 1907; and Teresa, born in 1905. The picture was taken at the Allen Studio. Later, Alex worked as a barber in Potsdam. (Courtesy of Ruth Garner.)

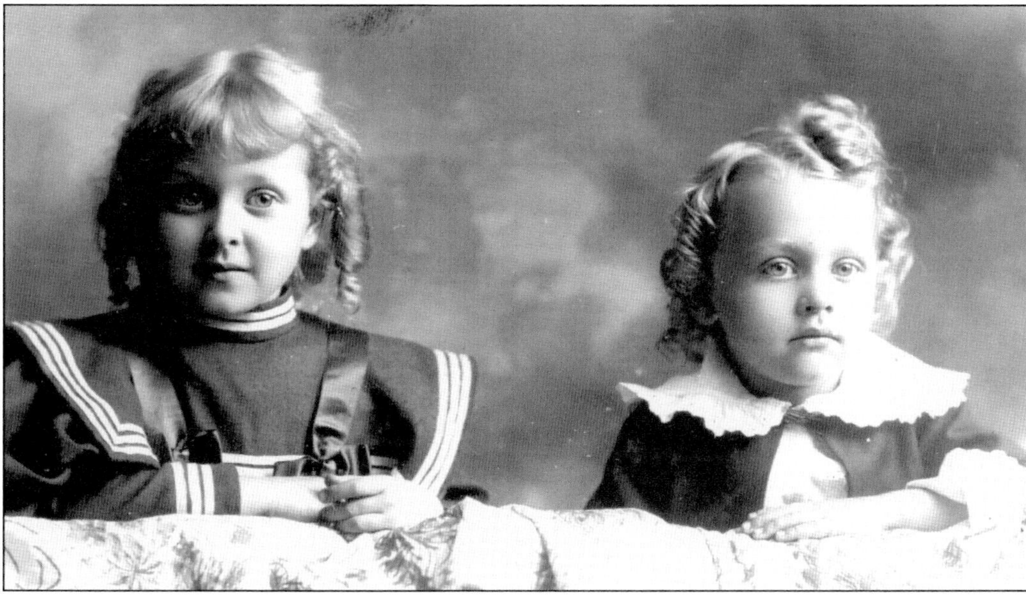

SISTER AND BROTHER FROM NATURAL DAM. Eula (born 1893) and Winfred McKenney (born 1897) were the children of Ida and John McKenney. Winfred married Mildred Maybee and had four children, Jean, Manley, Roberta, and Dick. They lived in Canton. Eula married James McCormick, who at one time was a St. Lawrence County Sheriff. Eula taught piano and lived a long life, residing in Canton and in later years, Gouverneur. Eula and James had two sons, James and Malcolm. (Courtesy of Malcolm McCormick.)

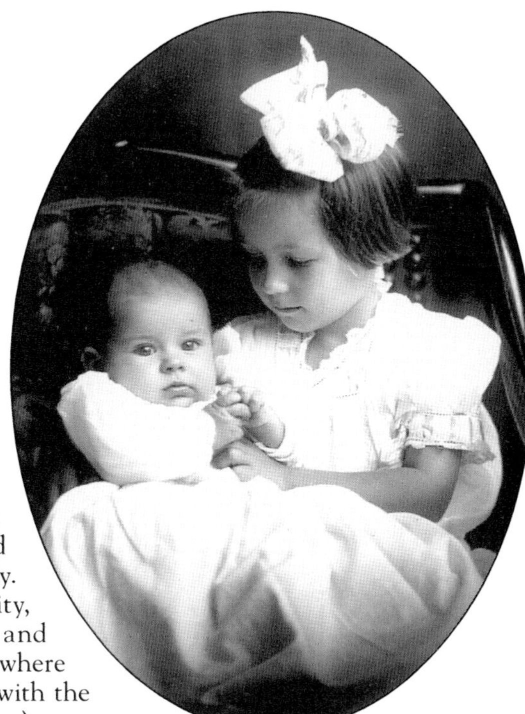

SISSON SISTERS. Margaret Thompson Sisson (1906) and Barbara King Sisson (1910) were the daughters of F. T. E. Sisson Sr. and Sarah Thompson Sisson from Malone. They lived in Potsdam among a large extended family. Barbara eventually moved to New York City, where she worked with the Red Cross, and Margaret went to Sante Fe, New Mexico, where she made her living as a pianist and worked with the Sante Fe Opera. (Courtesy of Robin Wilkinson.)

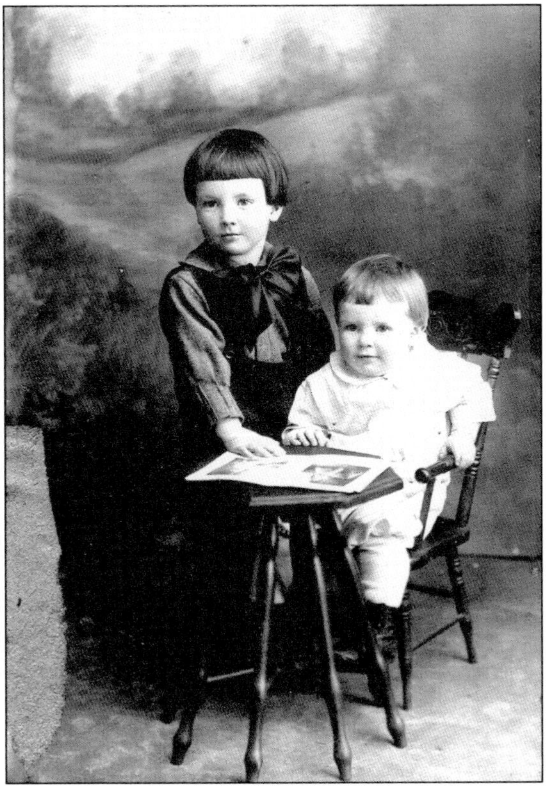

TWO LITTLE BOYS SHARING A BOOK. Brothers Donald (left) and Robert MacLeod of Canton posed for this picture in 1920. They were the children of Bill and Bernice Toomey MacLeod. The MacLeod family owned a large house on the right side of East Main Street where they ran a tourist home at one time. The house is no longer standing. The brothers served overseas in the Army during World War II. After the war, Donald worked for many years as a desk clerk at the Hotel Harrington. Robert (Bub) moved to Herkimer, New York. (Courtesy of Patricia Dominie.)

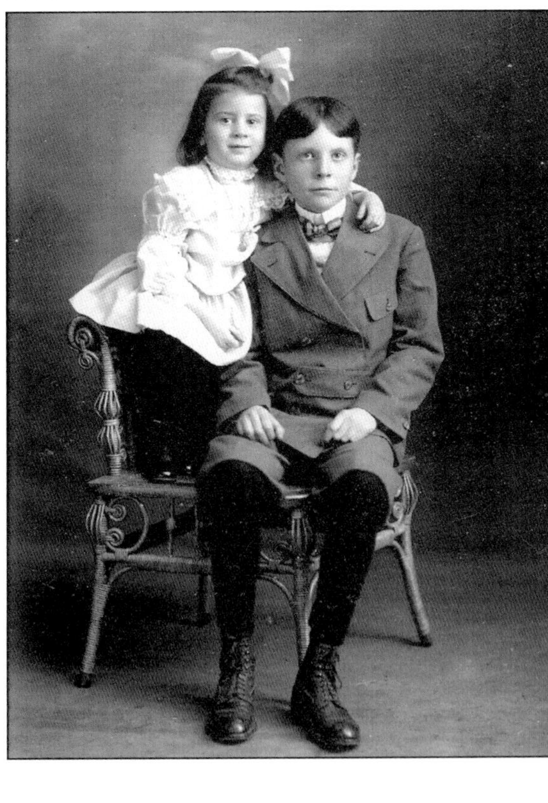

MARSHALL SIBLINGS. Standing on a chair is Edyth Marshall, with her older brother, Charles, beside her. The siblings were born on a farm outside Gouverneur that specialized in raising Ayrshire cattle. They were the children of John and Mary Belle Marshall. They attended Gouverneur schools and both went on to further their educations. Charles was a captain in the army in World War II. After the war he moved to Tucson, Arizona, and worked for General Electric. He married Elizabeth Hollister and they had two children. Edyth was a hospital superintendent and married George Elmer of Canton; they had one son. (Courtesy of the Elmer family.)

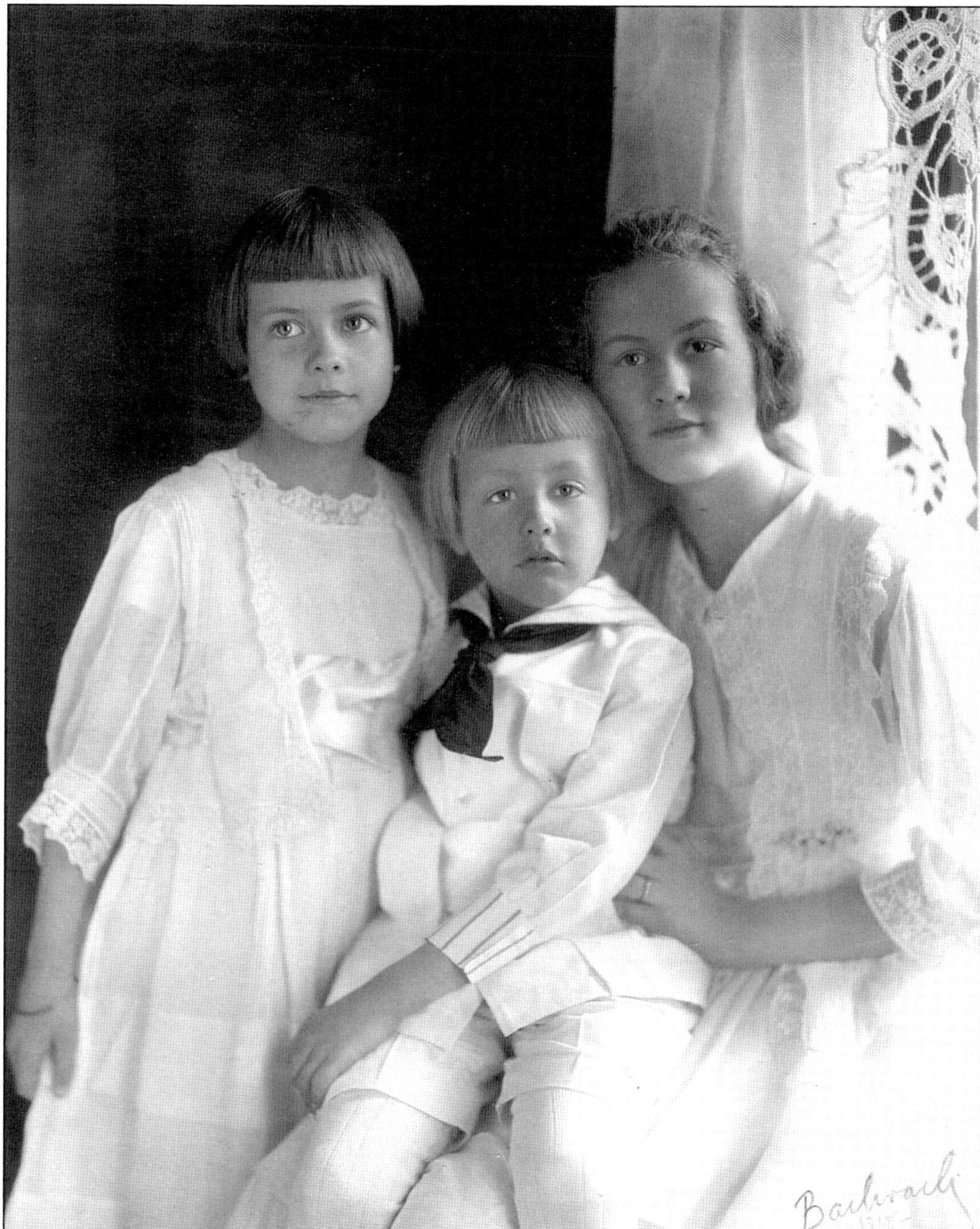

POTSDAM, 1918. This portrait is, from left to right, of Barbara King Sisson (8 years old), Francis T. E. Sisson Jr. (5 years old), and Margaret Thompson Sisson (12 years old). Frank, as Francis was generally known, was the only sibling to stay in St. Lawrence County. He was a graduate of the University of North Carolina at Chapel Hill. He worked with the family-owned Raquette River Paper Company and he also sold insurance. He was a member of the Potsdam Hospital Board of Trustees for 24 years and president for 10 years. He was also a member of the St. Lawrence County National Bank Board of Directors. (Courtesy of Robin Wilkinson.)

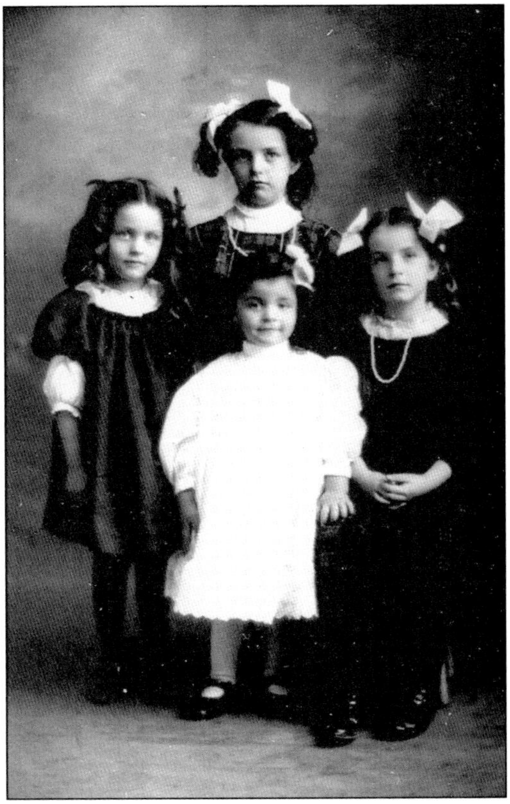

The Armstrong Sisters. These are the children of Judson and May Walker Armstrong. The girls, so elegantly dressed for their portrait and adorned with hair ribbons and necklaces, are Ola, Vanesha, Doris, and Carrie May. All four became wives and mothers. Two sisters graduated from St. Lawrence University, one became a nurse, and it is thought that the fourth sister was a housewife. (Courtesy of Mary Ruth Judd.)

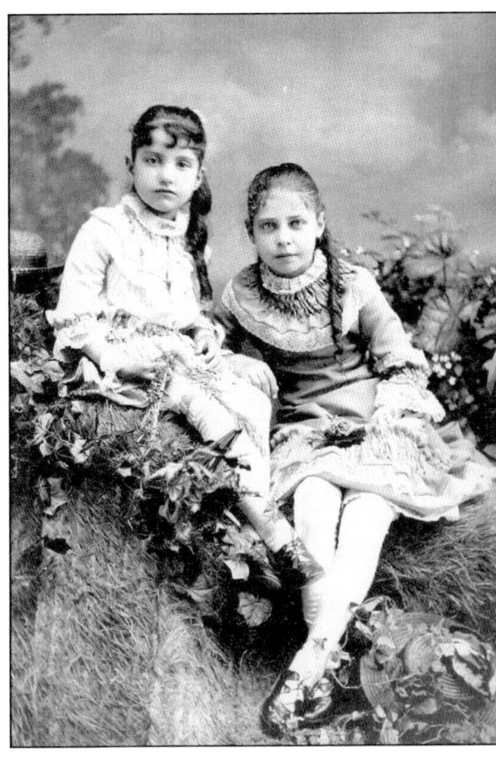

In the Good Old Summertime. The Thomas Studio took this picture of sisters Nora and Blanche Hodgken of Gouverneur in June, 1882. The unique setting that shows the girls posed on bales of hay, adorned with leaves and flowers, is most innovative, displaying the photographer's talent and creativity. (Courtesy of SLCHA.)

Three

CHILDREN AT PLAY

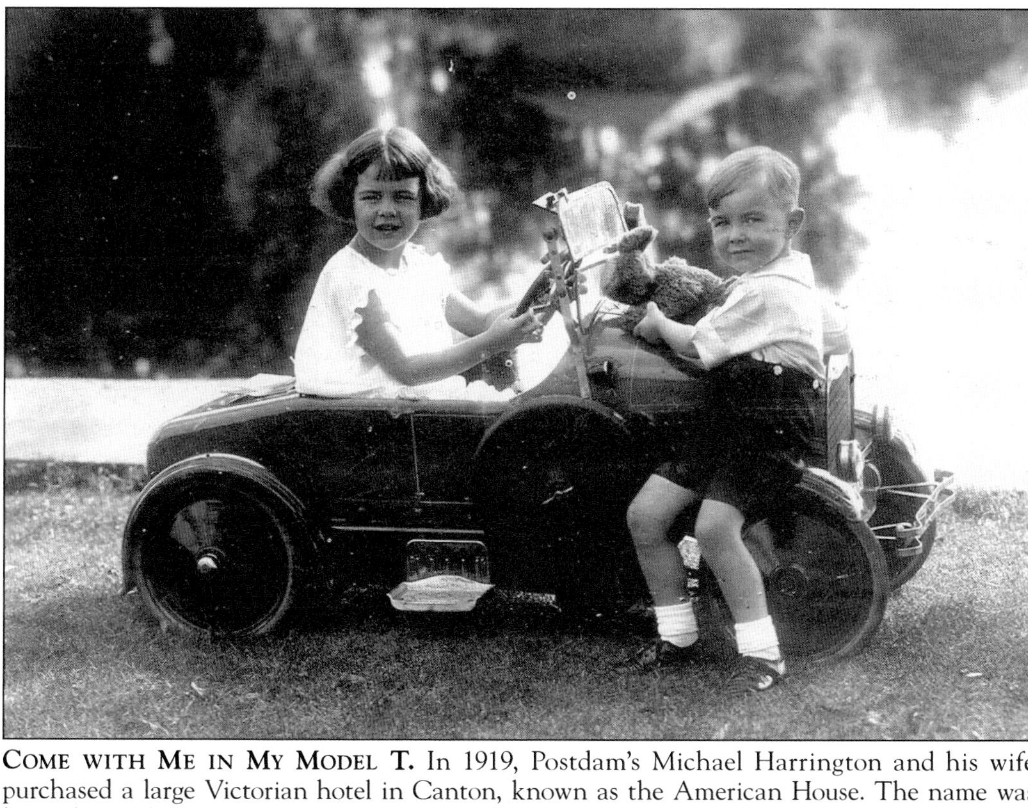

COME WITH ME IN MY MODEL T. In 1919, Postdam's Michael Harrington and his wife purchased a large Victorian hotel in Canton, known as the American House. The name was later changed to the Hotel Harrington. Playing on the hotel grounds on their new roadster are the two older Harrington children, Jean (five) and Jack (three). The roadster featured a running board, spare tire, and rumble seat. The 1920s were a time of peace and prosperity, and expensive toys were in vogue. In later years, Jean became a wife and mother of two, and Jack performed on Broadway. (Courtesy of Patricia Harrington Carson.)

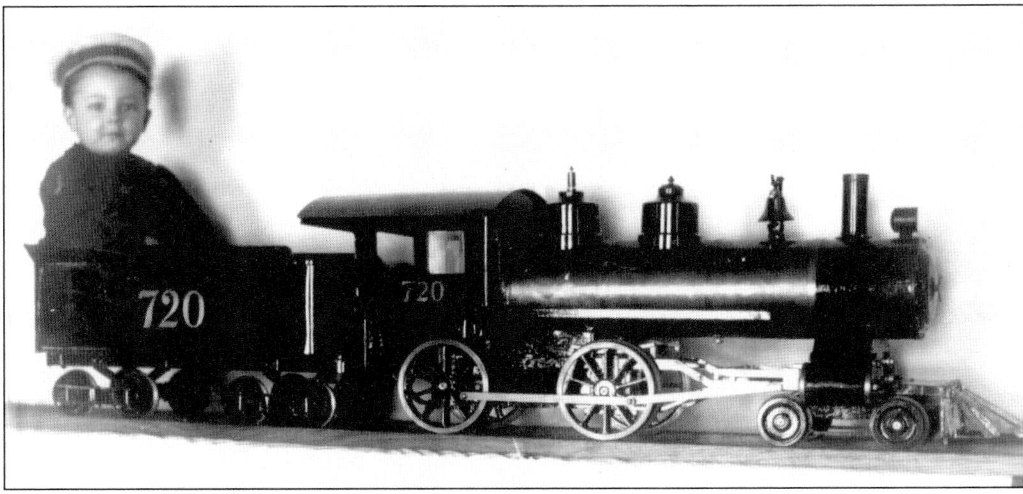

CHILDHOOD DREAMS. Young Silas Malterner of Canton sits aboard his personal locomotive. In later years, Silas became a railroad engineer and machinist with the railroad. The railroad was integral to transportation and economic development of this time period (1850–1920). It was the predominant method of travel. On September 3, 1859, a travel agent in Potsdam sold 805 tickets. The Northern Railroad of New York was built in the 1850s to connect New England with Lake Ontario by way of Ogdensburg. Later trains could not compete with the convenience of highway, air and bus travel. Passenger service on the Rutland disappeared in 1960. (Courtesy of St. Lawrence County Historian's Office.)

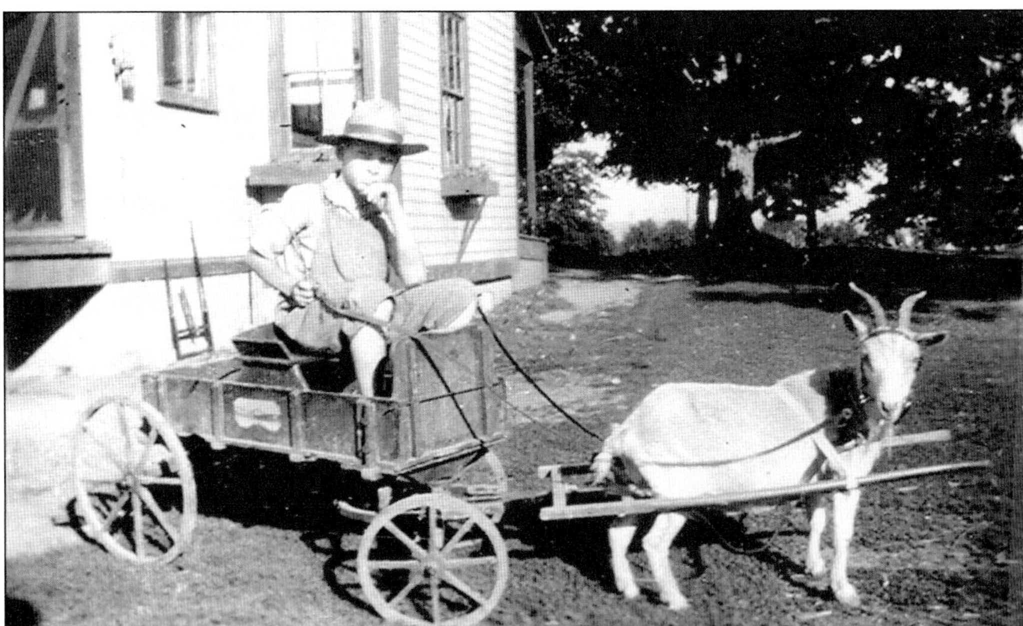

HOME DELIVERY. At 10 years old, Mark Hanna is ready to make his deliveries in his handmade cart drawn by one of the family's goats. His wagon was named "Fast Express." The Hannas' farm was in the Lisbon area. Mark's wagon was a favorite plaything, and with his loyal big-eyed companion, he was able to deliver fresh vegetables to friends on nearby farms. (Courtesy of Elsie Taylor.)

Biking Is Great Fun. Dorothy M. Clements (born 1914) and her uncle, Frederick R. Clements (1904), are having great fun on a tricycle on what appears to be a beautiful summer day. Both went on to graduate from St. Lawrence University in Canton. Dorothy worked as a teacher before her marriage to Peter Krug in 1937. Their family eventually moved to Syracuse and later to Maywood, New Jersey. (Courtesy of Bill Hull.)

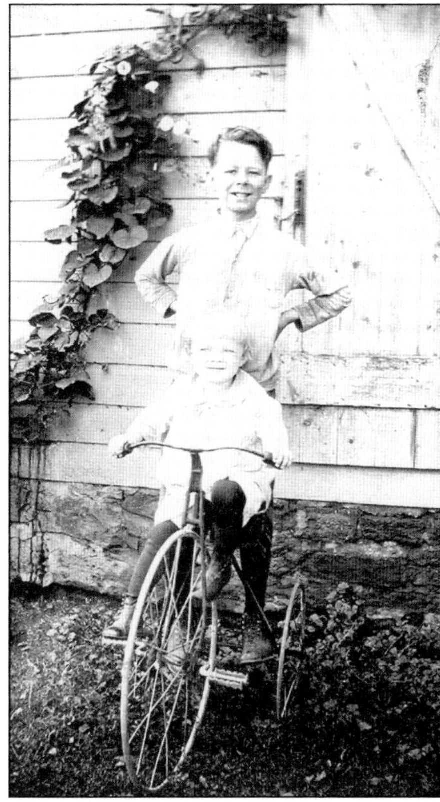

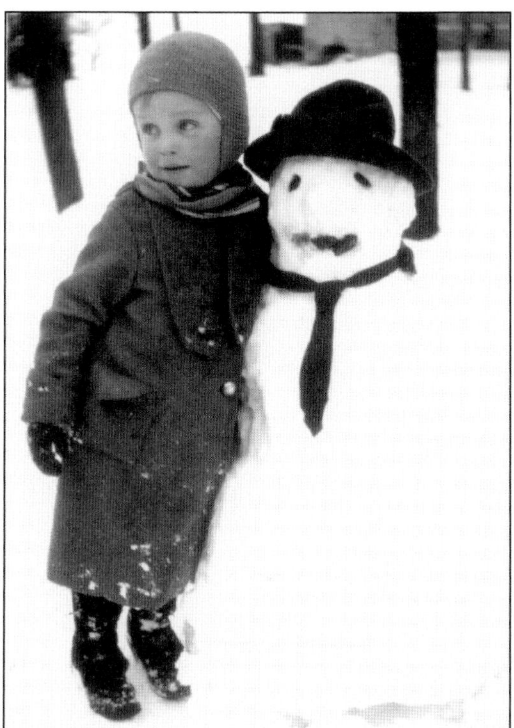

Snowman. James F. McCormick Jr. was born in 1921. He graduated from Canton High School and played trumpet with a professional dance band (Joe Caliparis) through his years at St. Lawrence University. He enlisted in the U.S. Air Force in 1942 and flew liaison reconnaissance in France and Germany through World War II. In 1945, he was stationed at Brooksfield, Texas. While en route to Washington, D.C. to take part in a program of events honoring Gen. Henry Arnold, McCormick was killed. (Courtesy of Malcolm McCormick.)

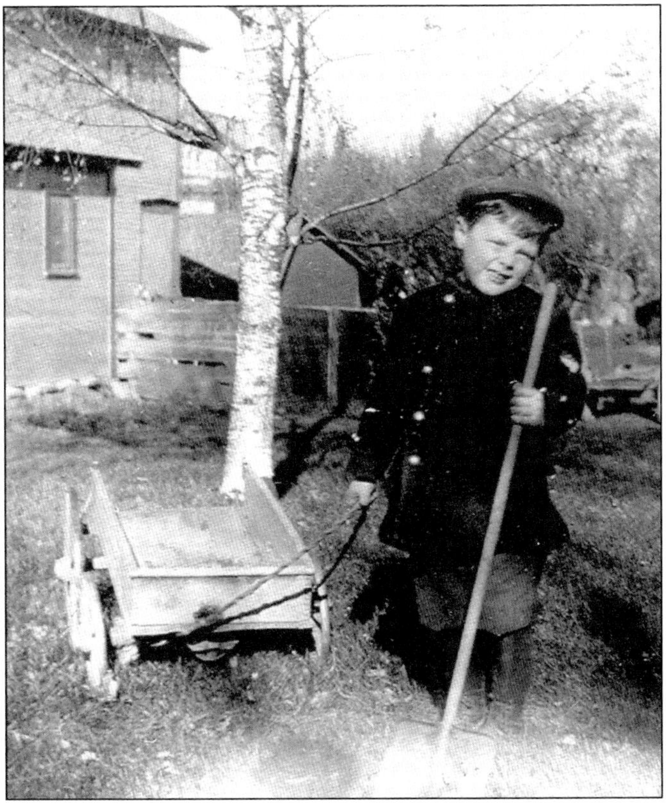

Hopkinton Landmark. Clark Chittenden is pictured with his wagon outside the family's granary and feed mill that was part of the Chittenden General Merchandise in Hopkinton. The store was a local landmark for 150 years. Clark married Sara Clark in 1927 at her family home at 80 Main Street in Potsdam. He ran the store and was later town supervisor of Hopkinton and chairman of the county board of supervisors. (Courtesy of Varick Chittenden.)

J. Henry Rushton and Buddies. J. Henry Rushton (center front) was one of Canton's better-known personalities. He was born in Edwards in 1843. As a youth he spent most of his time hunting and fishing. In 1869, he hiked to Cranberry Lake to go trout fishing. While there he met up with two Canton businessmen, Joseph Ellsworth and Milton D. Packard. This chance meeting paved the way to his future career in boat and canoe building. His workshop, a large four-story building, was located on Water Street, now known as Riverside Drive, in Canton. At the Chicago World's Fair in 1893, Rushton displayed a full line of his work in full scale and in miniature forms. By this time he had achieved world fame as a champion canoe builder. (Courtesy of SLCHA.)

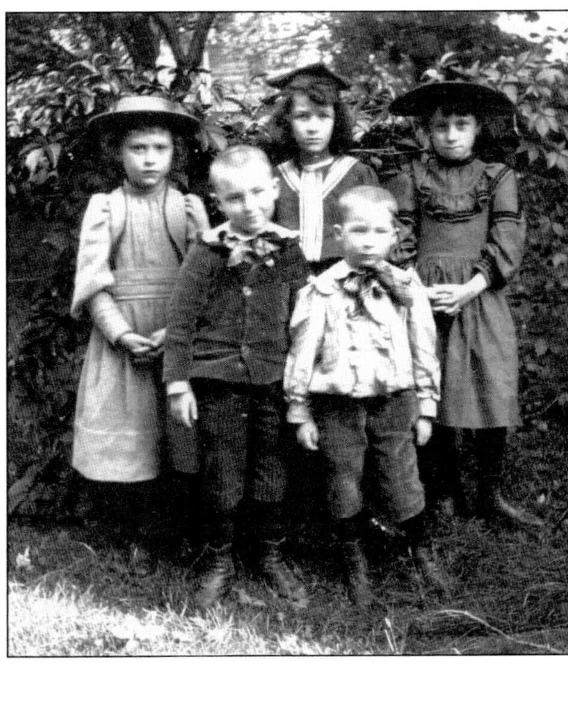

COUSINS FROM WEST STOCKHOLM AND DOWNERVILLE. Cousins Ruth Demmon and William Benjamin had their picture taken at the George Bartholomew Studio in Russell in 1908. William, the son of Stanley and Lillian McCauslin Benjamin, was born in West Stockholm, in 1904, in the Benjamin homestead, which still stands in a prominent position facing the river. The Benjamin family owned the St. Lawrence Creamery in Potsdam which was operated by William until the mid- to late 1900s. Ruth was born in Downerville (presently an abandoned settlement in the town of Russell). Her parents were U. S. and Anna McCauslin Demmon. She married Gerald Kerr of Fine and taught in many rural schools. (Courtesy of Jean Given.)

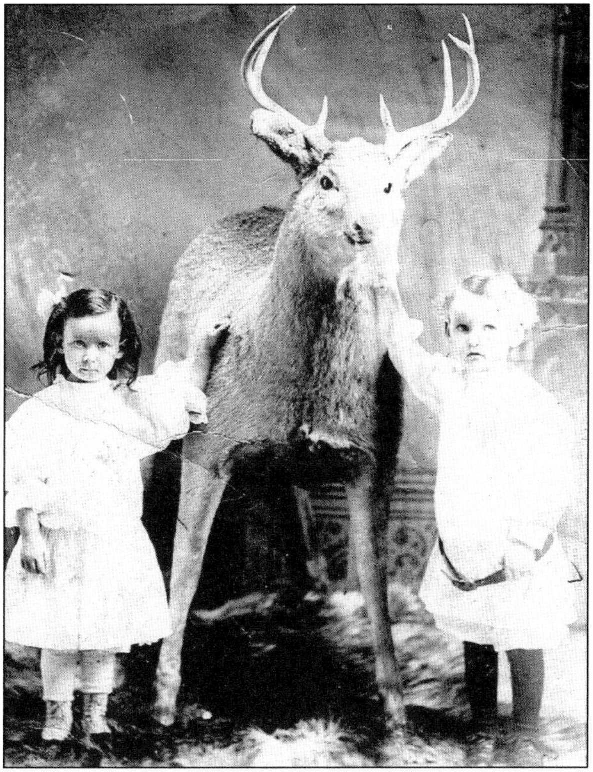

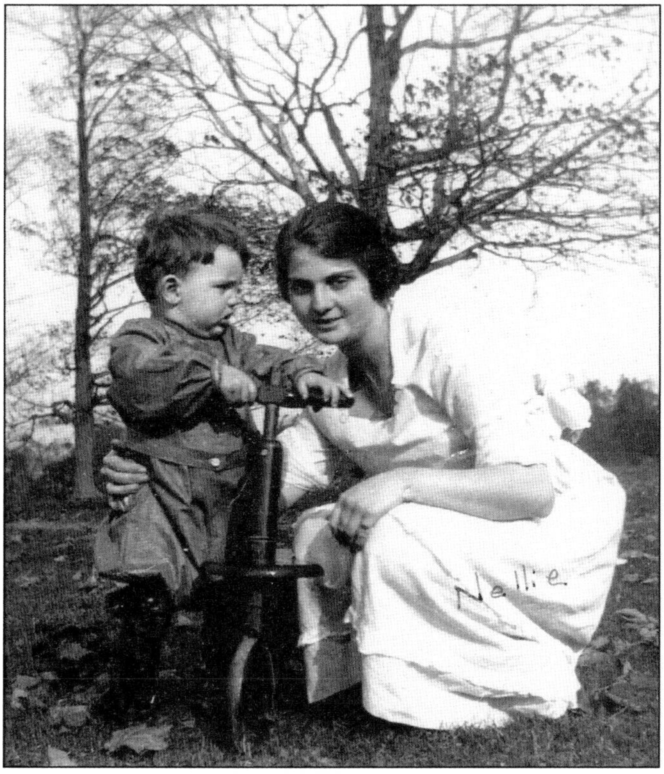

BORN 1900 IN HAMMOND. Nellie Phillips is shown here with a little friend who is holding on to his scooter. Nellie was the daughter of Dyer and Harriet Beasley Phillips from Lisbon. Her father, a stone mason, came from England and owned a stone quarry in South Hammond. Later, the family ran a farm near Ogdensburg. There were 15 children in the family. Nellie became a schoolteacher later in life. She died in 1975 and was buried in White Church Cemetery in Lisbon. (Courtesy of Elsie Taylor.)

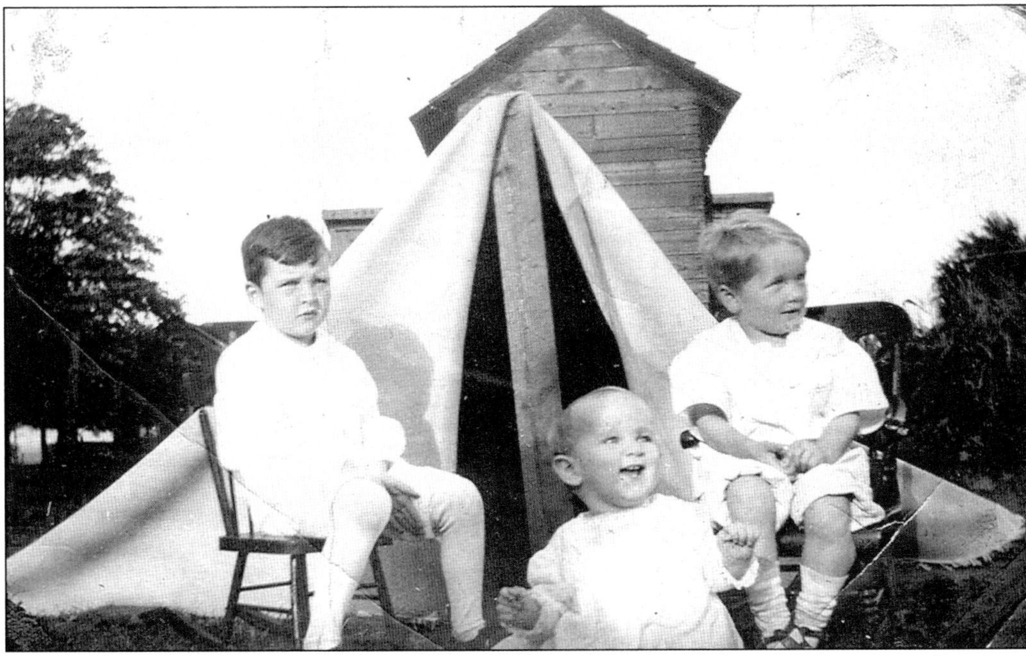

A Colorful Uncle. Robert (left), Leo (center), and Bernard Flynn are enjoying their time outdoors. They always looked forward to visits from their Uncle Patrick, who had moved to New Haven, Connecticut. Patrick earned the reputation as the family's black sheep because of the bootlegging enterprise he operated. He traveled in style, complete with a bodyguard and chauffeur in a silver Cadillac that had bullet holes in the car's exterior. Patrick had a twin sister Jane who was known for her piety, which was thought to be her attempt at ameliorating the eternal punishment that no doubt was coming Patrick's way. (Courtesy of Barbara Lee.)

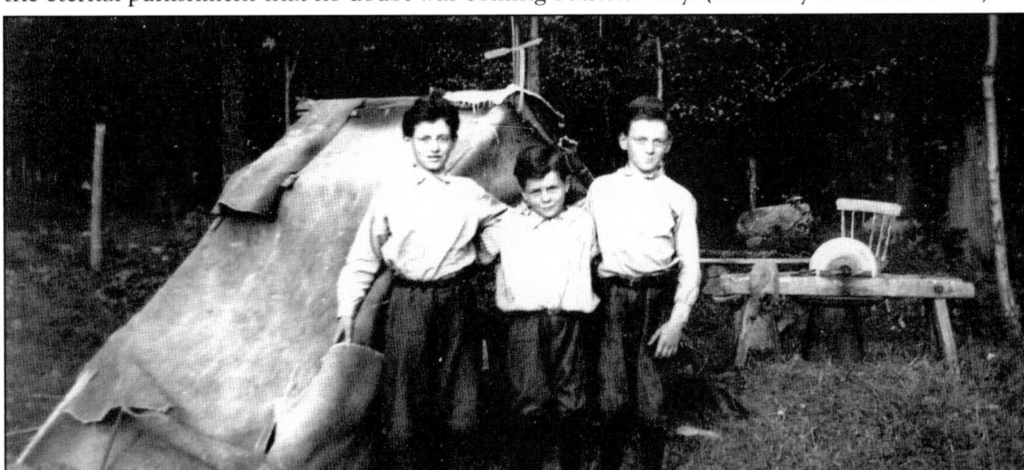

Backyard Camping. Kenneth (left), Fay (center), and Leland Young of Hermon are having a great time camping in the summer of 1919. Note the foot-operated grindstone used for sharpening axes, knives, and other tools in the background. The boys were the sons of Frank F. and Katie Oakes Young. All were born in the town of Hermon. Kenneth (born 1910) married Esther Helena Bice and had three children. Fay Hubert (born 1912) married Helen Marie Ehlers and had two children. Leland (born 1908) married Elizabeth Alice Conger of Brier Hill and had eight children. (Courtesy of Norman Young.)

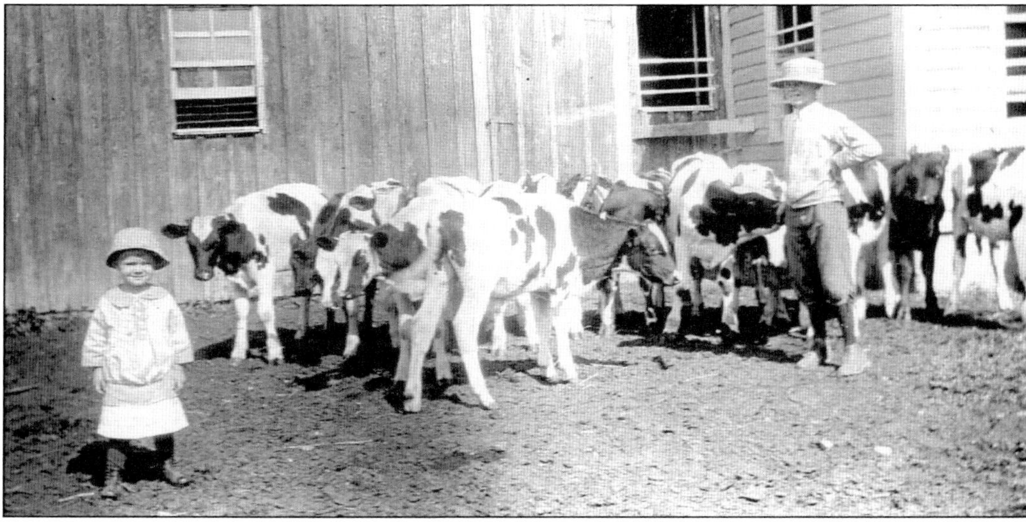

HOLSTEIN CALVES. Dorothy M. Clements, born in 1914, is shown here with her uncle Frederick R. Clements, born in 1904. They are tending the newborn Holsteins. Dorothy was the daughter of Ralph and Fanny Engert Clements of Dannsville. Fred graduated from St. Lawrence University in 1931 and became principal of Oswegatchie High School. This photograph was taken at the W. W. Clements Farm in Lisbon. (Courtesy of Bill Hull.)

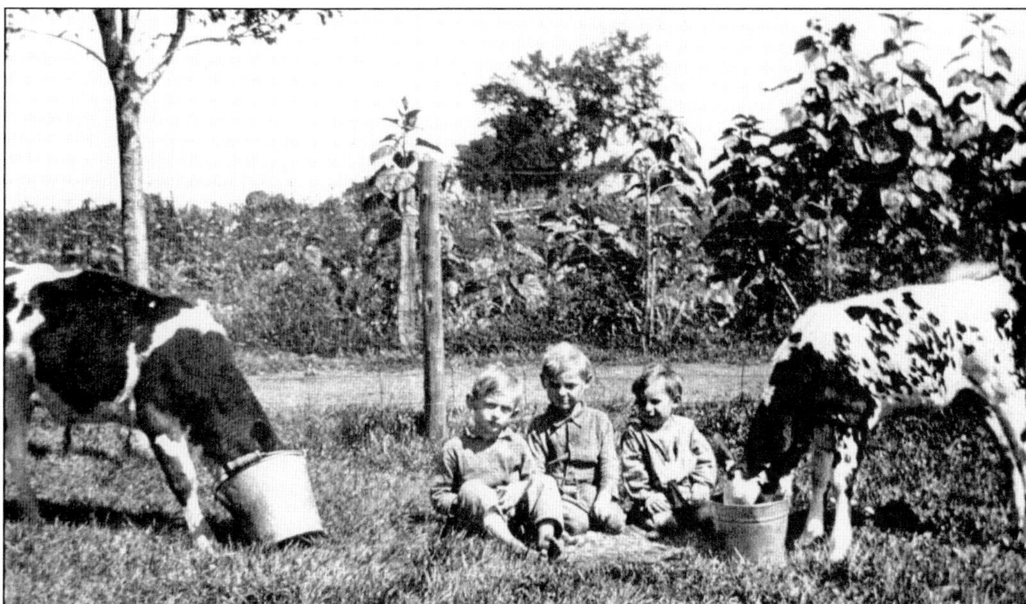

THE FAMILY FARM. This pastoral setting shows one of the many aspects of St. Lawrence County, and helps to reveal the charm of these children. In the early days, local residents, as well as incoming immigrants, owned and raised their families on various-sized dairy farms. In 1898, the most common cows to be found in the county were Ayrshires, Jerseys, Holsteins, Guernseys, and Durhams. The farms were self-sufficient and met most of the needs of the family. Dairy products, meat, vegetables, honey, wool, berries, maple syrup, and building materials were all available locally. Adults and children worked long hours, and the farm was passed down from generation to generation. (Courtesy of SLCHA.)

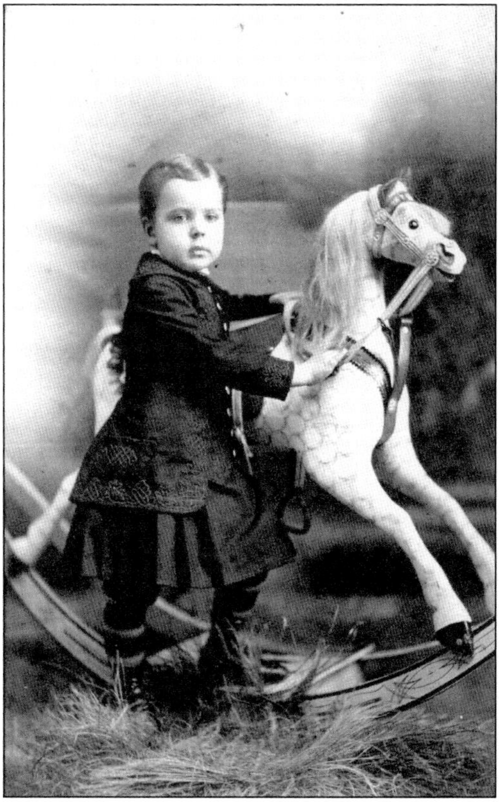

TREASURED TOY. Canton's young Charles Dean Laidlaw appears to treasure his rocking horse. He was the son of C. D. Laidlaw of 5 Pine Street. It is said that as a youth he walked a Jersey cow to pasture each day for Alvin Wallace, a neighbor on Park Street, who paid him 35¢ a week. Charles graduated from St. Lawrence University in 1926, and pursued a medical degree after leaving Canton. (Courtesy of SLCHA.)

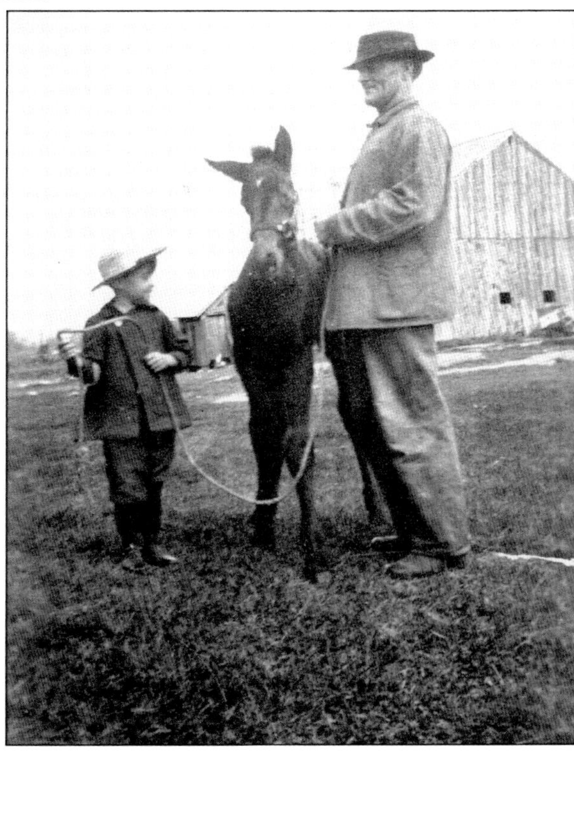

PYRITES FAMILY FARM. This is a picture of Johnny Toomey and his nephew, Bernard, at the family farm on the Pyrites Road around 1900. Johnny and brother Dennis, sons of Daniel and Katherine Hayes Toomey, learned blacksmith skills from their Irish immigrant father, and continued to run the family farm after Daniel's death. Five generations of Toomey sons lived on the farm into the 1970s. (Courtesy of Pat Dominie.)

MY KINGDOM FOR A HORSE. Harlan and his older brother, Bill Infantine Jr., are seen here as happy as can be riding their pony. It was a time when families could keep a pony in the village, as many of the homes had large backyards or adjoining fields along with barns. The Infantine home was on Gouverneur Street. The Infantine children would oftentimes ride their ponies in parades, as well as just around the neighborhood. (Courtesy of Marilyn Mintener.)

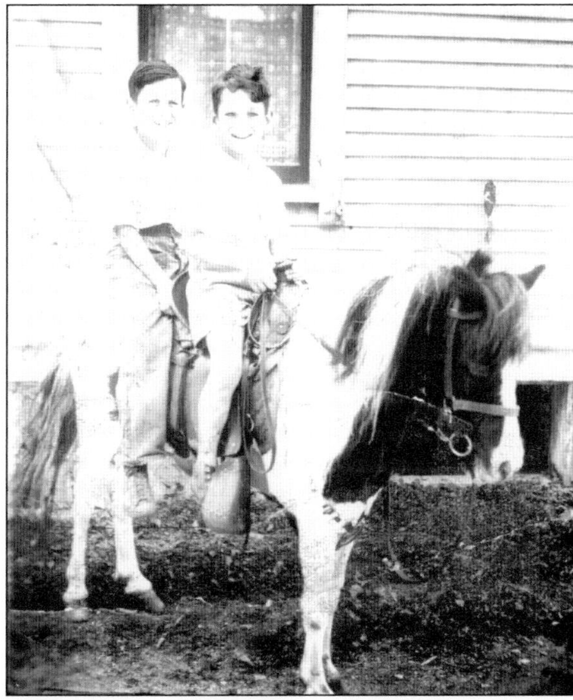

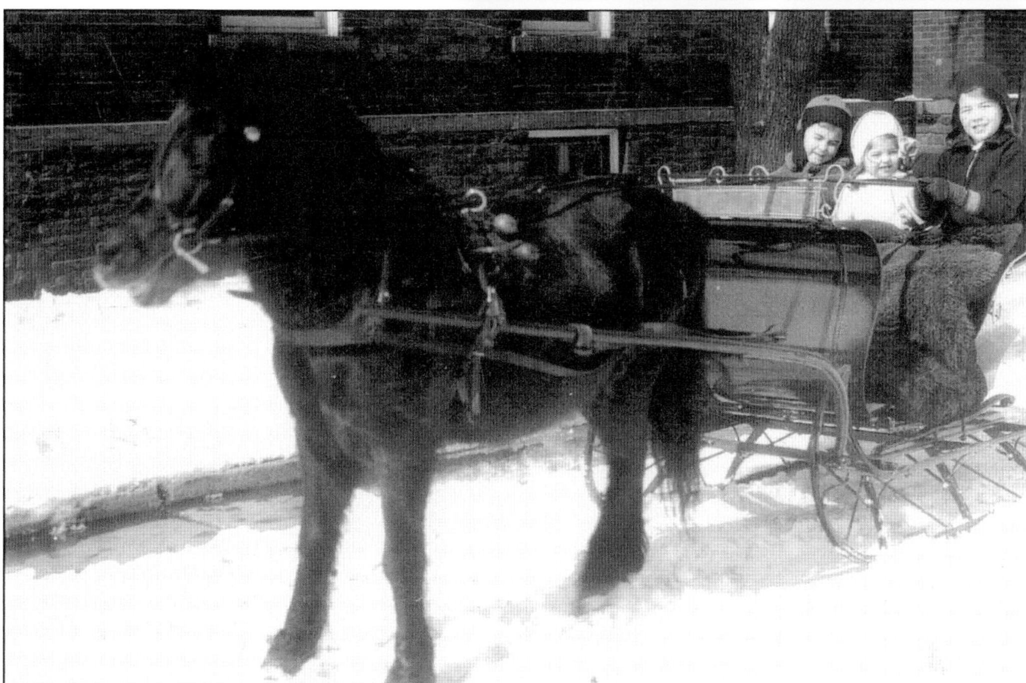

OH WHAT FUN IT IS TO RIDE. Warmly dressed and ready to ride, covered with a fur robe, are the three Harrington children, Jean (left), Jack (center), and Patty. They are riding in a sleigh drawn by their Shetland pony Brownie. The children are off to traverse Canton's snow-covered roads. This was a familiar outing for them, and Brownie knew their route by heart. This photograph was taken by Dwight P. Church. (Courtesy of Patricia Harrington Carson.)

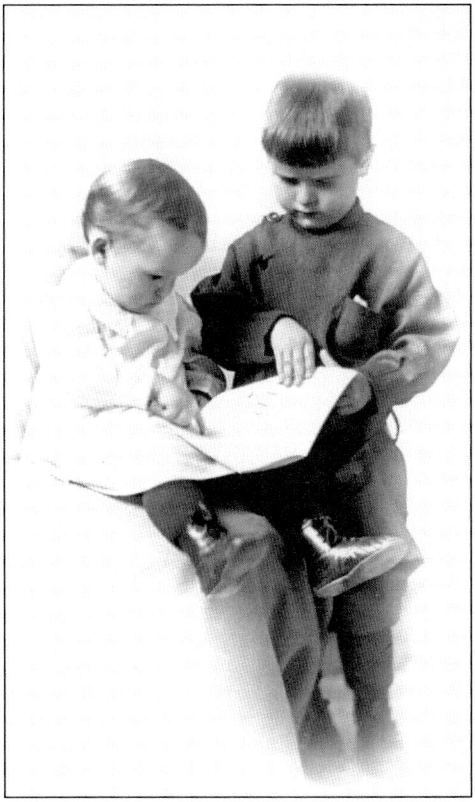

GUNNISON AND ELLSWORTH. Walter Gunnison is pictured here sharing a book with his older cousin, Joseph C. Ellsworth. Joseph was the grandson of Joseph B. Ellsworth, who owned and ran the Ellsworth shoe store, and the son of J. Stanley, who took over the store from his grandfather. The store was located almost directly across the road from the red-brick Ellsworth family home, next to the town hall. Young Joe graduated from St. Lawrence University as did his wife, Ethel Sanford. She was the daughter of Dr. Frank and Mrs. Sanford. The couple had three children. (Courtesy of SLCHA Archives.)

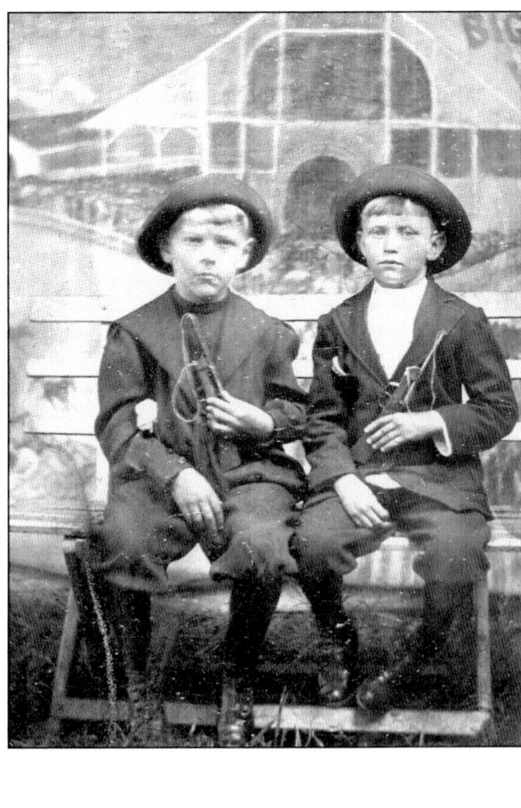

A DAY AT THE LAKE. This picture was taken at the St. Lawrence County fair in Canton around 1910. These two boys took time out to have their picture taken. The two friends are Milo Dean (left) and Harry Collins who came from Clare to take in the horse races and shows. Milo was the son of Herbert and Nellie Clintsman. Herb and Nellie were caretakers for the state of New York at the Cranberry Lake dam from around 1910 to 1960. (Courtesy of Gary Bushaw.)

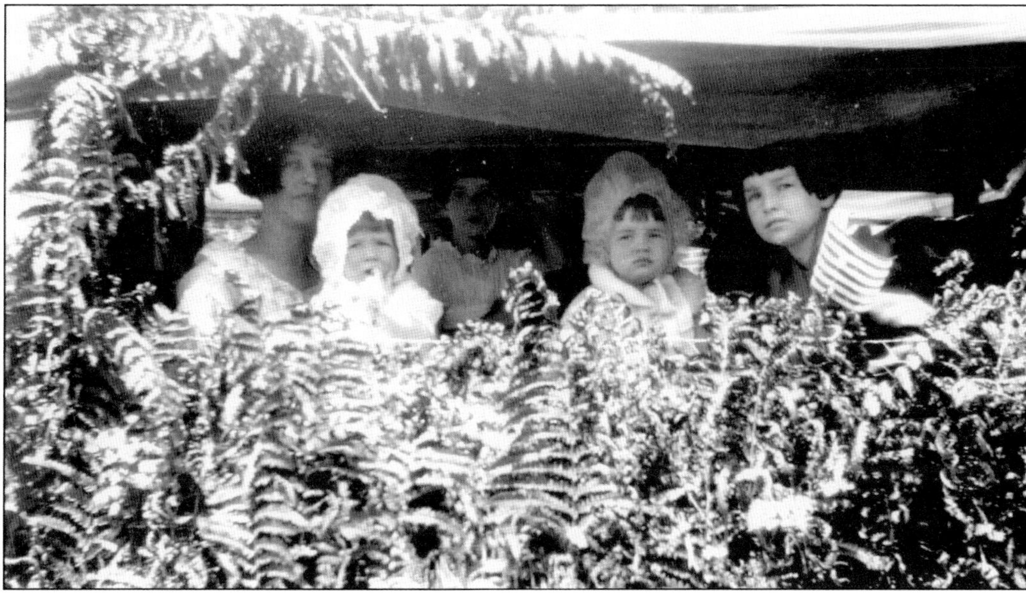

THE GLORIOUS FOURTH, 1925. Parades and festivities abounded in the 1920s. These Canton children are all dressed up for the occasion, riding in a lavishly decorated float which was sponsored by the Sullivan Garage on lower Main Street. The children are ready to join the bands and the other floats. The little girl to the left, in the white hat, is Mary Margaret Sullivan, one of the daughters of the garage owner. (Courtesy of Patricia Harrington.)

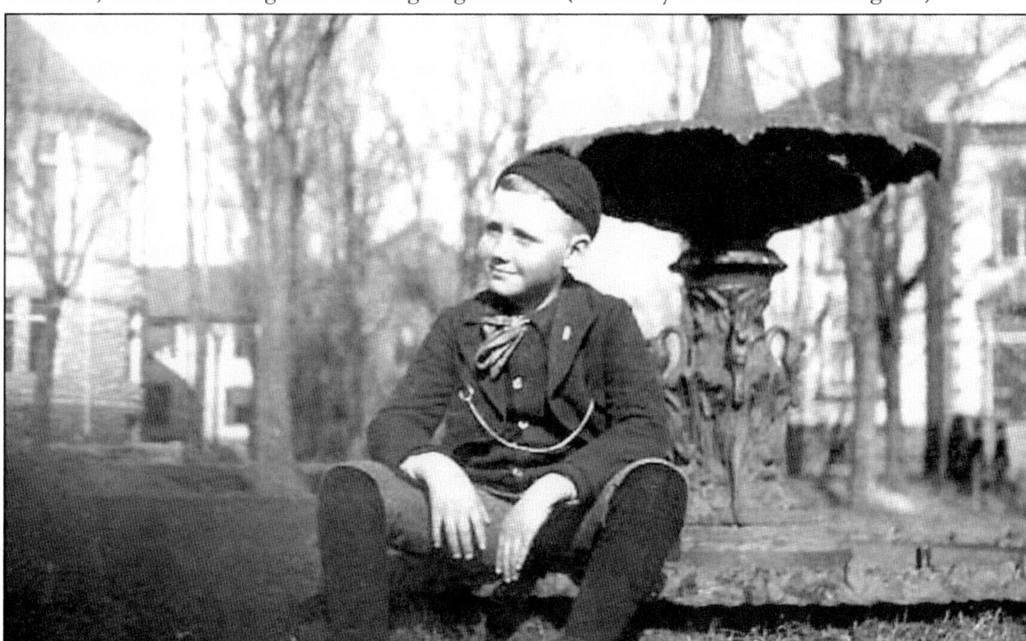

FUTURE DR. CONKEY. Young Ogden Conkey, the son of Mr. and Mrs. George Conkey, enjoys a day in the sun in the little park, which was then located on the corner of Court and Pearl Streets. At the time, the Conkey home stood across the road. Ogden later became a doctor, living and practicing medicine in Jackson Heights. In later years, he and his family spent many summers in the family home. (Courtesy of SLCHA.)

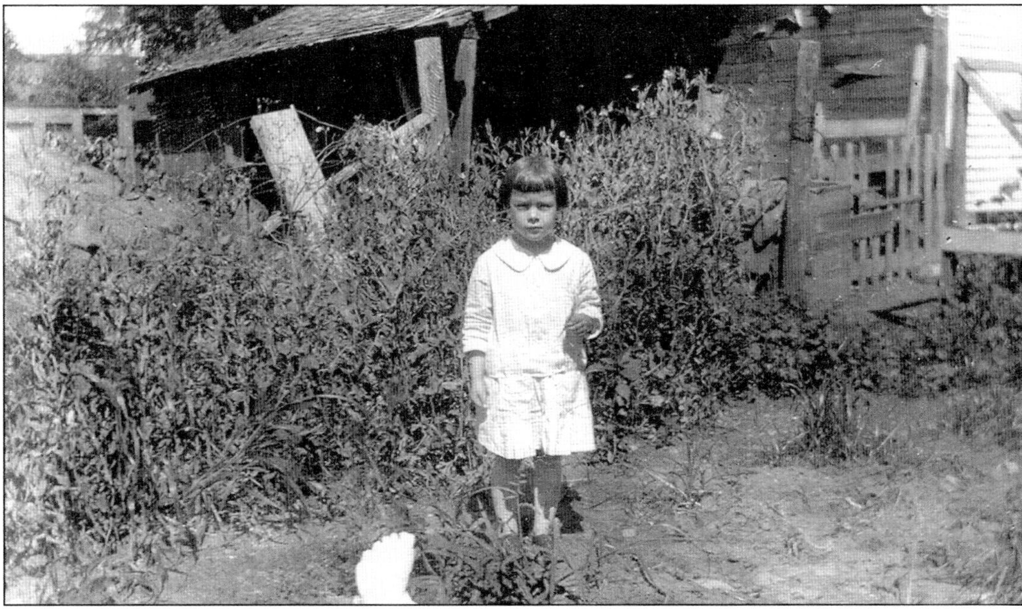

In the Barnyard. Virginia Ruth Chase was born on March 6, 1918. She is the daughter of Giles Aquila Chase and Edith Hall of Massena. Virginia attended Massena Schools and graduated high school in 1935. She graduated from the University of Kentucky in 1940 and worked at Alcoa and Eastman Kodak Company. She married Earl W. Huff in 1957 and they had three children—two sons, David and Douglas and a daughter, Janice. Virgina's siblings are Giles Elihu, Lester H., William, Irene, Annette, and Mildred Chase. (Courtesy of the Chase family.)

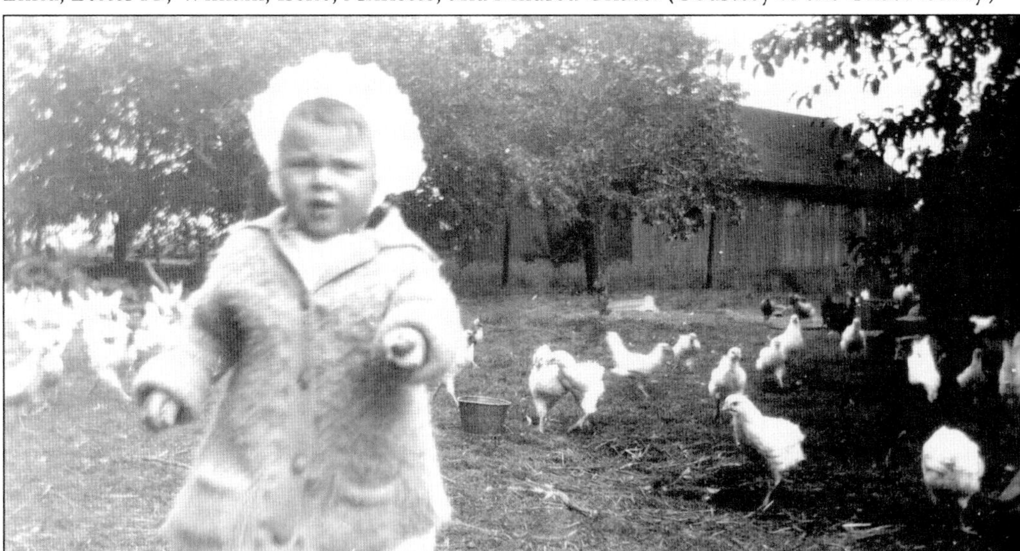

Catch Me If You Can. Little Carol Jean looks like she is trying to outrun the chickens. Perhaps she started out feeding them, but because there were so many of them, she quickly changed her mind. Children who grew up on farms in days gone by usually had their own daily chores, and feeding the animals was a favored one for the young. Dressed in a warm wool sweater and bonnet and running for all she was worth, Carol Jean and her friends make a great picture. (Picture courtesy of SLCHA.)

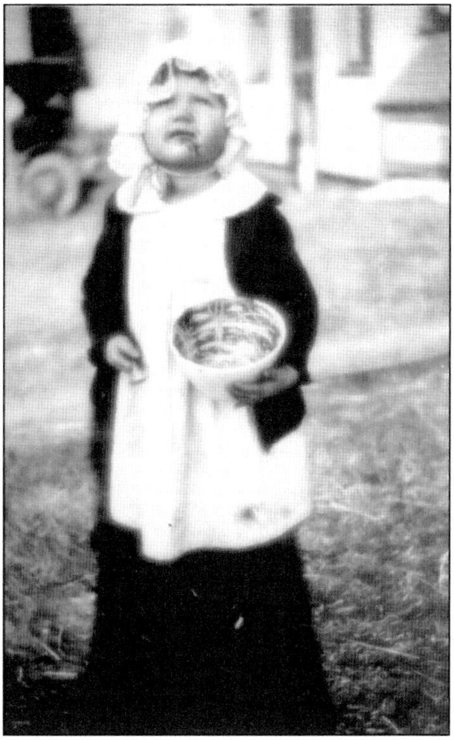

MARY RUTH BEAMAN ON THE FAMILY FARM IN RICHVILLE. Mary Ruth was born in Malone in 1918. In this picture she seems to be enjoying some chocolate pudding. Today Mary Ruth resides with her husband, Herb Judd, in the Judd family homestead on Farnes Road in Canton. They are both active members of the St. Lawrence County Historical Association. The Judd Gallery in the museum is named in their honor. (Courtesy of Mary Ruth Judd.)

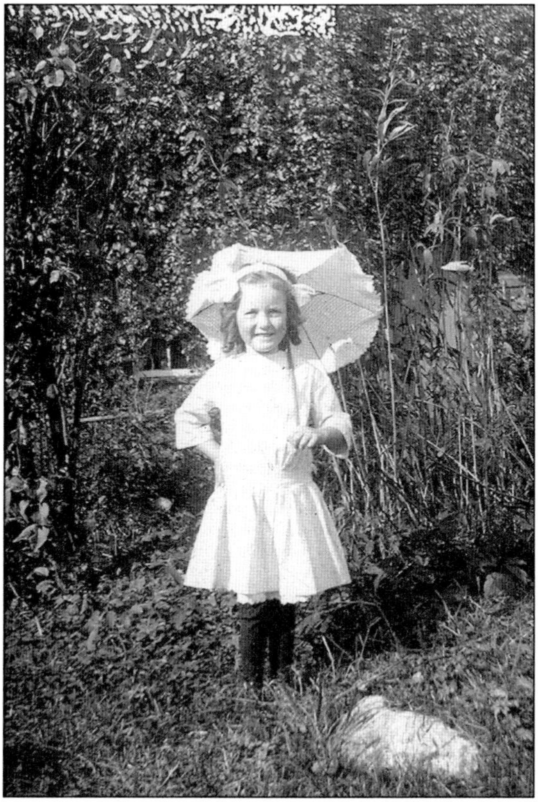

ENJOYED FISHING FOR TROUT. The picture is of Leta Clintsman standing in her backyard on a sunny day with her parasol in hand. Leta was the daughter of Albert "Bert" Clintsman and Addie Hull of Cranberry Lake. Leta enjoyed fishing with her father and mother. It was not unusual at the time to catch an 18-inch trout below the dam in Cranberry. Unfortunately, in 1916, Leta perished in a house fire, shortly after this picture was taken. (Courtesy of Gary Bushaw.)

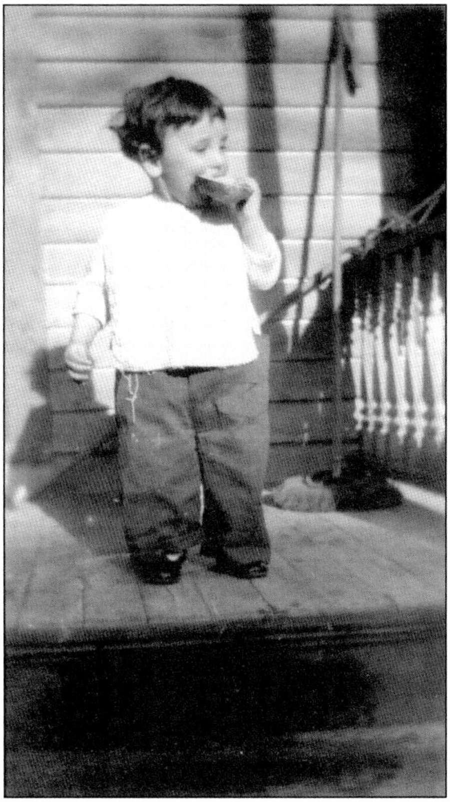

How Sweet a Boy. Enjoying his apple on a sunny day in 1920 is Edgar A. Newell. Edgar was the son of Albert P. and Ella Waterman Newell of Ogdensburg. This photograph was taken on the steps of the family home on Washington Street. The Newells later moved to 414 Green Street next to the Jewish Synagogue. Edgar became the chief financial officer of Newell Company. He spent his secondary school years at Deerfield Academy, attended Williams College, and graduated from Clarkson College of Technology in Potsdam, New York, in 1940.

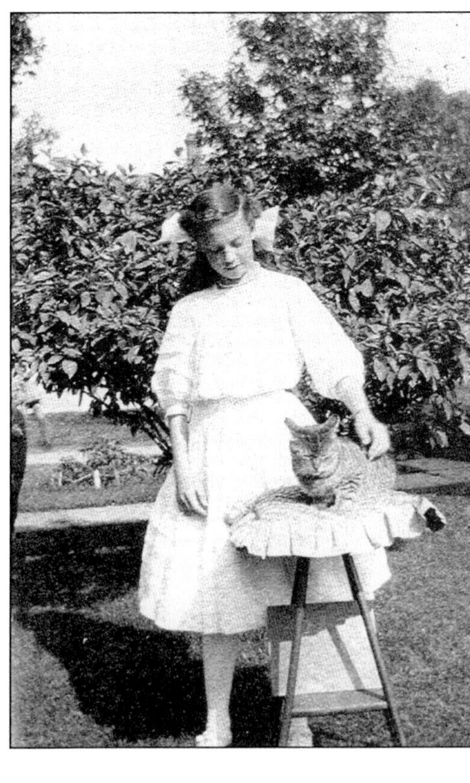

Little Girl with a Big Cat. This picture of Burnetta Sealy was on a postcard that she wrote to an aunt and uncle in Massachusetts in 1907. Burnetta and her sister, Emily, were the daughters of Walter and Lorena Sealy and lived on Cottage Street in Potsdam. Walter Sealy was mayor of Potsdam in the 1880s, and Burnetta and Emily raised their respective families there in later years. Burnetta wrote on the postcard that they were busy and expecting lots of company as "there is a circus here Thursday." (Courtesy of Dianne Hansen)

Four

FAMILIES

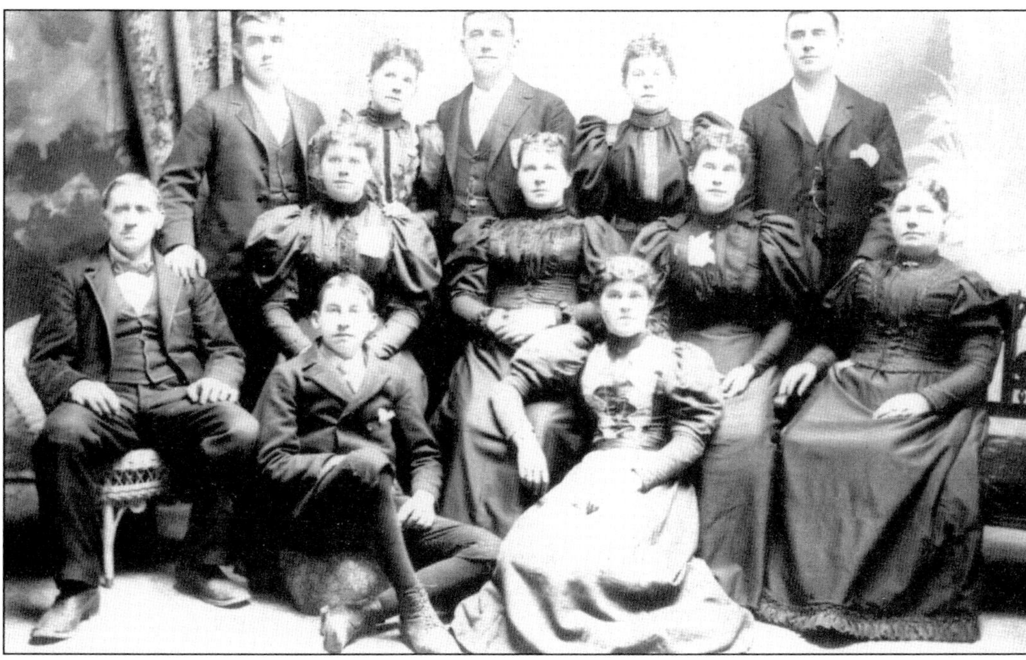

THE CASEY FAMILY. John Casey was born in Bantry, Ireland, in 1836, and immigrated to the United States in 1855. He and his wife Mary settled on a farm on Route 11 in Potsdam and raised 10 children. Shown here are, from left to right, (first row) Jeremiah, and Ella (Ford); (second row) John (their father), Hannah (Sullivan), Nora (Sullivan), Julia (Fitzgerald), and Mary (their mother); (third row) John, Katherine (O'Brien), William, Mamie (O'Brien), Patrick H. The names in parentheses are the married names of the women. (Courtesy of Nancy Casey.)

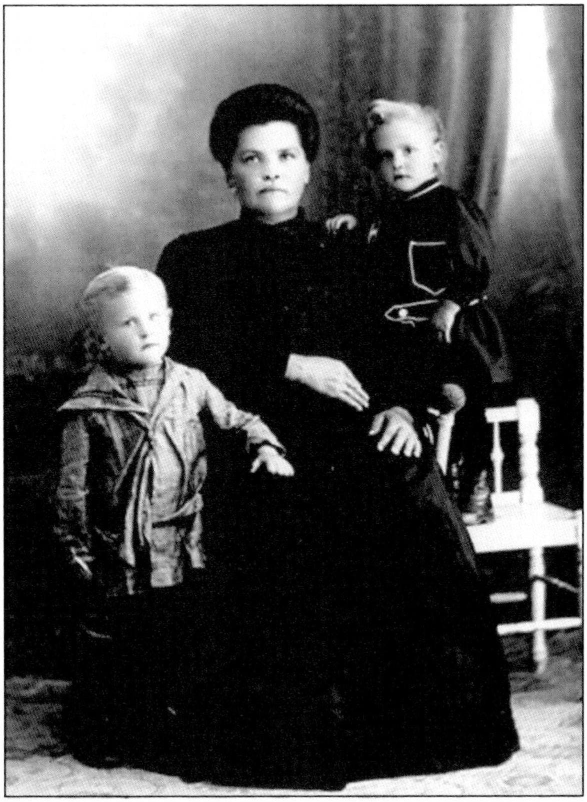

YOUNG WIDOW IN HELENA. Emma Beaulieu LaClair (1871–1922) poses with her two sons, Rufus (left) and Ernest. The photograph was taken in 1910, shortly after her husband, Wilfred, died. Wilfred and his brother, Joseph, were the sons of Francis LaClair and Felicite (Bissaillon) LaClair of Hogansburg. (Courtesy of Tom LaClair.)

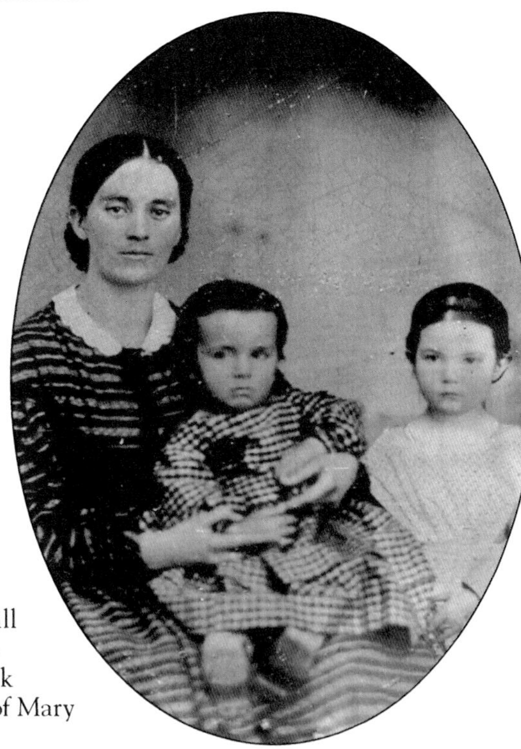

GO WEST, YOUNG MAN. Little William Walker seems content to sit in the arms of his mother, Emeline Spencer Walker, with his sister, Ruth, sitting close by. Brought up in Richville, the two children were the oldest of 13 siblings. After their mother's death, Ruth stayed home and took care of her brothers and sisters. Will ran away from home and ended up in northern Montana. Will died while out West and was brought home to be buried with his parents. Ruth married Frank Beaman and had one son, Daniel. (Courtesy of Mary Ruth Judd.)

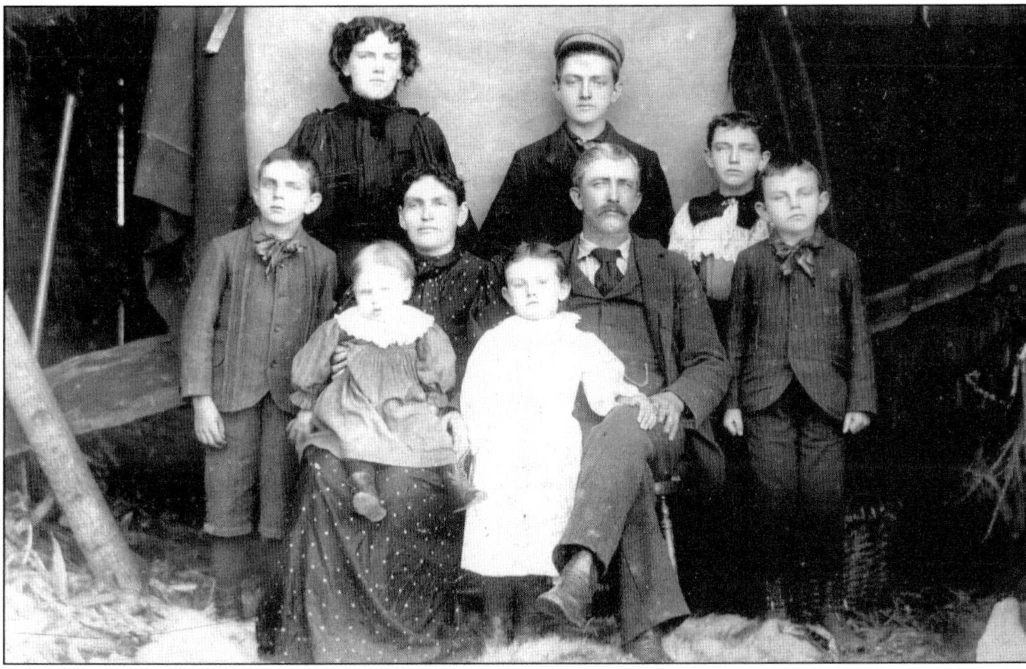

St. Lawrence River Dairy Farm. Here is a photograph of the Lorenzo and Mary (Curtis) Honeywell family. It was taken around 1895 on their farm on the border of St. Lawrence and Jefferson Counties. Lorenzo is the grandson of Richard Honeywell, who operated a farm, which eventually was sold to make up the property of the New York State Psychiatric Hospital at Ogdensburg. Mary and Lorenzo are seated in front of the barn. Their children, clockwise from top left, are Lena Belle, William Albert, Maribelle, Fred Harrison, Lulu May, Lovisa Grace, and Dow. Children still to come were Margaret Pearl and Elmer Clarence. (Courtesy of Parks Honeywell.)

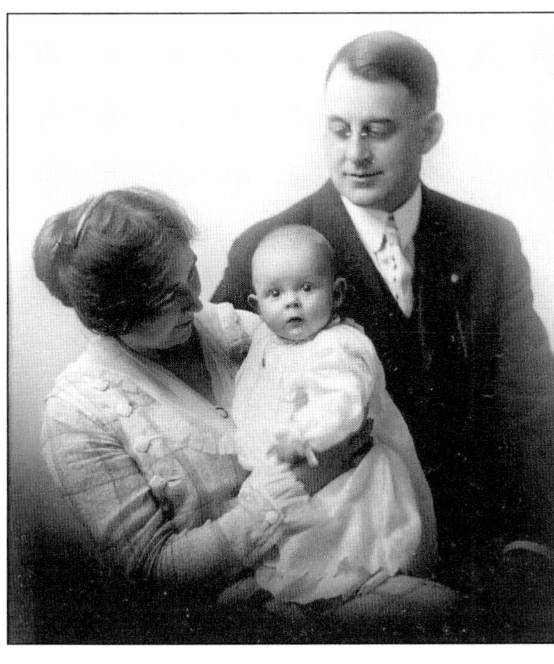

Young Family. Walter Safford is posed here with his wife and their baby daughter, Eleanor. Walter and his brother, Rowland, owned a high-class dry-goods store on Canton's Main Street, where Rowland's wife, Ella, was one of the clerks. Eleanor and her younger sister, Helene, were very fashionable. There were many good years in the business and personal lives of the Saffords, however, in the middle of the Depression, Walter committed suicide in the basement of the store. (Courtesy of SLCHA.)

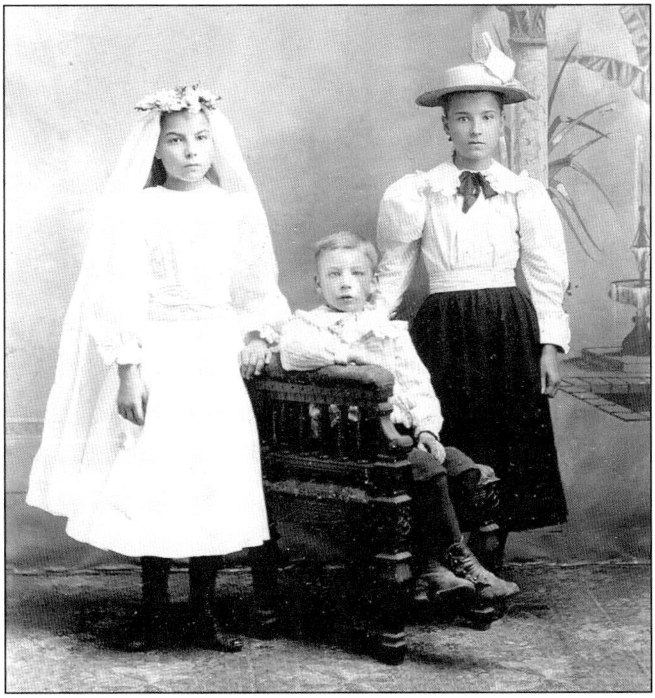

CONFIRMATION DAY. Ready to be confirmed in her white dress and veil is 12-year-old Isabelle Dame. She lived on Sisson Street in Potsdam. Joining her in the picture is her brother Bertram, and the other girl is thought to be Isabelle's sponsor. They were communicants of St. Mary's Church in Potsdam and confirmation day was a very important day for the family. (Courtesy of Ruth Finnegan Garner.)

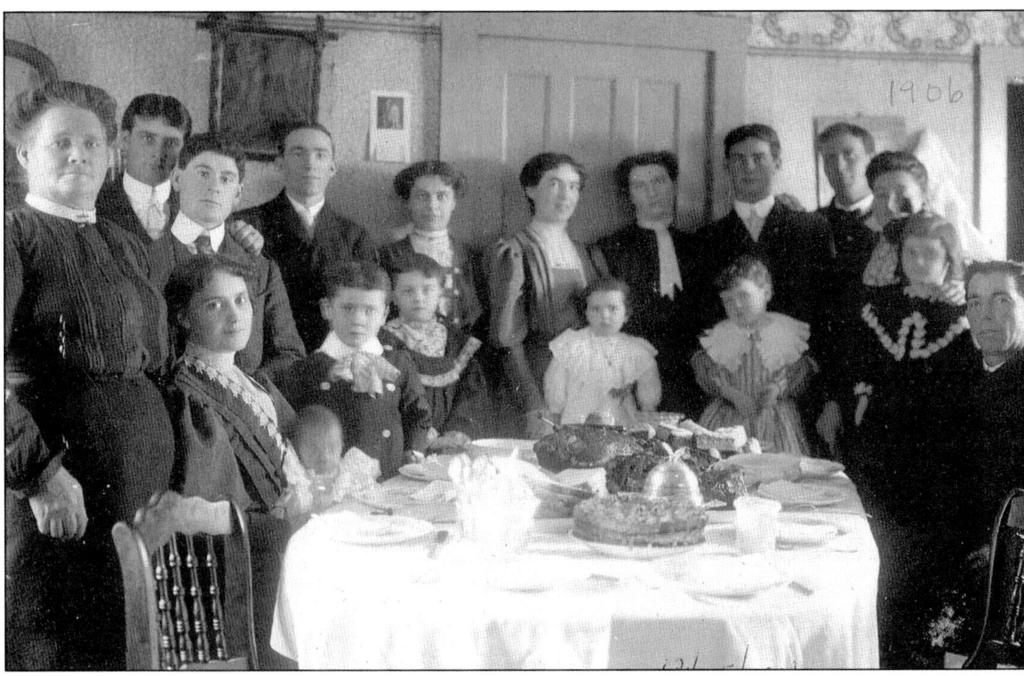

HOLIDAYS ARE FAMILY TIMES. Here is the Kiah family at a holiday dinner in 1906 at the home of Lillian Kiah, who lived in Ogdensburg. Some of those in attendance are the hostess, her brother Chauncey, Elizabeth Penfield and her baby Eva, Alexander Kiah and their little one, and Maryetta McDonald Kiah along with other family members and friends. In those days, there were no finer celebrations than Thanksgiving and Christmas dinners and get-togethers. (Courtesy of Monica LaRose.)

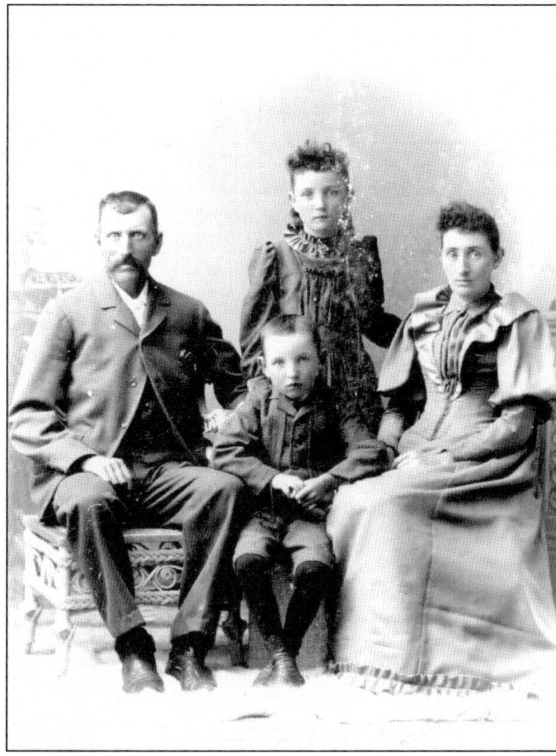

BORN IN ROSSIE. This picture is of the Whalen family. Father John, mother Maria, Charles John, and Nellie. The children were born in Rossie and grew up in Gouverneur. Charles worked in the monument business and moved to Canton before World War I to join Carl Witherbee in forming Witherbee and Whalen. In 1923, he married Fleeta Arlina Powers in Gouverneur. They made their home in Canton at 38 Park Street. They had two children, Robert and Mary. (Courtesy of Mary Jo Whalen.)

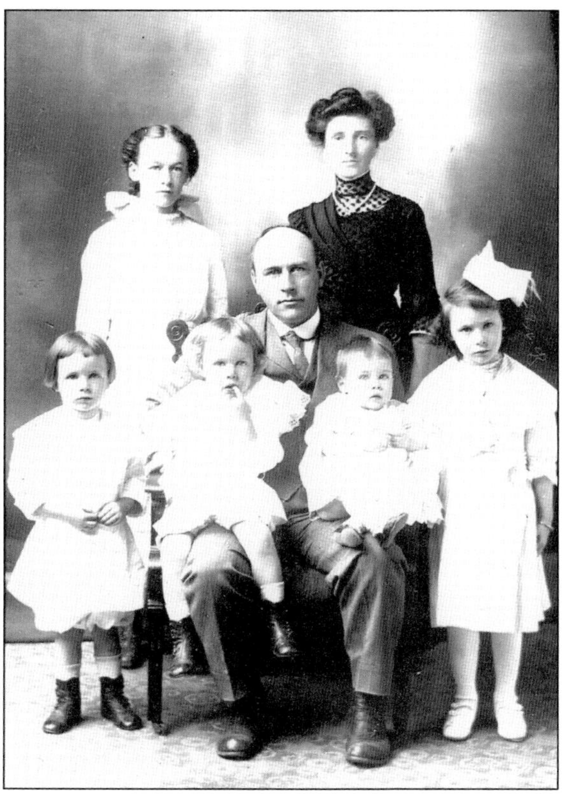

CHASE FAMILY PORTRAIT. Gathered together for a family portrait are father Giles Aquila Chase (born 1872) in the center, with, from left to right, (first row) Giles Elihu (1909), Lester (1910), Irene (1912), and Annette (1907); (second row) Mildred (1900) and mother Edith (1878). Another daughter, Virginia, was born in 1918. Edith was a schoolteacher in Massena and Giles Aquila was a lawyer who had graduated from Cornell University Law School in 1899. He was a U.S. commissioner and a children's court judge. (Courtesy of the Chase family.)

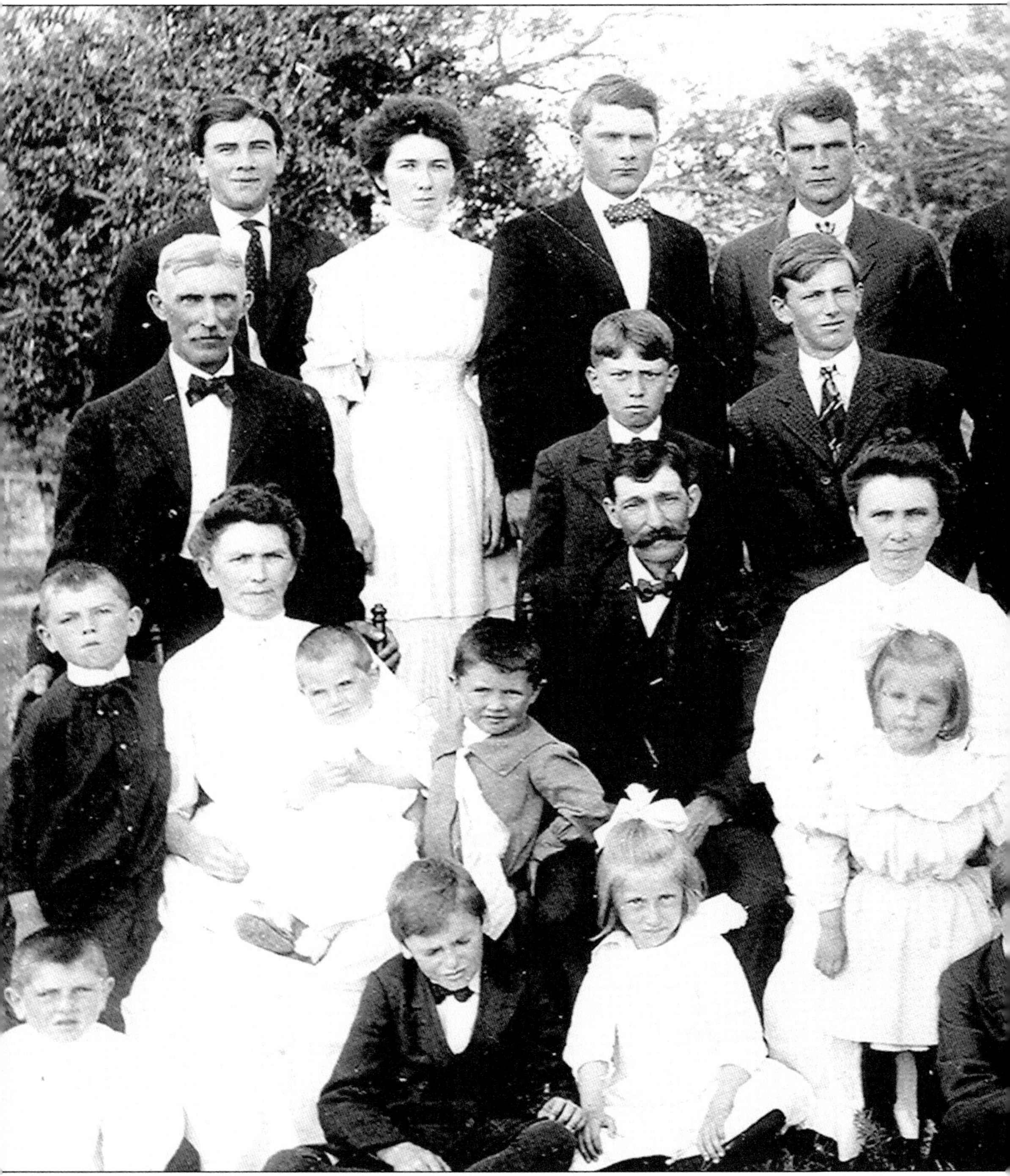

SULLIVAN FAMILY, 1908. Jeremiah and Mary Casey were born in Bantry Bay, Ireland. Jeremiah came to the United States first and bought farmland. In 1867, he sent for his wife ,Mary Casey Sullivan, her sister, Julie Casey O'Leary, and two daughters. The Sullivans had 13 children. The children became teachers, a school principal, a district attorney in Queens County, North Country farmers, and an undertaker. The third-generation children are Tom

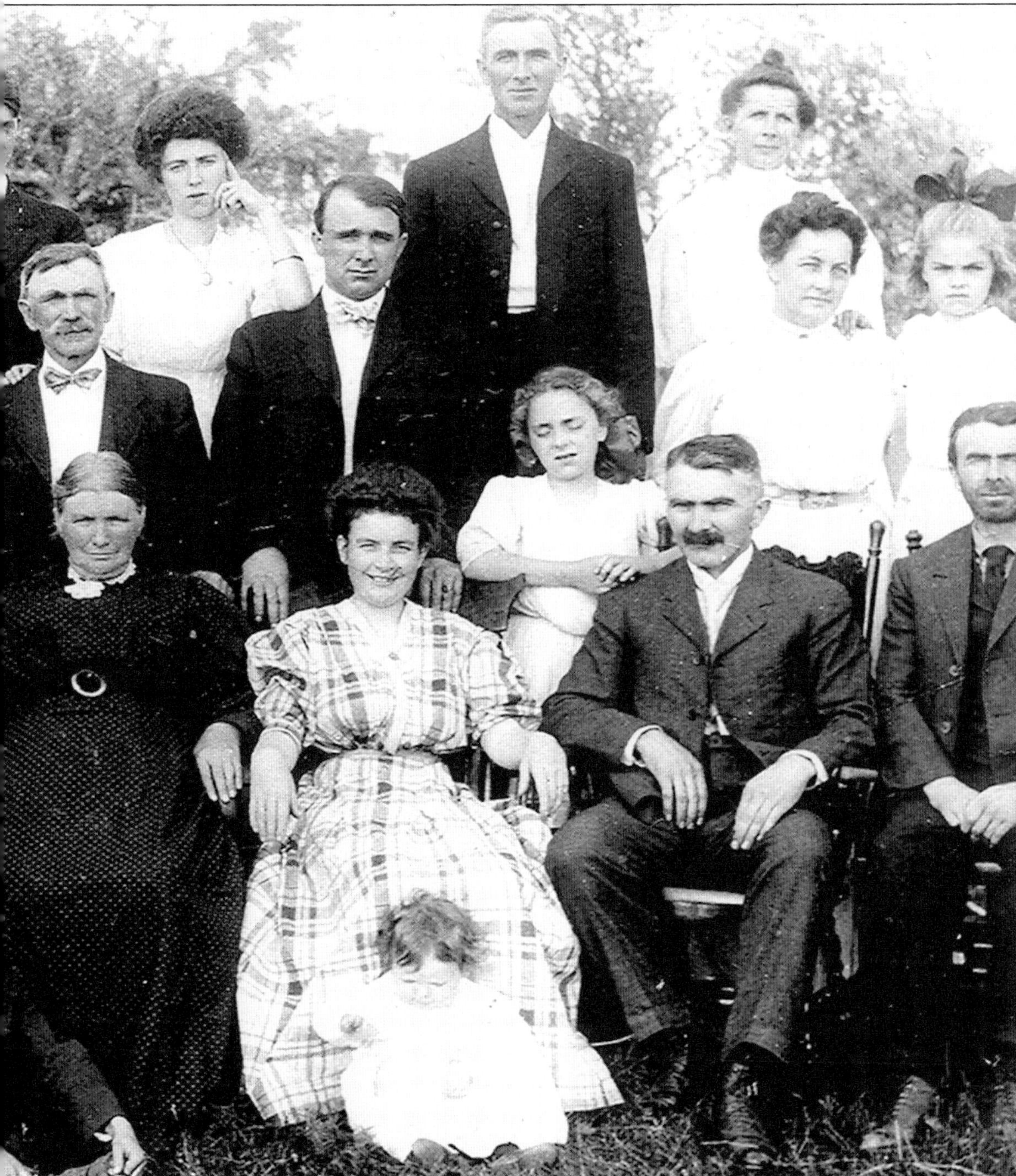

Fay, former postmaster in Massena; Ed Fay (on lap), former businessman in Potsdam; George Fay, former businessman in Massena; Francis Fay, who died at a young age; Emmett O'Leary, former businessman in Canton; Ann O'Leary (O'Brien), teacher; Mary O'Leary; Charles O'Leary; and Lavern Sullivan. Fourth generation family members live throughout St. Lawrence County as well as in other areas of the country. (Courtesy of Peg Podgurski.)

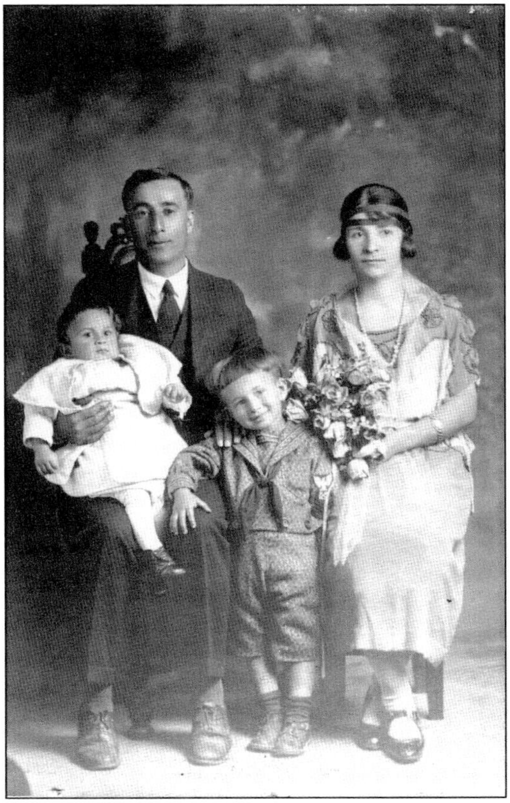

Armenian Presence in Massena. This is a photograph of the Balukjian family. Shown here are Karaken (father), Serpouli Davoudian (mother), Sarkis K. (born in 1921), and Albert A. (born in 1923). The Balukjian family, among many others from Armenia, came to the United States in 1913 to escape religious persecution in their homeland. The men planned to look for work in New York City. They encountered an Alcoa agent who told them of work in Massena. Word spread and by the mid-1920s there were 300 members of the Armenian community living in Massena. Many of them moved to other states when work was cut back during the Depression. (Courtesy of Sarkis Balukjian.)

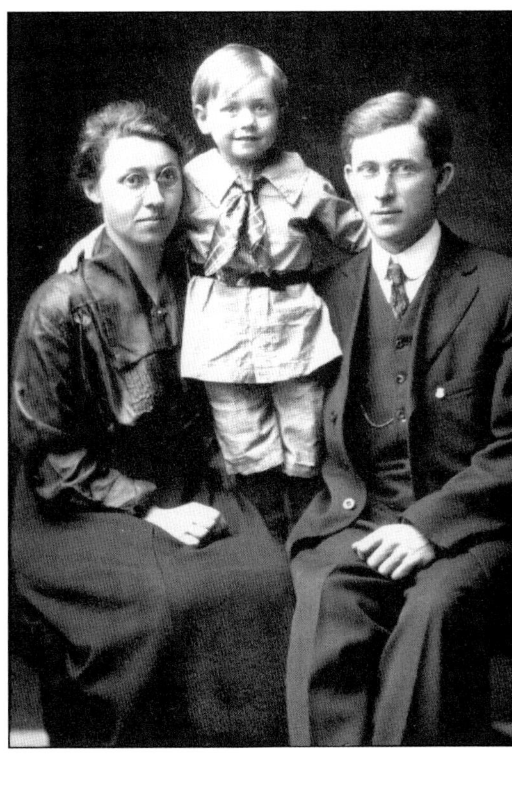

What a Little Man. So finely dressed and so sweet of face is little Herb Judd. Herb and his parents had made a visit to the Allen Photographers Studio in Potsdam. Holding on ti his parents, the world seems to be his oyster. Herb has lived all of his life on the family farm in Canton where he was born. He attended the area country school, Canton High School, and then graduated from St. Lawrence University. Today he and his wife, Mary Ruth, live in contentment in the old homestead. (Courtesy of Herb Judd.)

SALVATION ARMY FAMILY. Milton Mills Brooks was born in DeKalb in 1856 and died in 1918. Two of his children are shown in this picture—Judson Milton Brooks, who was born in 1895 in Russell, and Ethel May Brooks, who was born in 1888 in Richville. Ethel's mother, Lizzie Bradford, was Milton's first wife; Judson's mother, Sadie Stamper, was Milton's third wife. They were in the Salvation Army. Ethel lived in Oxbow where she began a journal of her life, which has been copied and shared with many branches of the family. Later she moved to Niagara County where she married G. Albert Hull. (Courtesy of Bill Hull.)

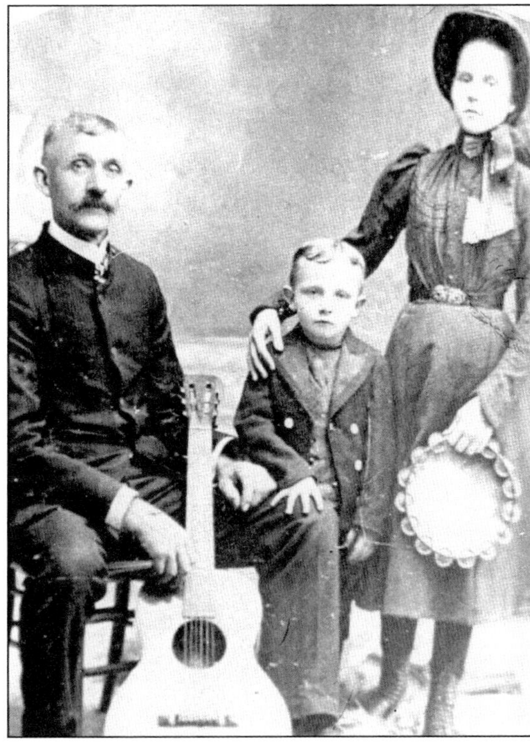

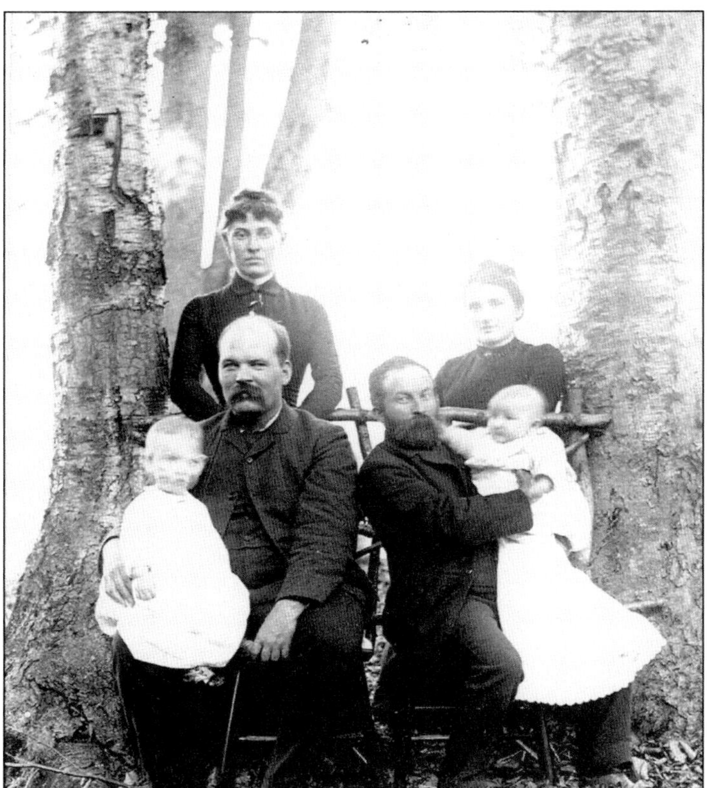

SKILLED CRAFTSMEN. Seated on the left in this picture are Judd W. and Mrs. Rushton and their child, and on the right are J. Henry and Mrs. Rushton and their child. The Rushton brothers grew up in Canton. Judd owned a sash, door, and window factory, and J. Henry became famous for his canoes and small boats. The Rushton name has become world famous. The J. Henry's home was located on Hodskin Street and is still standing. His four-story boat-building factory was nearby on Riverside Drive. His constant companion and loyal helper was his wife, Leah. One of Rushton's most popular canoes was the *Indian Girl*. (Courtesy of SLCHA.)

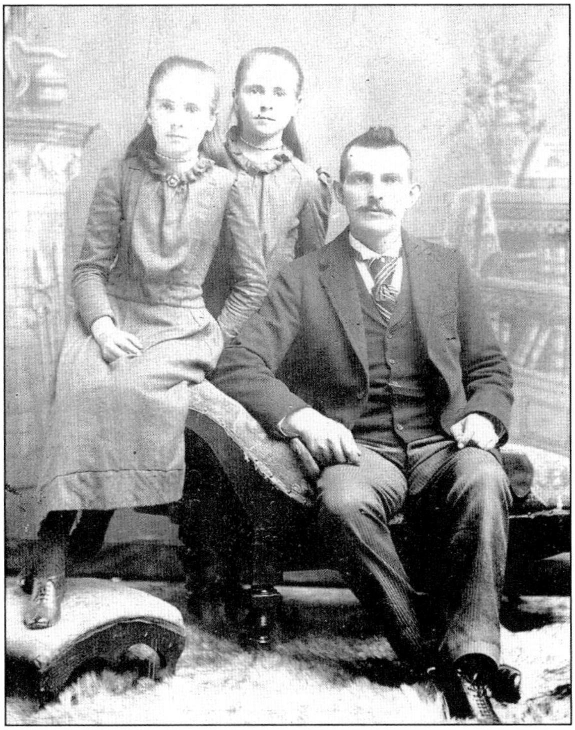

DAN BUTLER AND TWIN NIECES. Dan Butler was born in 1865 in the Brasher Falls area. He is shown here with his twin nieces. The girls were born in 1880 and lived in St. Lawrence County. On the left, Charlotte (Lottie), married Henry Quenelle and lived in Massena where she was a businesswoman and active in politics. She had three children, Paul, Norma, and June. Letetia married Cornelius Mahoney and lived in Brasher Falls. She taught at the White School and the public school in Winthrop for many years. She also had three children, Dan, Kathleen, and Eileen. They have grandchildren residing in St. Lawrence County. (Courtesy of Peg Pogorsky.)

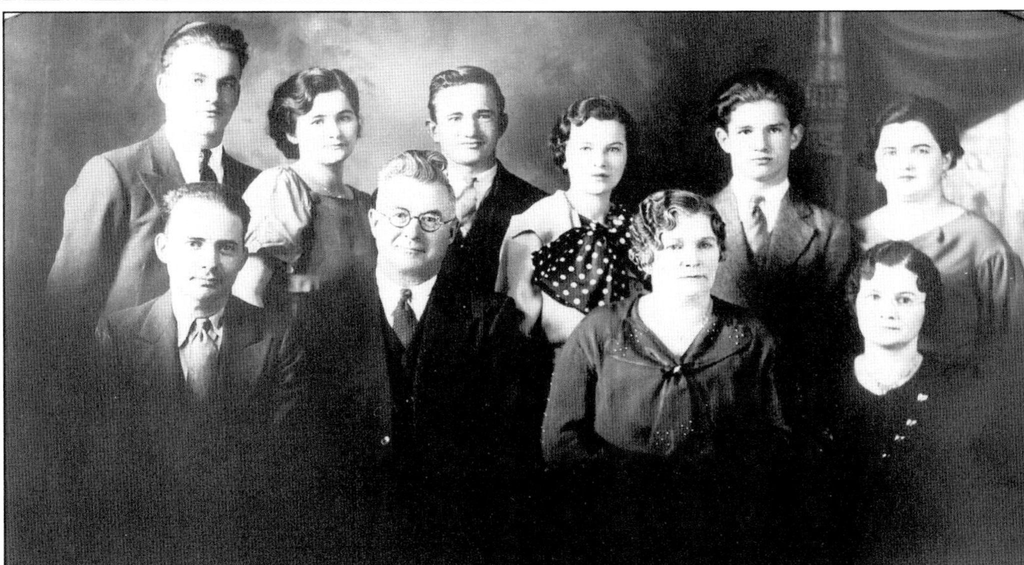

THE ALEGNACE MARTIN FAMILY. Alegnace Martin came from Clarence Creek, Ontario, to work in a lumber camp in the Malone area. In 1903 in the village of Malone, he married Clara Denise Mainville, who was also from Clarence Creek, Ontario. After having three children in the United States they moved back to Ontario in 1924. That same year Alegnace came back to the United States to take a job at the Copeland Steel Corporation plant at Ogdensburg, and his family returned permanently in 1925. Shown here, from left to right, are: (first row) Clarence, Alegnace Isidore, Clara Denise Mainville, and Stella; (second row) Joseph Ephraim, Rolland, Vincent, Zanita, Maurius, and Claire. (Courtesy of David Martin.)

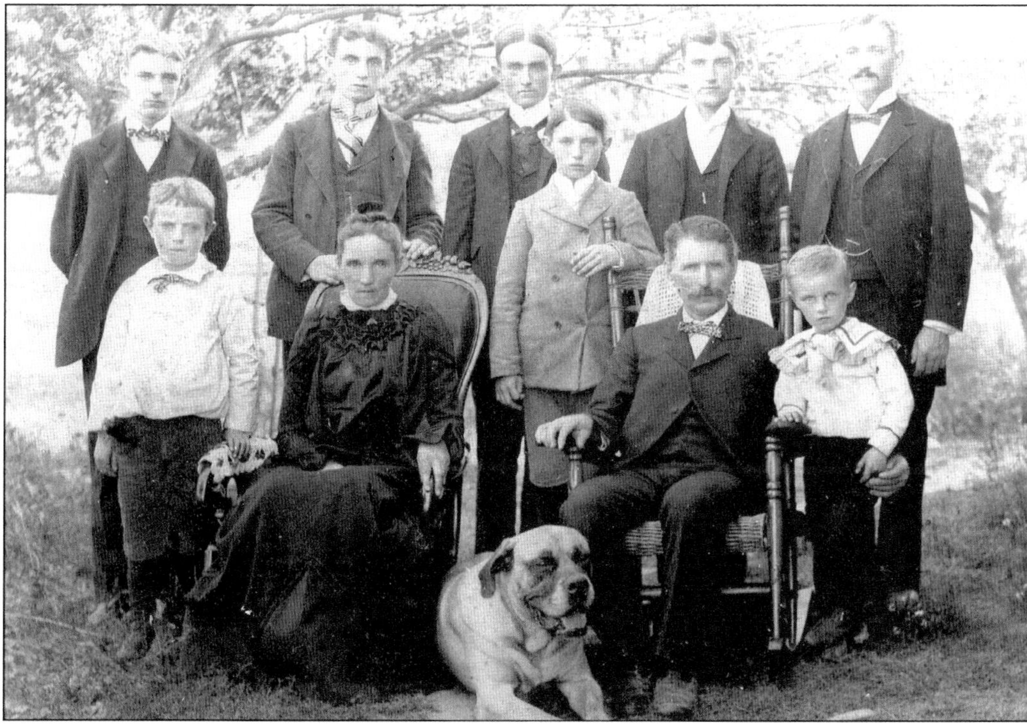

BOYS TOWN AT ITS BEST. Nine sons were born to Matthew and Ellen O'Donoghue Hayden of Canton. Pictured here are Francis, Charles, William, Matthew, John, Clarence, Clifton, mother Ellen, father Matthew, Harold, and the dog Jack. One son, Martin, died at birth. Matthew supported his family by first working at a tannery and then as an engineer at a Canton steam mill. The original family home on Buck Street is no longer standing, but the present-day Hayden homestead is on a lot in front of the original house. (Courtesy of Pat Hayden.)

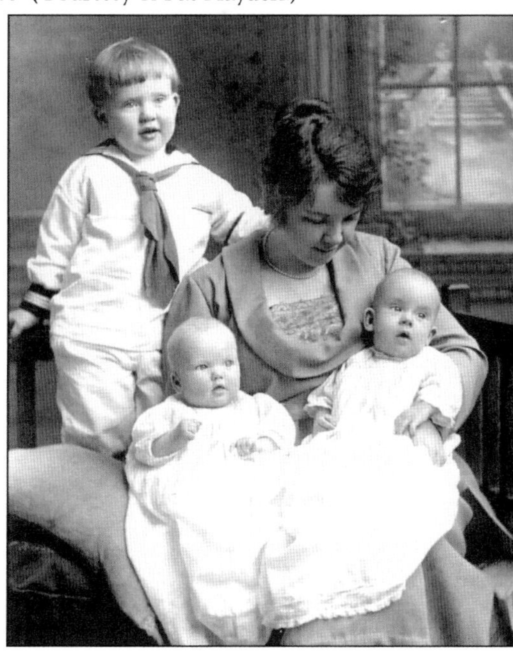

SONS GRADUATED FROM CLARKSON COLLEGE. Walter Louis Baker, born in 1916 in Potsdam, and twins Philip Eastman and Phyllis Elizabeth Baker, born in 1918 in Ogdensburg, were the children of Emily and Roy Baker. Walter (Bud) was a long-time resident of Potsdam with a career as an officer of Elliot Hardware Company. Philip was a bank officer with Key Corporation in Syracuse, and Phyllis was a homemaker. (Courtesy of David Baker.)

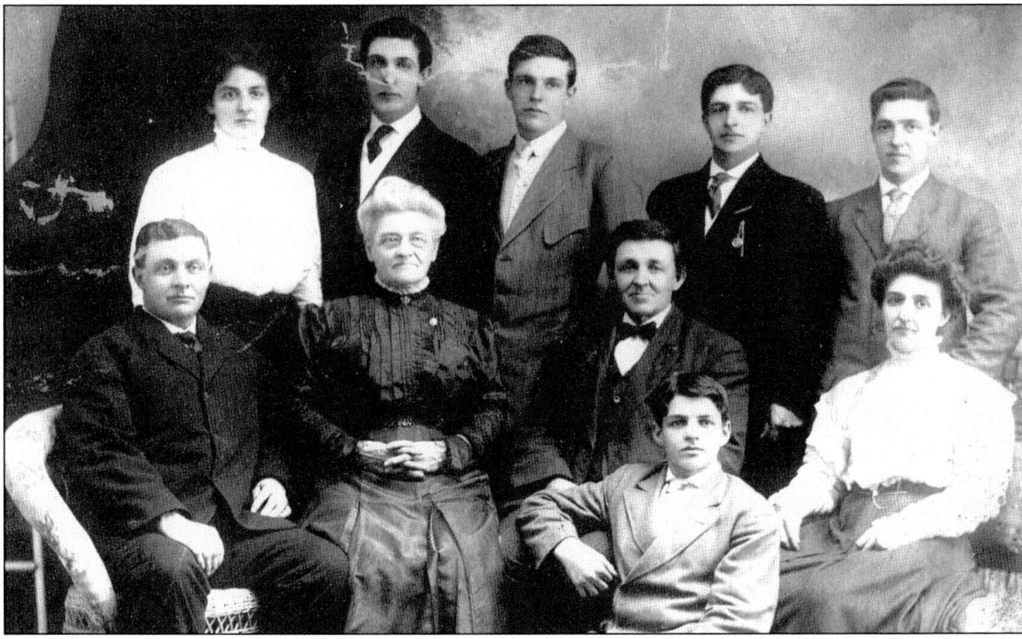

HOME ON THE FARM IN PIERREPONT. The Charles and Alice Tupper family lived on a dairy farm on County Route 24 outside Pierrepont. There were eight children in the family. Pictured with their parents, who are seated on the left, are, from left to right, (first row) Stanley, Arthur, and Grace; (second row) Ruth, Lester, Charles, George, and Ray. The children attended school in Pierrepont. Arthur stayed at home and took over the running of the family farm. (Courtesy of Sally Tupper.)

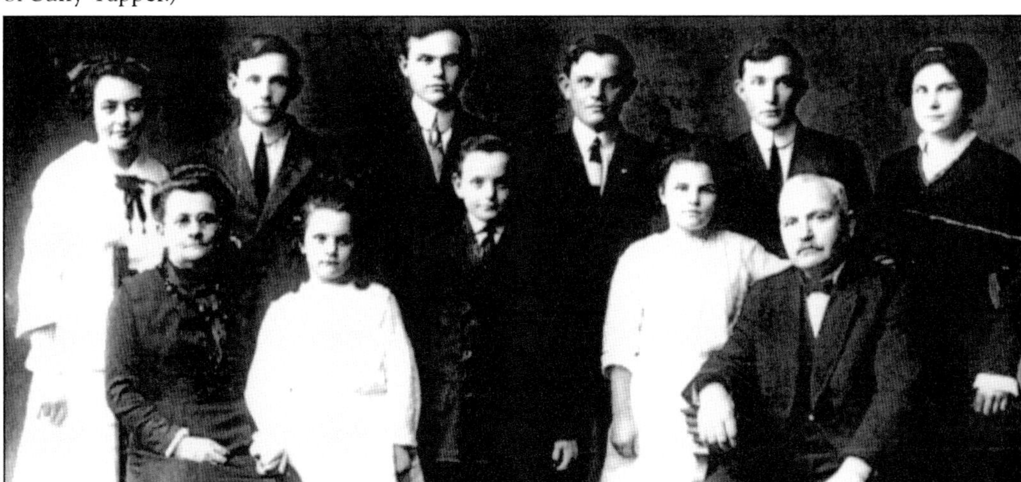

OVERCAME BAN ON EDUCATION. Margaret McKenna grew up on a dairy farm outside of Potsdam. She is shown here in a family group with a hand on her father's shoulder. She was one of 10 children, one of whom died as a baby. Her parents were James and Mary Brannen McKenna, both children of Irish immigrants. According to genealogy research, their grandparents had suffered through a ban on education while children in Ireland. James stressed the need for education to his children and was very proud when Margaret graduated from Potsdam Normal (now SUNY Potsdam). Margaret taught school for many years and was dearly loved by her students. (Courtesy of Joan Barrick.)

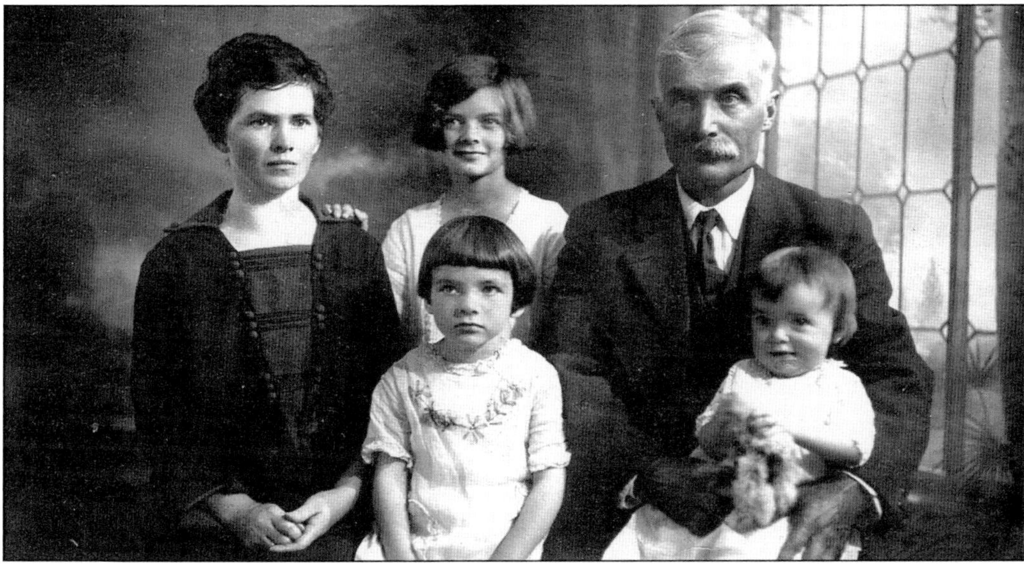

LIVED ON A FARM NEAR COOKS CORNERS. This is a picture of Almon and Celia Irish Phillips and children. Elva, the oldest daughter, is standing in the back. Sitting in front are her younger sisters, Rena on the left and Jessie on the right. Another daughter had not yet been born. She was to be named Lillian. Almon was born in West Parishville. He was a farmer and woodsman. He and Lucelia Irish of South Colton were married in June, 1904. The couple settled on a farm near Cooks Corners, where they lived for most of their lives. (Courtesy of Elva Billings.)

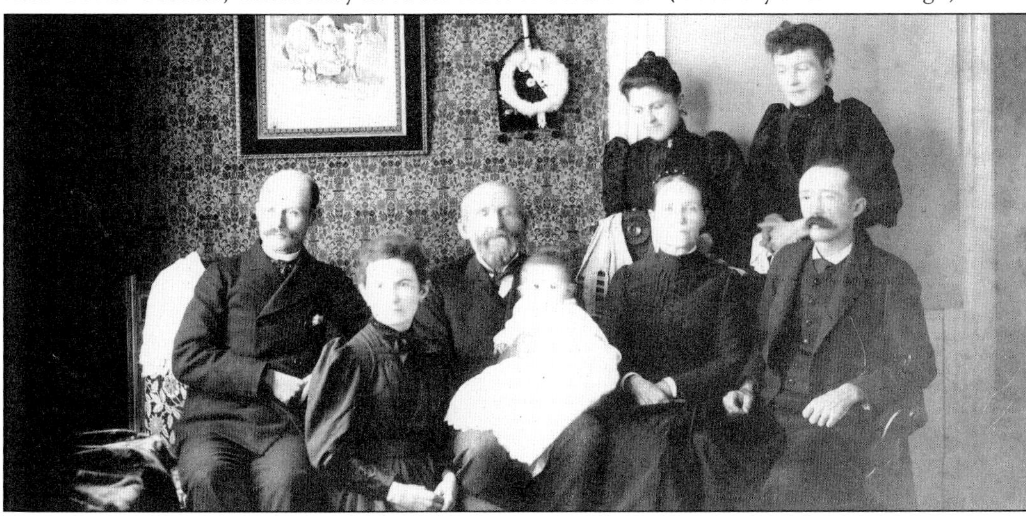

THE SYKES FAMILY. The Sykes were successful farmers. Their farm was located on Middle Road, which led to Madrid, a few miles from Canton. The photograph shows, from left to right, (first row) R. E. Sykes, Mrs. Fred Sykes, Edwin Sykes, baby Edwin G. Sykes, Mrs. Edwin Sykes, and F. A. Sykes; (second row) Mrs. R. E. Sykes and Nellie Sykes. Richard Eddy Sykes became president of St. Lawrence University in 1919. He was one of Canton's better-known citizens. The stone residence on the St. Lawrence University campus is called Sykes Hall and was named in his honor. He was the first president to occupy the present president's residence. His brother, Fred, ran the farm for many years and then his son, Edwin, took it over. Edwin and his wife, Dorothy O'Neil, were both St. Lawrence University graduates. (Courtesy of St. Lawrence University Archives.)

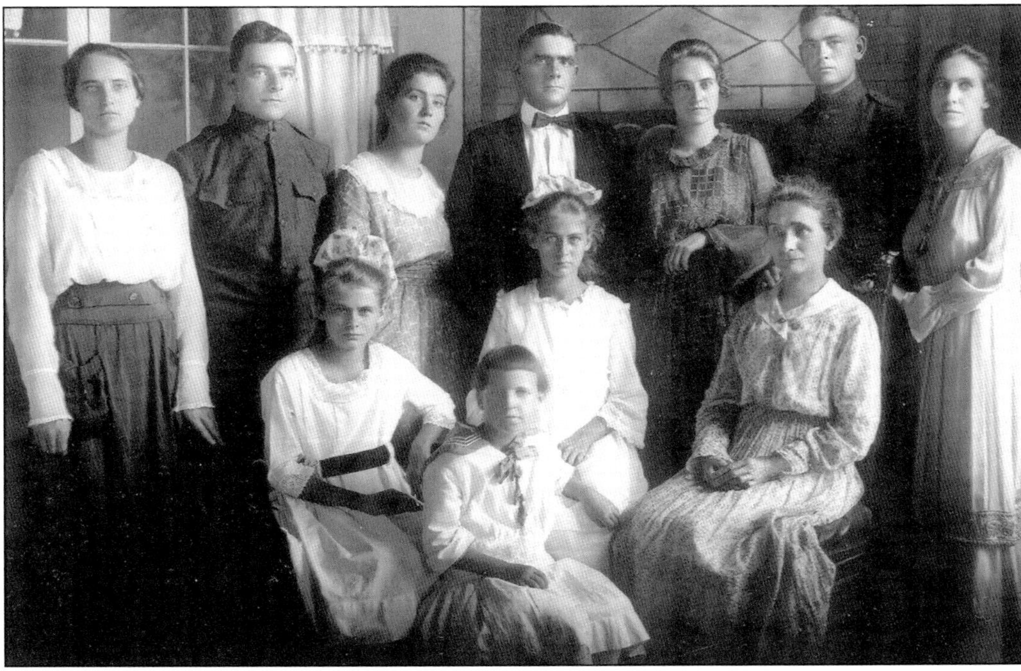

THE McTURKS BEFORE AND AFTER THE WAR. The first picture shows the McTurk family in 1917. Thomas Jr. and William McTurk are dressed in their World War I uniforms. It was taken just before the boys left for war. The second picture shows the brothers having returned from war and the family is together again. Thomas came from Dundee, Scotland, around 1887. A Mr. Babcock, a farmer on Rock Island Road in Gouverneur, paid his passage. Thomas married Jessie Stewart in 1890. On May 21, 1906, he became an American citizen. Thomas and his sponsor, George Holmes, traveled to Canton by train. Upon Thomas's naturalization, Jessie automatically became a citizen. He was employed by the Talc Mines outside Gouverneur. (Courtesy of Ellen Burns.)

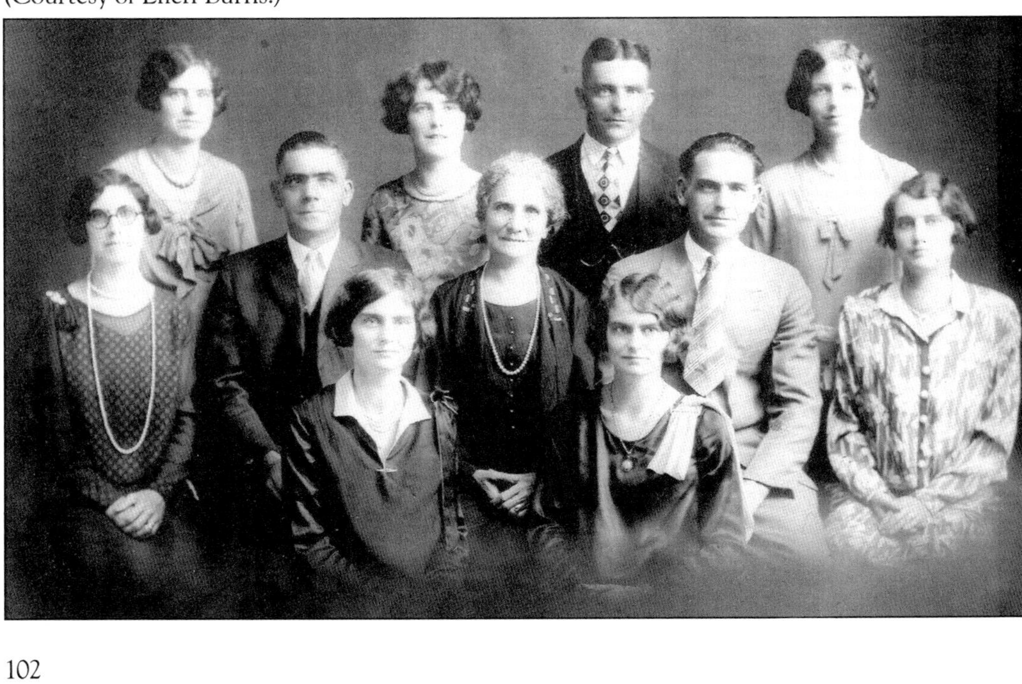

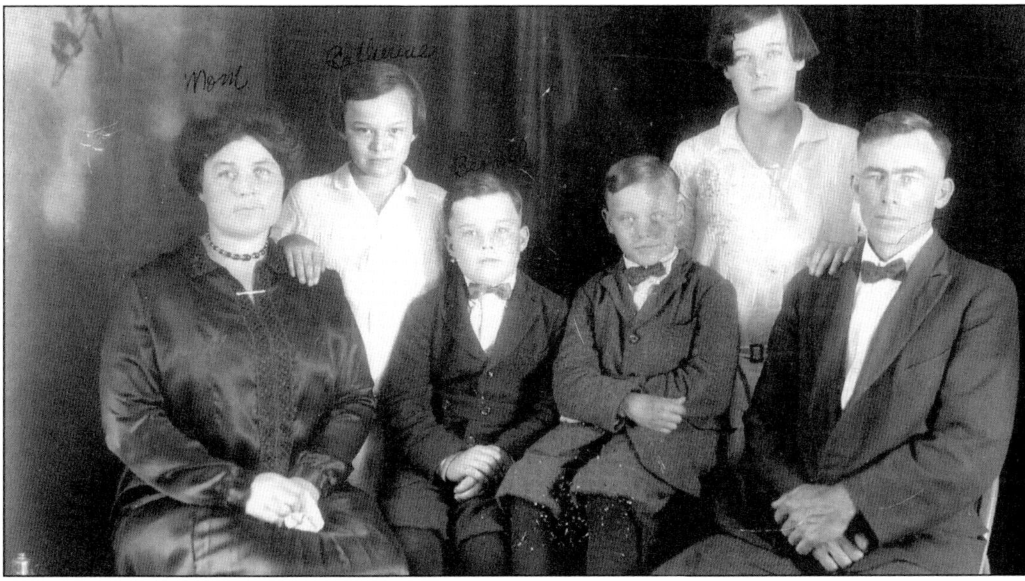

JINGLEVILLE ROAD IS HOME. The Stephen Ragan family is gathered at the homestead in 1928 for this photograph. Shown here, from left to right, are mother Mary (Mamie) Maroney Ragan, Catherine, Bernard, Stephen, Mary, and the patriarch, Stephen. The family always resided on the Jingleville Road, outside of Canton, where they ran a farm. A son, John, died of pneumonia following a case of measles when he was seven. Daughter Catherine died in her thirties in a fire at the Kingston farm down the road where she was living and working. There was much sadness in the family—out of the 11 children born to them, four, including twin girls, died as babies. (Courtesy of David Ragan.)

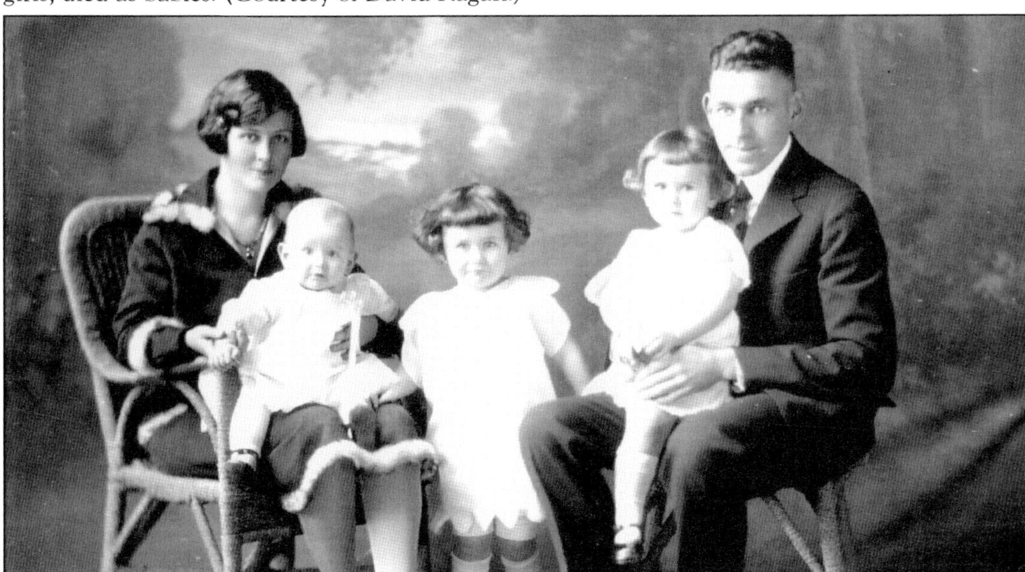

OWNED CLARK'S STORE. Carl and Florence Langdon Clark of Canton are sitting with their three children, from left to right, little Langdon, Mary, and Lillian. In the years to come, two more children, Ruth and Lura, who were named for Florence's two sisters, would join the family. The family home was on Chapel Street, and Carl's thriving grocery store was located on Court Street. (Courtesy of Helen Clark.)

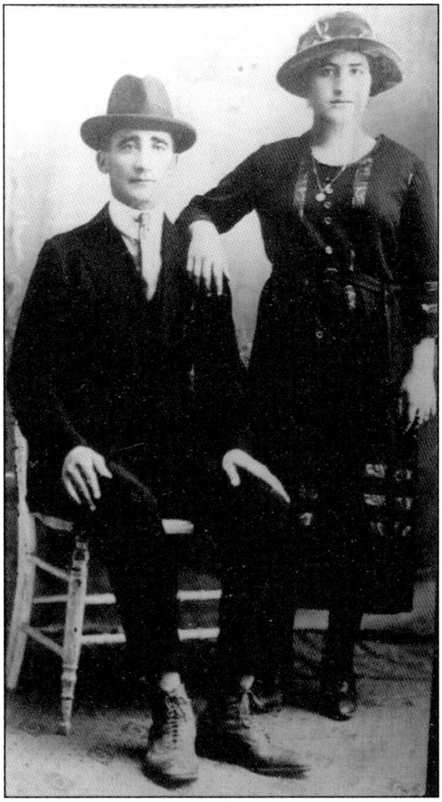

YOUNG BRIDE ARRIVES IN MASSENA. The photograph shows Antonio and Anna Catanzarite. Antonio came to the United States from Plati, Italy, when he was 12 years old. He stayed with his uncle, Joseph Romeo, and began work at Alcoa in Massena in 1905. Some 16 years later he went back to Italy to visit his mother, and met and married Anna Jermano on July 13, 1921. They sailed back to the United States, took a train to Massena, and lived there permanently. This picture was taken within a few days of their arrival. Antonio died in 1953, but Anna was 103 years old on April 13, 2005. (Courtesy of Mary Catanzarite.)

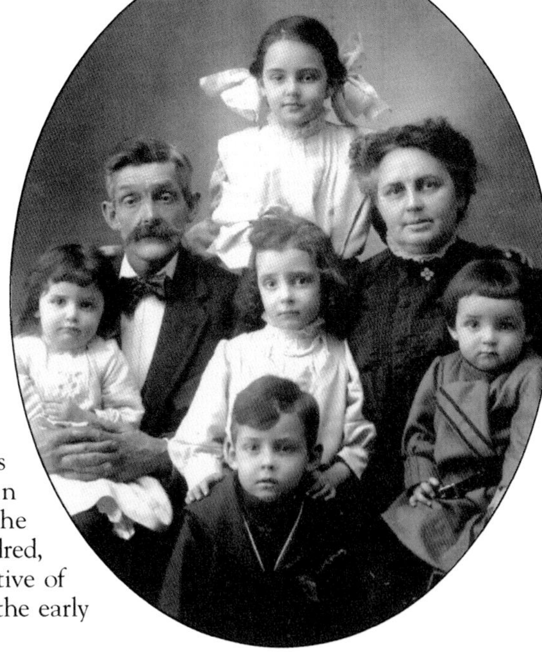

THE PELSUES OF STOCKHOLM. This is a picture of the Pelsue family. The parents are George (holding Luthera) and Lillian (holding James). The three children in the middle, from top to bottom, are Marion, Mildred, and Newton. George's grandfather was a native of Massachusetts, but moved to Stockholm in the early 1800s. (Courtesy of Carlton Stickney.)

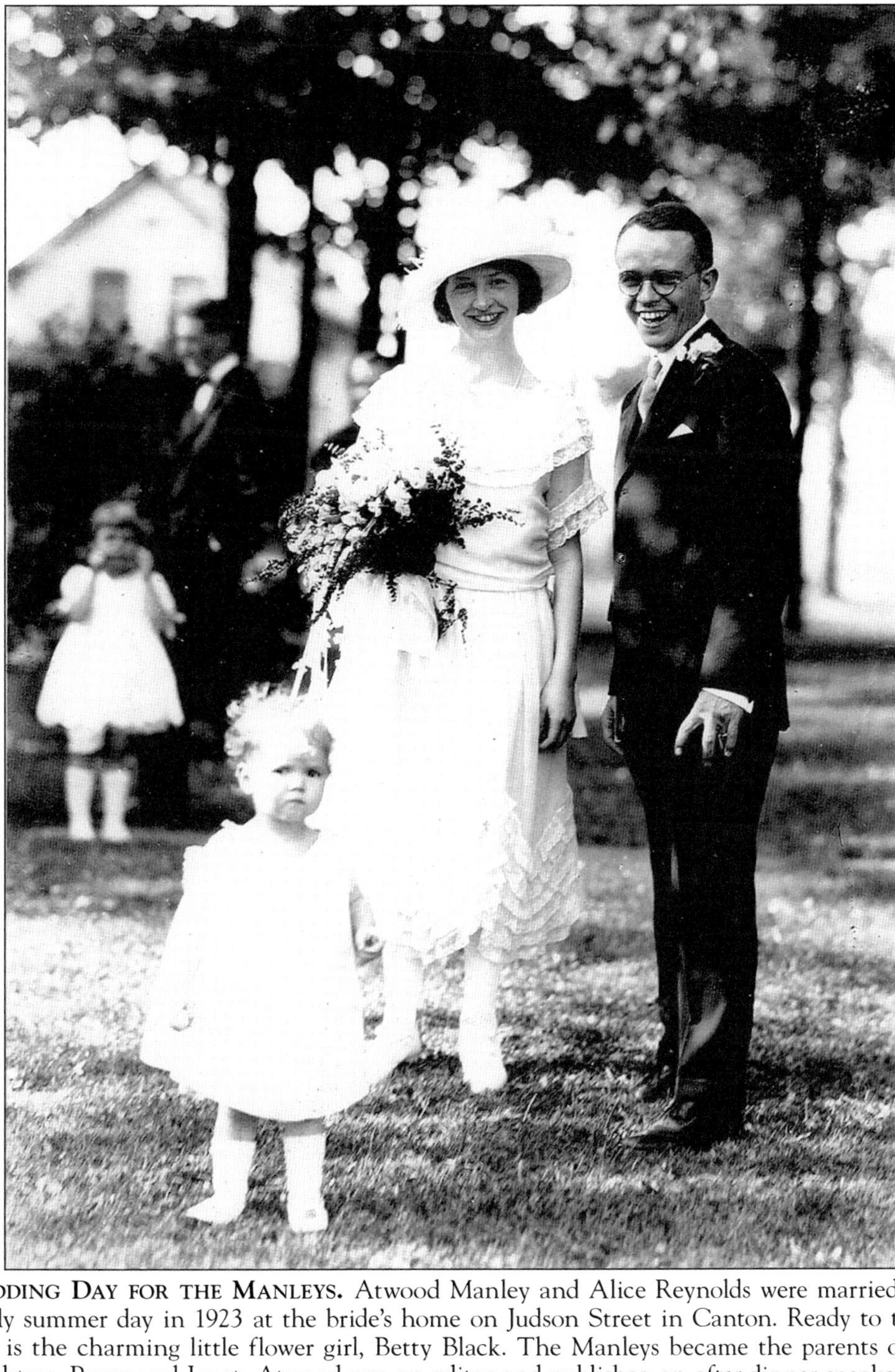

WEDDING DAY FOR THE MANLEYS. Atwood Manley and Alice Reynolds were married on a lovely summer day in 1923 at the bride's home on Judson Street in Canton. Ready to take a bow is the charming little flower girl, Betty Black. The Manleys became the parents of two daughters, Peggy and Janet. Atwood was an editor and publisher, an after-dinner speaker, and a renowned author. He wrote a book with Peg, his daughter, about Henry Rushton's canoes. Both Atwood and Alice were graduates of St. Lawrence University, and during their lifetime they contributed much to the university, as well as to the village of Canton and to many of its local organizations. (Courtesy of SLCHA.)

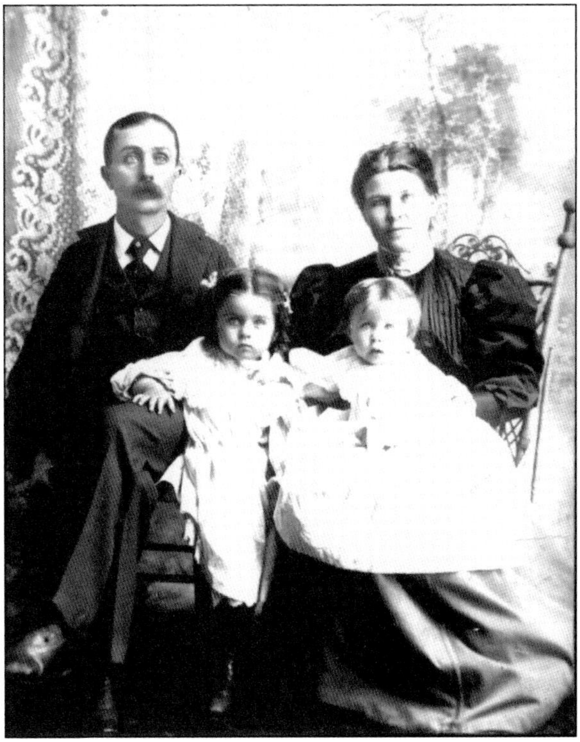

BITTERSWEET FAMILY PHOTOGRAPH. An early photograph (1899) of the Brothers family shows Joseph and Jenny Curtis Brothers with their daughters, Marion on the left and Mildred on the right. Shortly after this photograph was taken, Marion had a fatal sledding accident at the age of four. Joseph ran a general store and was postmaster at Brookdale.(Courtesy of Carlton Stickney.)

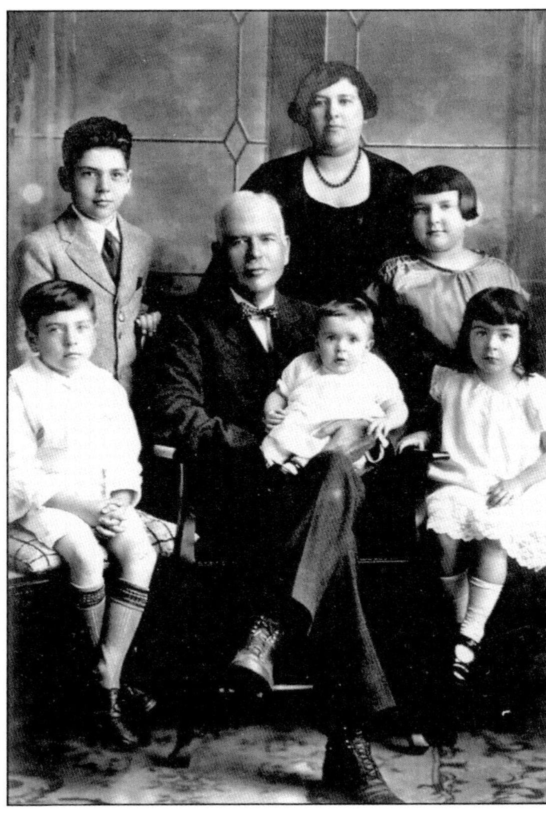

HEFFERNAN FAMILY. This picture shows the Heffernan family all together in their Court Street home in Canton in 1926. The patriarch, Richard, seated in the center, is shown proudly holding their newest child, Gerald. Mother Clara is standing in the back. Sons Walter (sitting) and Robert (standing) are joined by their sisters Mary (standing) and Little Rita (sitting). Mr. Heffernan was a lawyer and politician, and his son Walter followed in his footsteps, later becoming a lawyer and district attorney. Rita was a dance instructor for the Arthur Murray Dance Studio in New York City. Mary taught school and Robert was on the Chateaugay Village Council. (Courtesy of Rita Heffernan Foote.)

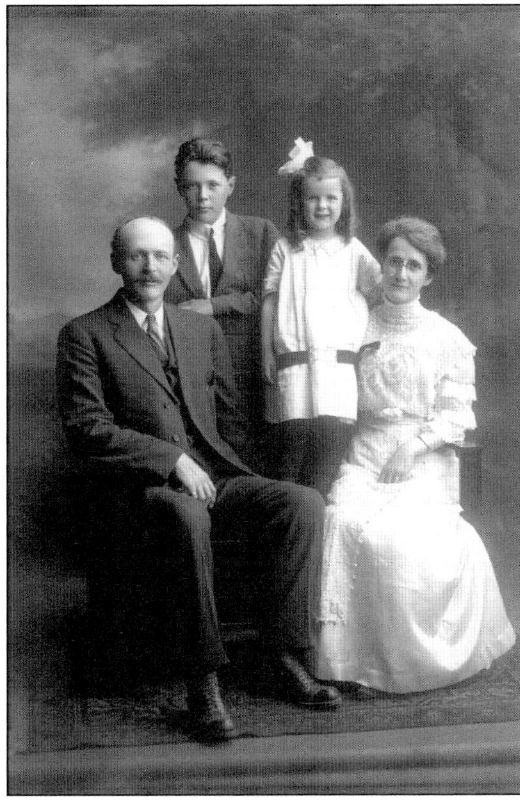

THE CHITTENDENS. The family of J. H. Chittenden of Hopkinton posed for this portrait in a Potsdam studio around 1918. Shown here are, from left to right, are J. H. Chittenden (merchant), Clark S. Chittenden, Charlotte Elizabeth Chittenden (Miller), and Gertrude Hoyt Chittenden (formerly of Parishville). (Courtesy of Varick Chittenden.)

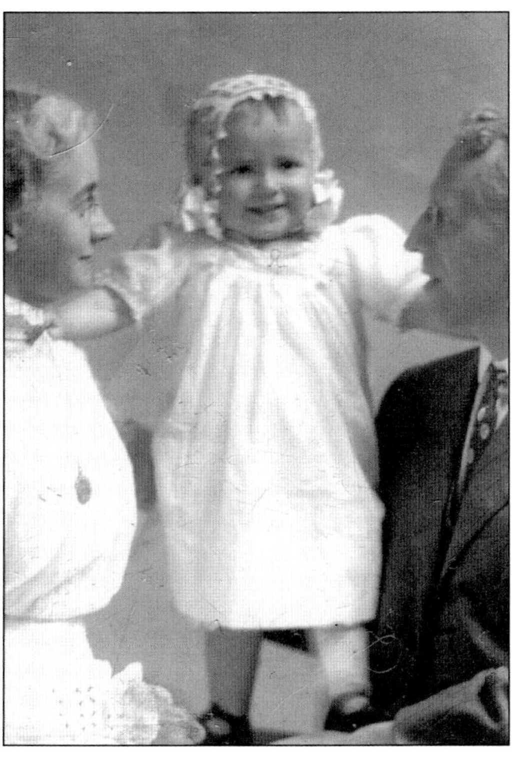

WEALTHIA KIPP WITH GRANDPARENTS. Wealthia is shown here with her grandfather, the illustrious artist of portraits and frescoes, Henry De Valecourt, and her grandmother, Harriet Kipp. Wealthia's father, Benjamin, was the youngest of Henry and Harriet's three sons. Benjamin was a photographer of note who had a studio located on Main Street in Canton. The Kip family home still stands on Chapel Street. Wealthia was an only child. (Courtesy of SLCHA.)

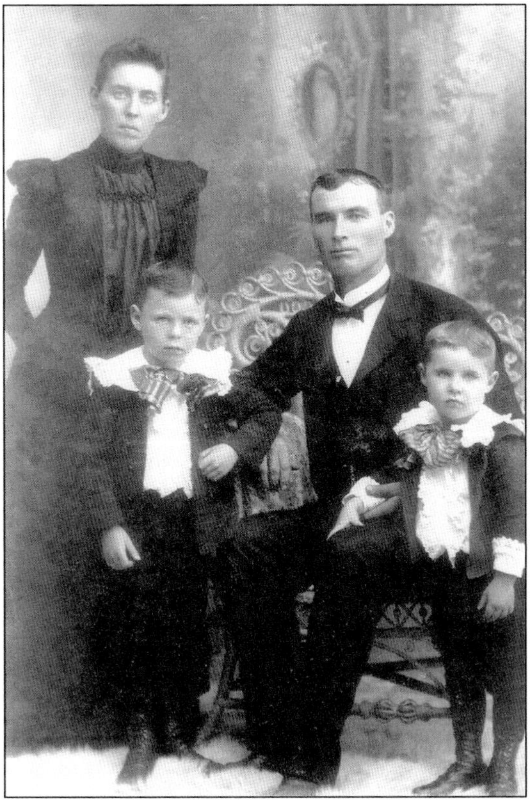

WOODBRIDGE CORNERS. This portrait is of the Cunningham family and it was taken at the Runion Studio in Canton in 1899. Shown in this photograph, from left to right, are Mary Ann Cunningham, John L., Owen L. Cunningham, and Leon Andrew. Mary and Owen owned several farms in the Lisbon area. Their main farm was on the north side of Woodbridge Corners. (Courtesy of Alan Cunningham.)

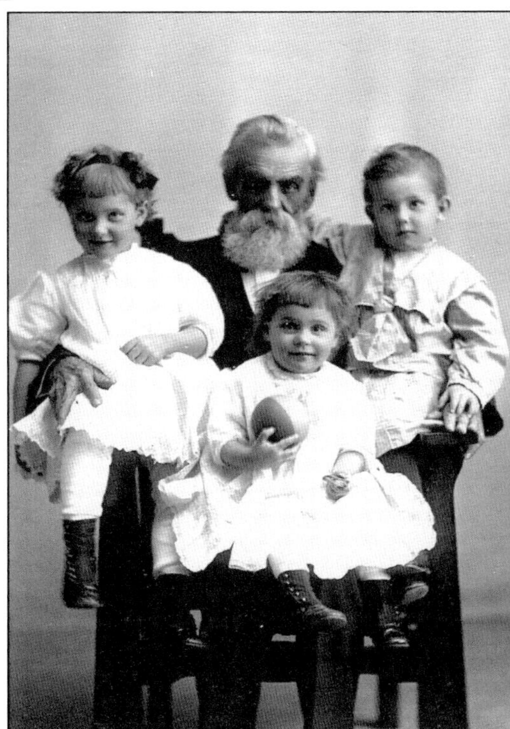

FLORIDA NATIVE TO MORRISTOWN RESIDENT. Sitting with their grandfather, J. Hurd Kooker of Pennsylvania, are Jeannette Mabel, born in 1907 (left) and her sister Helen Marjorie, born in 1909. They are the children of Mabel Giffin and J. Weir Kooker of Florida. They spent each summer in their cottage in Morristown. Pictured with them is their cousin, Harry Cressy. Jeannette's and Helen's father died at the cottage at the age of 32. Mother and daughters returned to Florida, but later decided to return to Morristown and make it their home. On June 14, 1922, Mabel married Walter Couper Witherhead and had two more children, Louise Constance Thode of Braintree, Massachusetts, and John Maurice Witherhead of Canton. (Courtesy of Marcella Lavarnway.)

WEDDING DAY. Andrew and Ellen Salina Lanphear Cobb look very classy on their wedding day in April 1877. Andrew was born in the 1850s to Stephen and Gertrude Bulson Cobb. Ellen, the youngest of 11 children, was born in Pitcairn on March 17, 1857, to John B. and Eliza Jenne Lanphear. Ellen's mother, Eliza, was the daughter of Prince and Olive Lincoln Jenne. Olive Lincoln Jenne claimed to be a first cousin of Abraham Lincoln. Ellen and Andrew lived most of their married life on a farm in Silver Hill in the town of Russell. Andrew was also a stonemason and both were very well educated for their time. (Courtesy of Jean Given.)

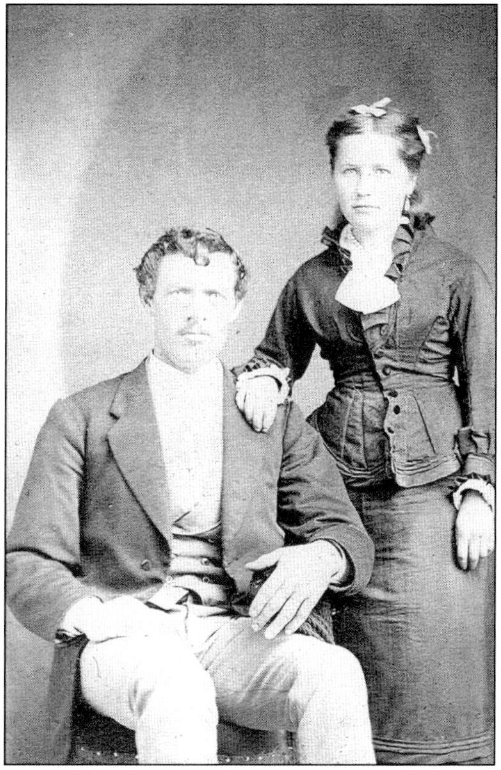

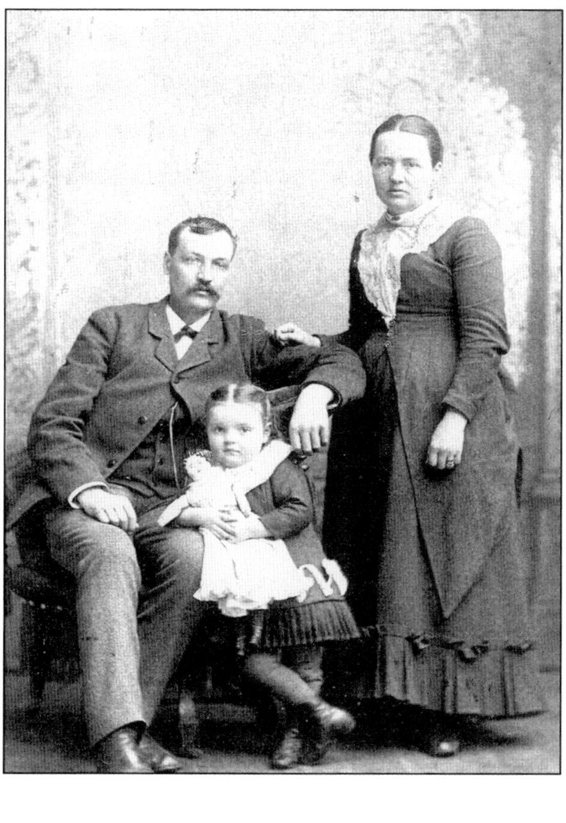

COUNTRY DOCTOR. Moses Smith was a very busy doctor in Colton. He is shown in this portrait with his wife, Lorena Smith, whose maiden name was Perkins. Their daughter, Myrtle, later married Eldon Bullis. She was the organist at the Zion church in Colton for 47 years. (Courtesy of Dennis Eickhoff.)

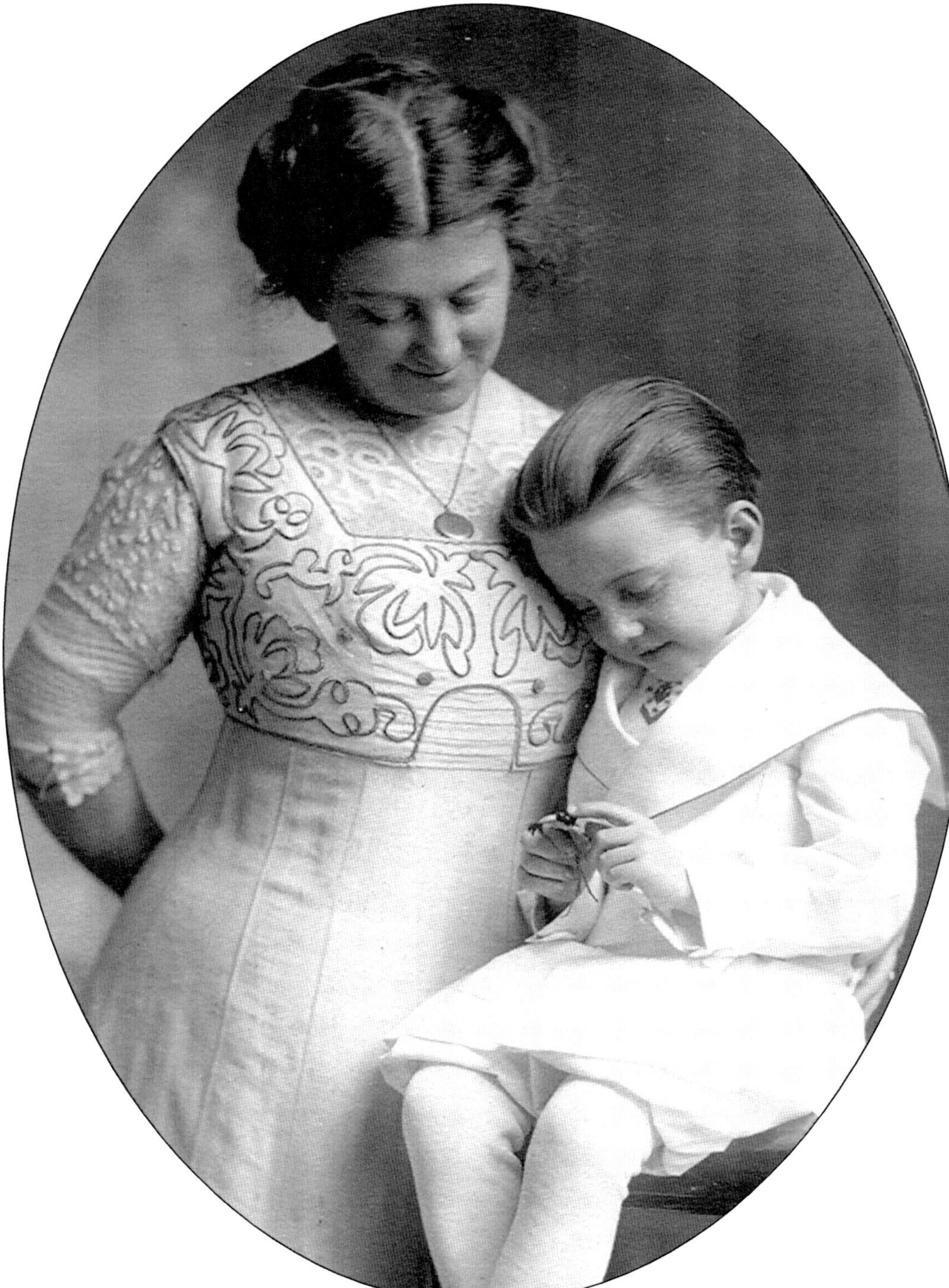

MOTHER AND CHILD. The lovely lady in this picture is Rose Taney Barnett, wife of Michael Barnett, with their handsome son, Joseph. The Barnett family lived in Potsdam. The parents performed together in the local opera house as actors and singers. Joseph attended schools in Potsdam and graduated from the University of Notre Dame in 1929. (Courtesy of Kate Newell.)

Five

OUTDOOR LIVING

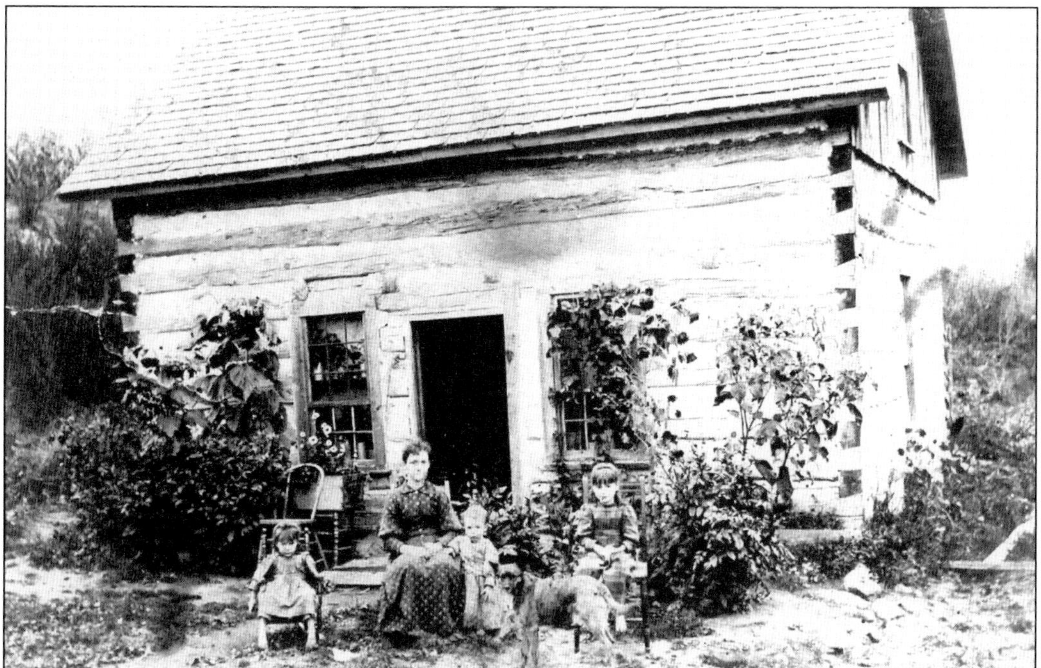

LOG CABIN IN THE LATE 19TH CENTURY. Pictured here, from left to right, are Mabel, Katie, Frank, and Maude Agnes Young. Mabel Irene Young was born in 1890 and married Ivan R. Taylor. They had 11 children, 4 of whom died in a house fire in Fowler in 1940. Katie Oakes Young (born 1867) married Frank F. Young and had 14 children. She lived most of her life in Hermon, Richville, Talcville and Syracuse. Frank W. Young (born 1892) married Ruby Austin and had seven children. He, his wife, and a hired man, Asa Brayton, drowned in the St. Lawrence River at Red Mills. Maude A. Young (born 1889) married Fred G. Carpenter and had 11 children. (Courtesy of Norman Young.)

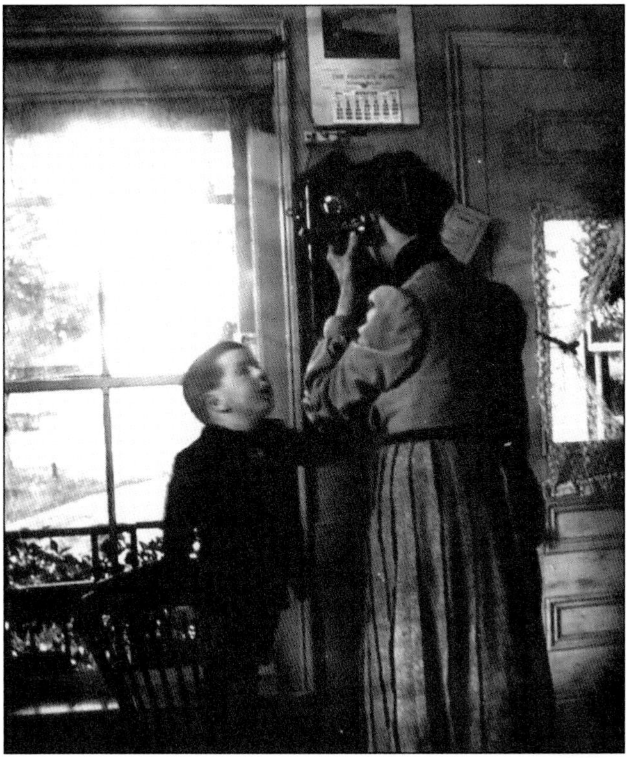

SOUTH EDWARDS. This is a picture of Leon Elgin Maine and his mother, Florence Fairbanks Maine. Leon was born in Hermon in 1877, and is about six years old in this picture. The calendar on the wall reads the Peoples Bank of Edwards. The Maine family was living in South Edwards at that time. Elgin owned the sawmill there and they had a farm about one mile south of the hamlet. This was most likely one of the first telephones in the area. (Courtesy of Stan Maine.)

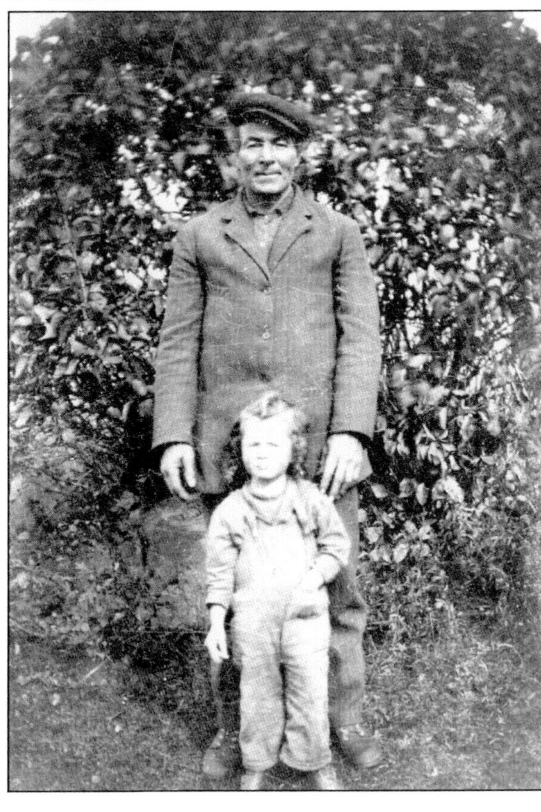

LUMBERJACK, FARMER, AND BLACKSMITH. This picture is taken in the town of Hermon in 1915. The photograph is of Frank F. Young (1863–1937). He was born in Vermont, but because his parents died young he moved to Malone with his grandparents. He came to St. Lawrence County in 1875 to work in the woods and later farmed and worked as a blacksmith. His son, Hubert, pictured with him, is one of fourteen siblings. (Courtesy of Norman Young.)

LEFT POLAND AND SETTLED IN PARISHVILLE. This is Mayer Sperling and his son Bernard (Bun), riding their horse Tony in 1929. Mayer came from Poland, with a stopover in Canada, before arriving in St. Lawrence County in 1915. He originally worked on a farm owned by Byron Parker near Parishville. Parker taught Mayer how to read and write in English using the *Watertown Daily Times* newspaper as a teaching tool. Mayer met and married Anna Bennett from Canton. In later years, he owned the successful Sperling Furniture Stores. (Courtesy of Peg Sperling.)

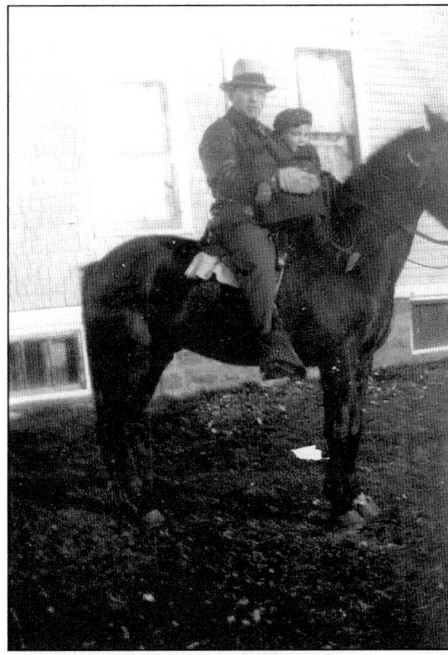

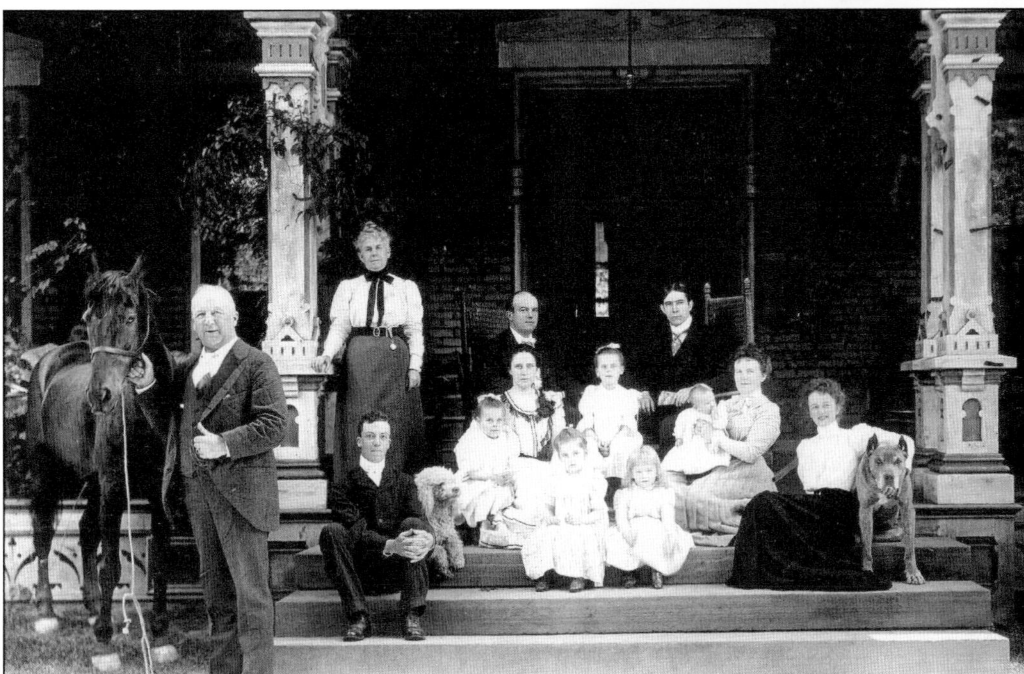

FAMILY GATHERING. Supreme Court Justice Leslie Russell and his family posed before their grand family home, which was located on the corner of Elm and College Streets in Canton. The home later became a St. Lawrence University fraternity, Beta Theta Pi. Judge Russell was fond of horses and had one join him in the family photograph. He always owned horses and entered one yearly in the county fair. Pictured with the judge are his wife, two sons, two daughters, seven grandchildren, and their pet dogs. (Courtesy of SLCHA.)

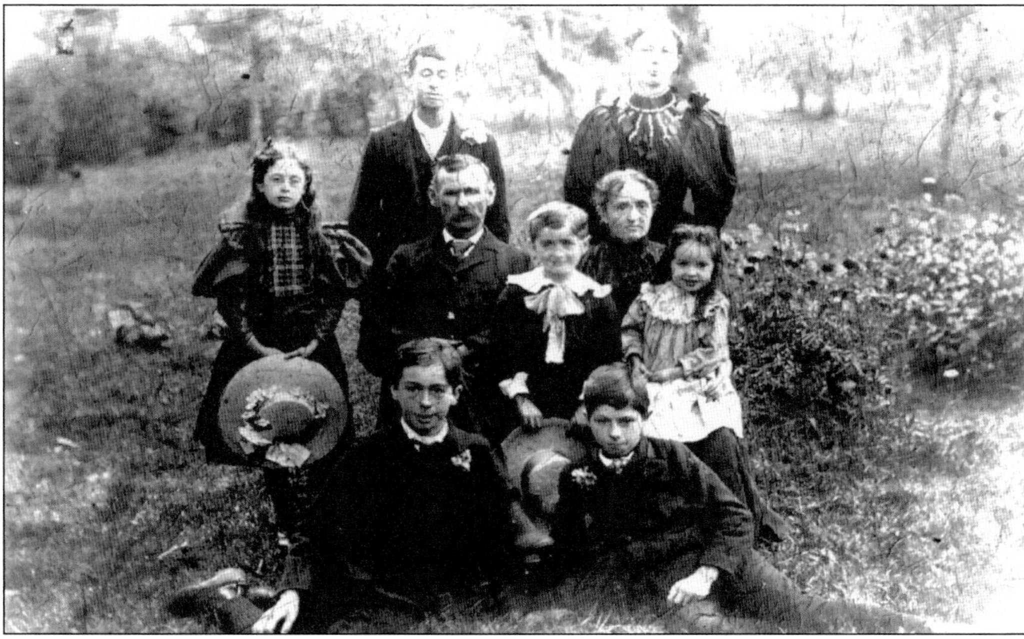

SERVED WITH THE 60TH REGIMENT. Sylvester Thompson was born at Woodbridge Corners in 1843 and later married Helen Mary McEwen. Sylvester served in the Civil War with the 60th Regiment, Company G, New York State Volunteers. He is pictured here with his family. They are, from left to right, (front row) Floyd and Howard; (second row) Alice, Sylvester (holding Harry), and Helen (holding Mary); (third row) Charles and Ruby. Sylvester died in March 1915 and was described in his obituary as "a very successful farmer, a man of sterling character, devoted to his home and family." (Courtesy of Marcia Ragan Thompson.)

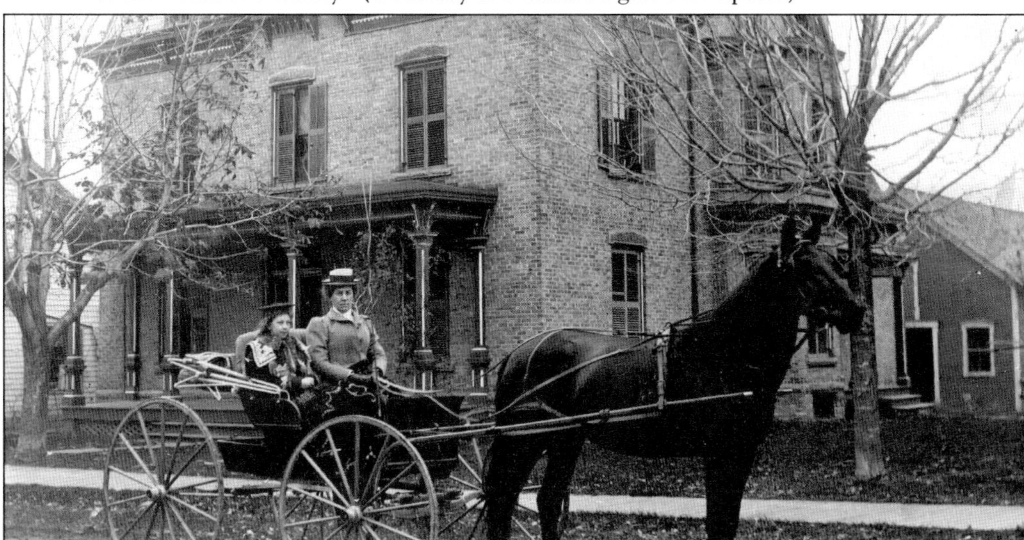

AN AFTERNOON OUTING. Mrs. Fred Merriman of Madrid is shown with her daughter Jessica. The picture is taken around 1904. Jessica graduated from St. Lawrence University in 1912. Their lovely home was built in 1879. Mother and daughter are dressed for an outing in their buggy drawn by their handsome horse. There is also a large carriage house behind their home. (Courtesy of SLCHA.)

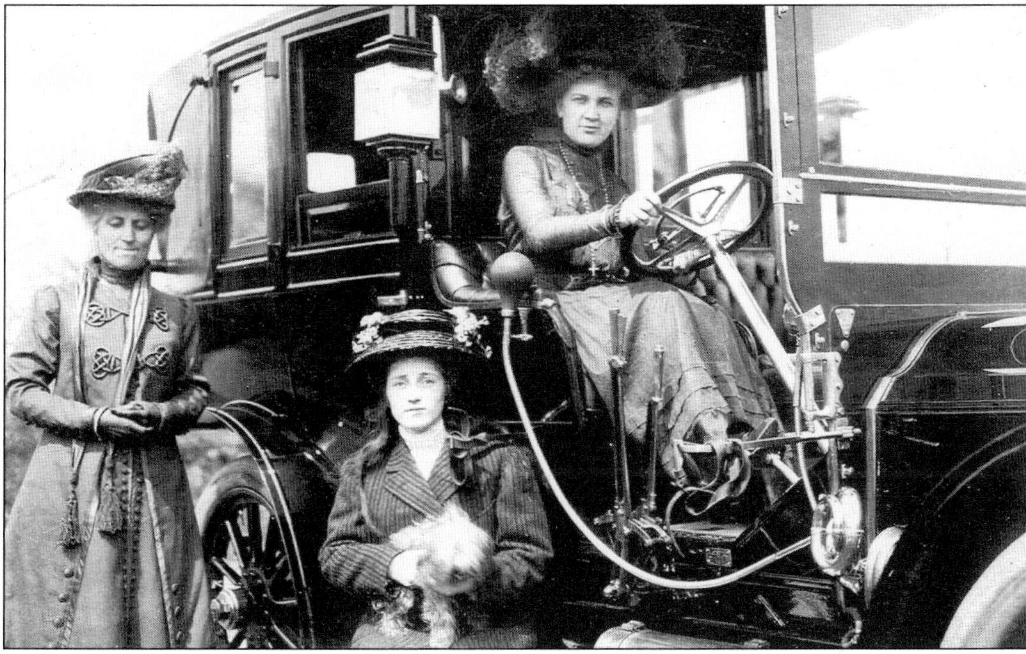

COLLEGE GRADUATE, PHILANTHROPIST, WIFE, AND MOTHER. Emily Eaton was born on September 7, 1865, in Middlesex, Vermont. She attended St. Lawrence University and met her husband, A. Barton Hepburn, while living in Canton. They began their married life in Canton, where their daughter, Beulah, was born. The family then moved to Washington where their second daughter, Cordelia, was born. Emily and her friend, Cora Dean of Gouverneur, were instrumental in the erection of Dean-Eaton Dormitory (for women) at St. Lawrence University in 1927. Many additional gifts were given locally from the philanthropic pair. (Courtesy of SLCHA.)

FAMOUS COLTON NATIVE. Alonzo Barton Hepburn was born on a farm in Colton on July 24, 1846, to Beulah Gray and Zina Earl Hepburn, a man of Scottish descent. Alonzo Hepburn had three older brothers. He attended St. Lawrence University and Fuller Academy in Oswego. Hepburn became an internationally known financier, president of Chase National Bank, and was also a New York State legislator. He endowed seven public libraries in St. Lawrence County in addition to being a benefactor to A. Barton Hepburn Hospital in Ogdensburg. (Courtesy of SLCHA.)

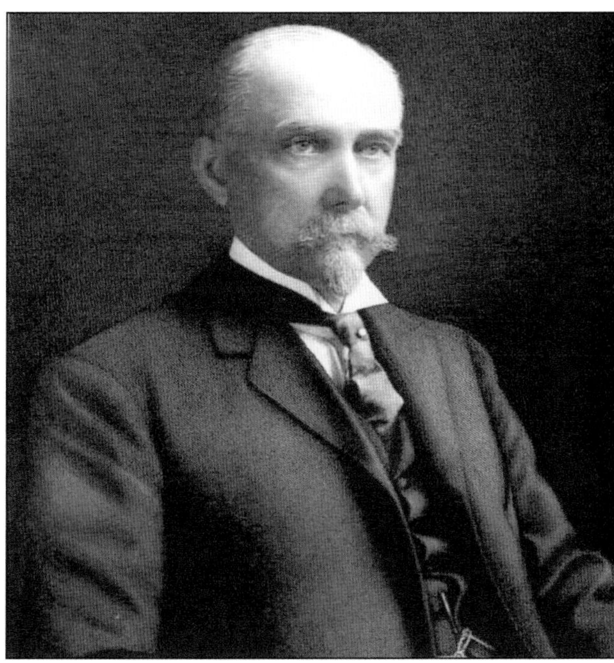

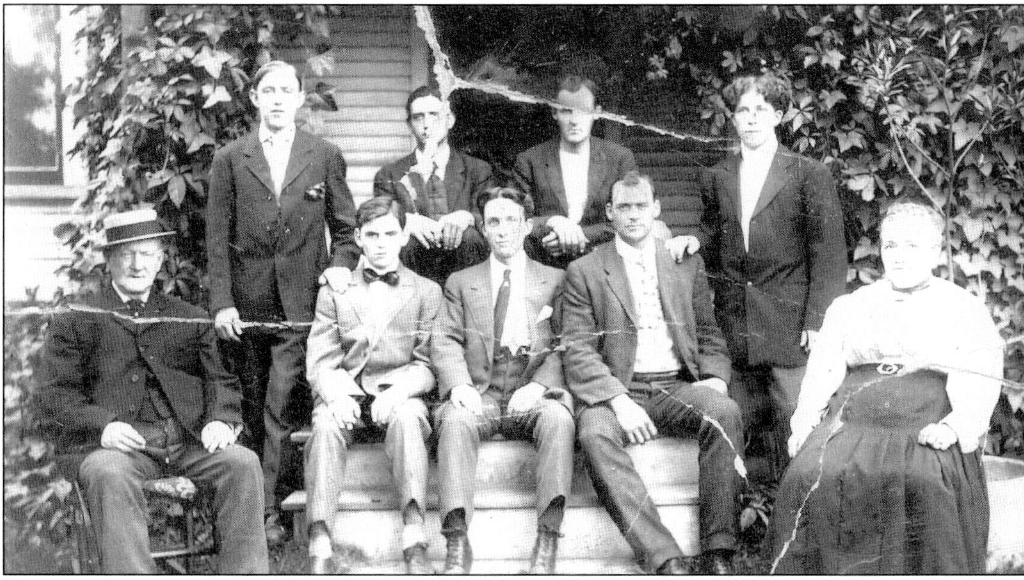

SEVEN SONS. Picture here is the Oliver and Laura Brodeur Eurto family. Oliver was born in 1845 in Dewittville, Canada, and moved to Dundee (on the international line between the United States and Canada in 1854). He married Laura in Malone in 1870 and in 1877 they moved to the Norfolk-Plumbrook area. The picture shows Oliver and Laura with their sons, Jack, Napoleon, Frank, Oliver, Joe, Andrew, and Herbert. Oliver is said to have changed the spelling of the original family name from Hurteau to Eurto. (Courtesy of Ruth Pharoah.)

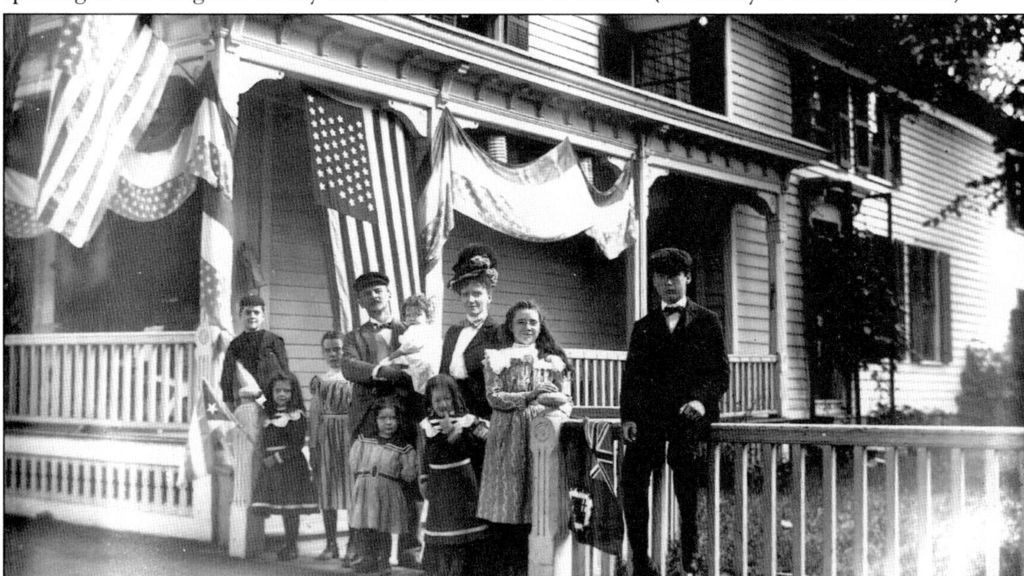

THE GLORIOUS FOURTH. The family of Alfred L. Jameson of Ogdensburg gathers to celebrate the Fourth of July in grand style amid the waving flags and buntings decorating the homestead. Their home was located on the corner of Washington and Elizabeth Streets. The holiday was celebrated with much pomp in this by-gone era with parades, speeches, and family reunions. Alfred Jameson was a banker and owned the Ogdensburg Music Store on Newell Block on State Street. (Courtesy of SLCHA)

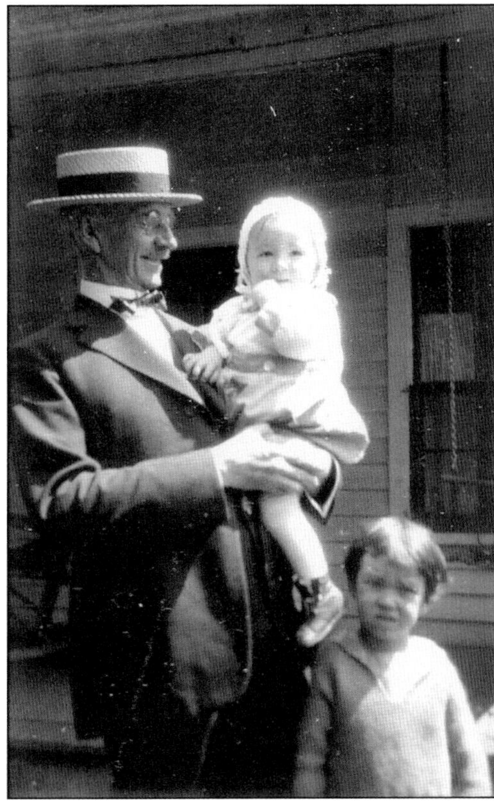

A Son of the Revolution. Ledyard Park Hale, a son of the Revolution, was born in the farmhouse on Hale Road that was settled by his ancestors in the 1830s. Ledyard became a well-known judge in St. Lawrence County and was also the head of the New York State Public Service Commission. He lived with his wife and two children in their large, red-brick home on the corner of Park Street and University Avenue in Canton. The building now houses the Kappa Delta Sigma sorority. He is shown in this picture sporting a straw boater with his grandson, Ledyard Park Hale, in his arms and another grandson, Ledyard Pfund, standing close by. (Courtesy of Ledyard Park Hale.)

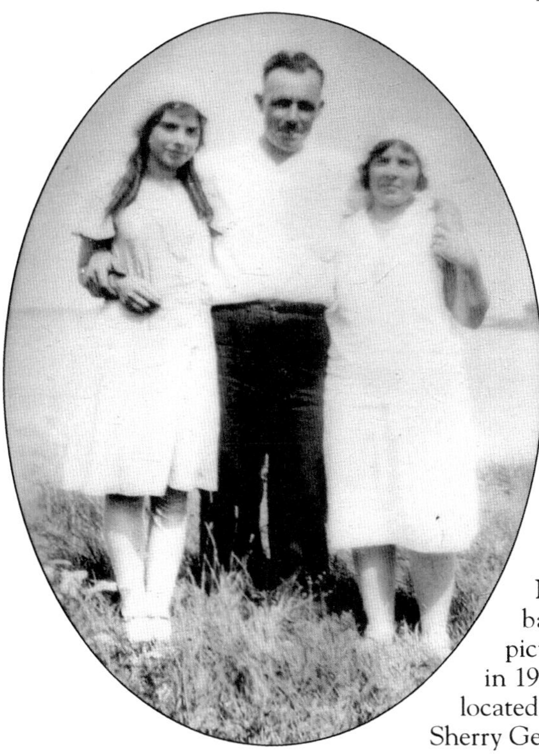

On the Banks of the St. Lawrence River. With the St. Lawrence River in the background, Lillian (left) and Marion are pictured with their father, John Edgar Conway, in 1925. The picture was taken at the family home located on James Street in Waddington. (Courtesy of Sherry Germano.)

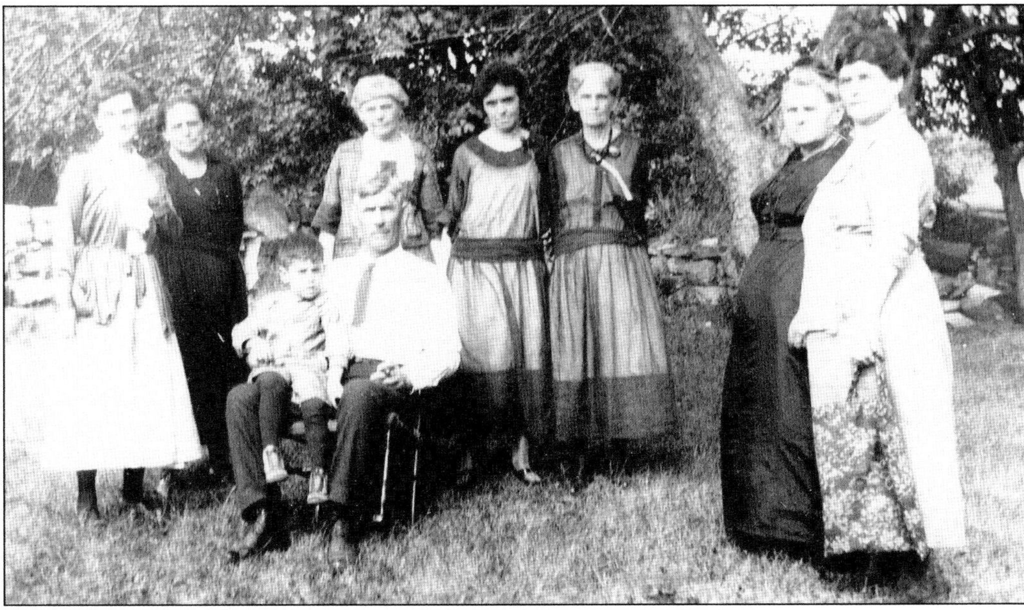

The Schermerhorn Place. The members of the James and Mary Ann Stratton Thrasher family are shown at their family home, where they were born and grew up. It is located at Oak Point on the St. Lawrence River in the town of Hammond. Standing here are, from left to right, Minerva Thrasher Fuller, Dell Gordon Scanlon, Mrs. Endsworth (a friend of the family), Katherine Dodds, Susan Thrasher Dodds (mother of Katherine), Matilda Thrasher Gordon (mother of Dell Scanlon), and Lydia Thrasher Luther. Seated is Thomas Scanlon (husband of Dell) holding their son, Thomas Scanlon Jr. James Thrasher died when Minerva was one year old. Thrasher's eight children were brought up by their mother, Mary Ann. (Courtesy of Jean Given.)

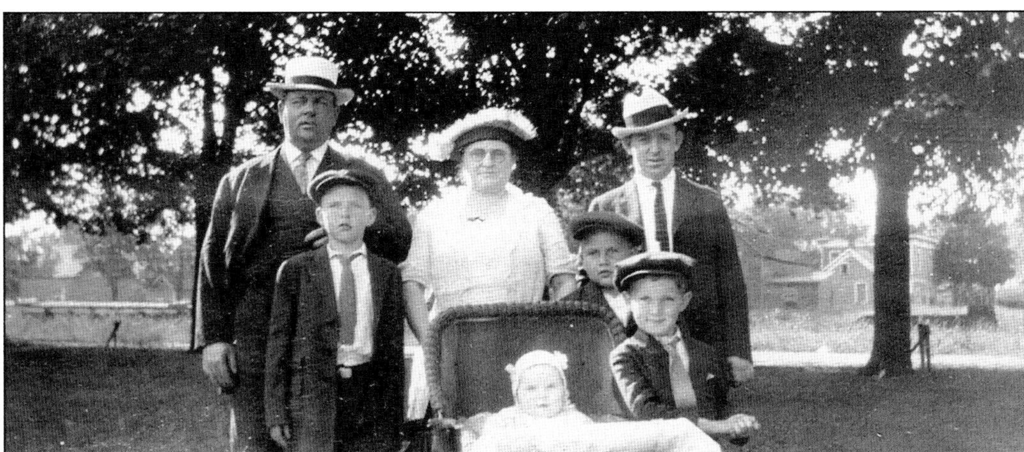

Fynns from Norwood. Shown here are, from left to right, as follows: (first row) Robert, Dorothy (in carriage), Bernard, and Leoback (second row) James Flynn (father), Pearl Kimball Flynn (mother), and Tom Riley (family friend). James Flynn's parents emigrated from Sneem, County Kerry, Ireland, during the potato famine. They arrived in New York with two children and had nine more, including James, after they settled in their new home. Pearl Kimball Flynn's family came from the Netherlands. James was a New York Central train engineer for his entire life. (Courtesy of Barbara Lee.)

Six

Groups and Schools

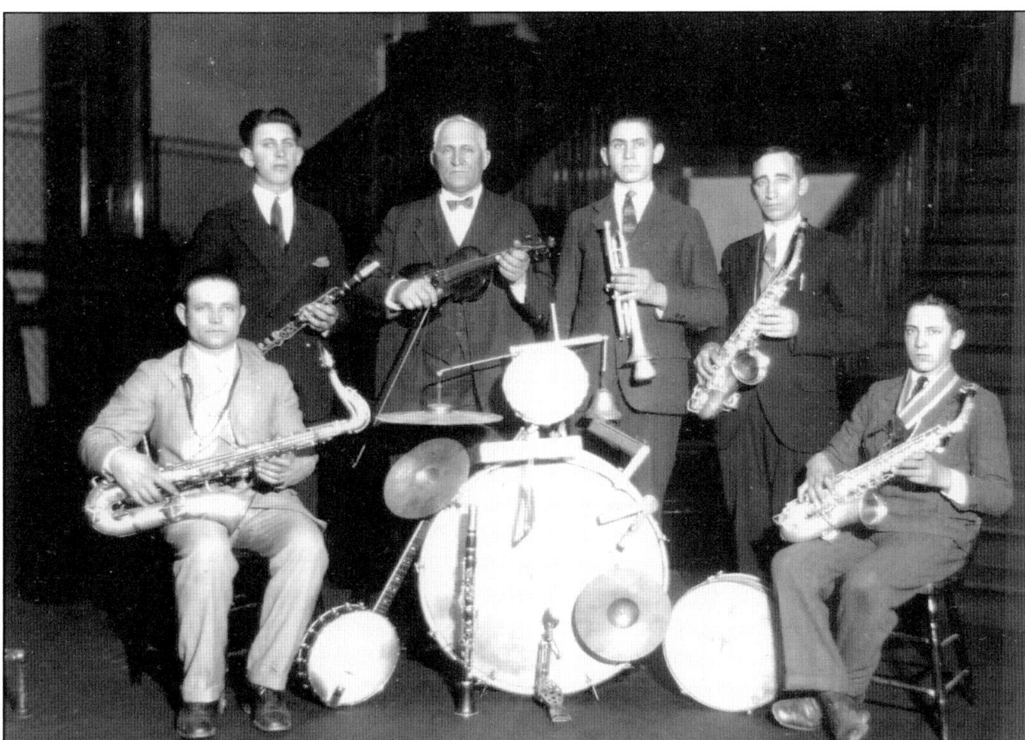

Band from Massena in the 1920s. The band played at numerous events in the Massena area. Shown here are, from left to right, are as follows: (first row) Ross Violi Sr. and Charlie Durant; (second row) Clayton Durant, Frank Durant, Guy Durant and Tony Catanzarite. The 1920s were a time when the world was enjoying the feeling of peace that followed World War I and the prosperity that was to come. The Charleston was all the rage and bands like this were in great demand. (Courtesy of Mary Catanzarite.)

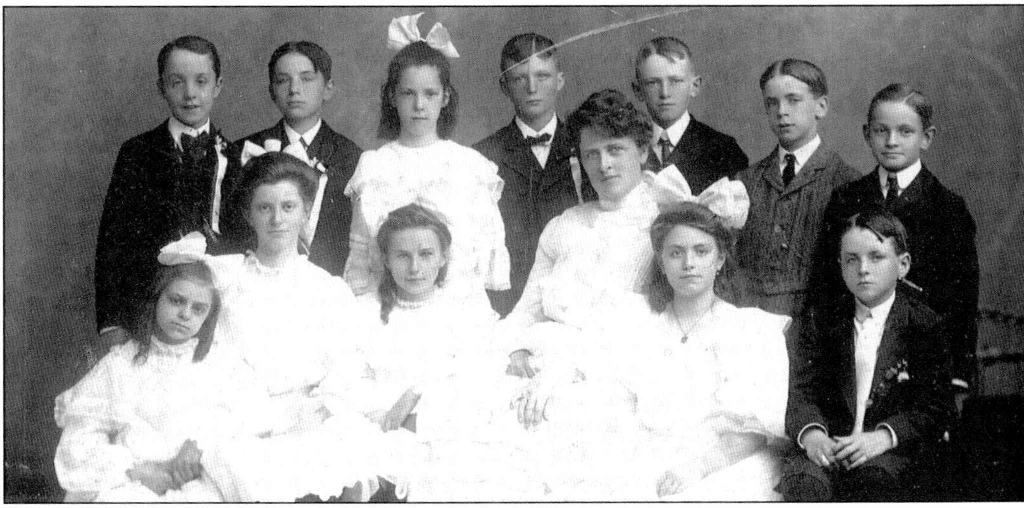

CLASS PICTURE. Pictured in this group of young people is James O'Leary, son of Ella and Patrick O'Leary. Born in 1891, he was one of six children raised on the family farm on Butternut Ridge Road in Potsdam. The picture was taken by Stone Studios located in Potsdam. These elegantly dressed children surrounding an adult, believed to be the teacher, are her students from the nearby school which the O'Leary children walked to daily. (Courtesy of Lawrence & Karen O'Brien.)

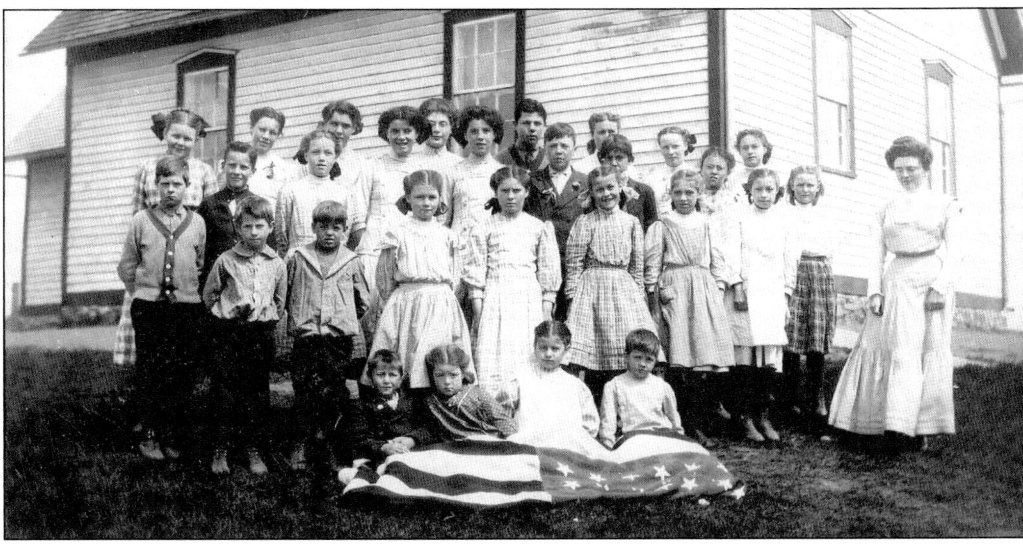

SCHOOLHOUSE AT LANGDON CORNERS. Pictured here are the students of the one-room schoolhouse near Langdon Corners on Pierrepont Road. The original schoolhouse was a stone building that came with the purchase of the land of Cinda and Peter Langdon. The wooden schoolhouse in the picture was built at a later date. Three Langdon girls from the family farm are in the photograph. Shown here, from left to right, are (first row) Clarence Cota, Lena Jardin, Gladys Kerky, and Merton Kerky; (second row) James Fuller, Frederick Bice, Myrtle Jardin, Mable Fuller, Florence Langdon, Lucia Blackmer, Gladys Cota, and Maude Bice; (third row) Nelson Jardin, Bower Rose, Frances Baker, Bernice Briggs, Bertha Briggs, Lee Potter, Thomas Farns, and Hilda Vaughn; (fourth row) Lura Langdon, Grace Rose, Mildred Briggs, Marion Farns, Glenn Aldrich, Ruth Langdon, Lula Rose, and Ruth Cota. The teacher, standing on the right, is Ella C. Donovan. (Courtesy of SLCHA.)

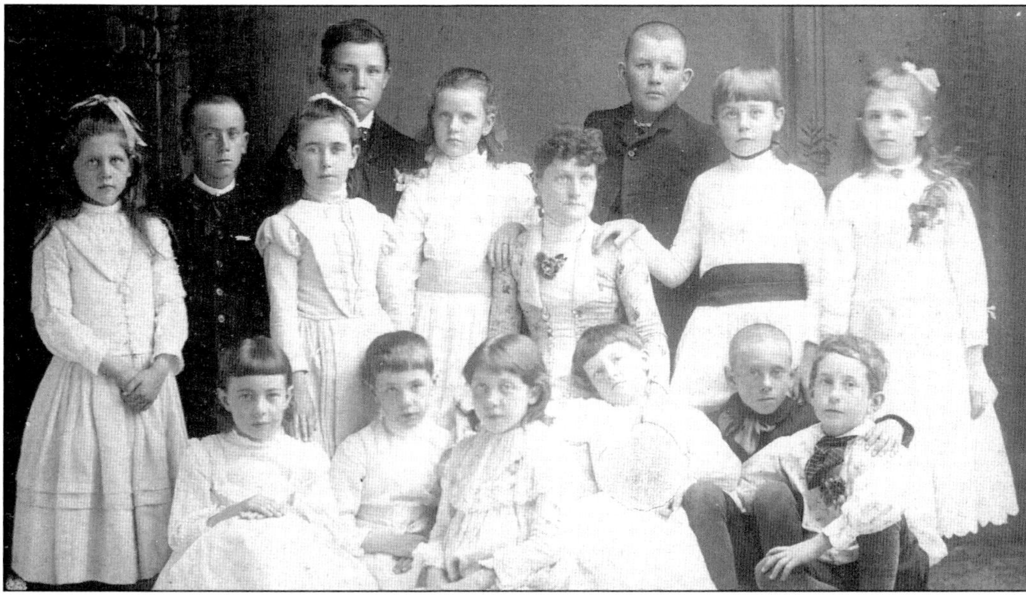

GRADUATION DAY AT MASSENA SPRINGS. It's graduation day in June 1889. Second from the left in the second row is Catherine Finnegan, who was born in 1877. Catherine and her family lived on East Hatfield Street in Massena Springs. She was the aunt of the eight-term mayor of Potsdam. In the early 1900s, the hamlet of Massena Springs drew visitors from all over the northeastern United States to frequent the springs for health and relaxation. Later, as the resorts faded, there were still many requests for mineral water. It was sold by druggists and mineral water dealers throughout New York state. (Courtesy of Ruth Finnegan Garner.)

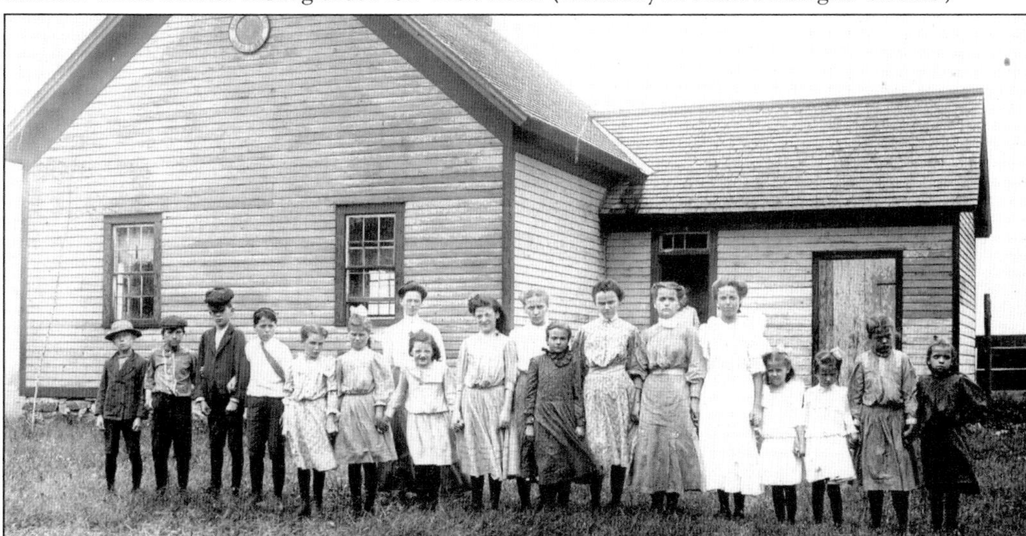

CRANE SCHOOL. The Crane School was in the Canton School District No. 15, on Canton Pyrites Road. The school dates back to at least 1845. Henry Van Rensselaer, who owned this land, leased it to the trustees of the school. When he sold his property in 1853, he reserved this parcel for the school. Lillie Fordham was the teacher in 1907–1908 and from 1916 to 1919. The school was in use up until the 1940s, and in later years it was purchased and transformed into a private home. (Courtesy of Beulah White.)

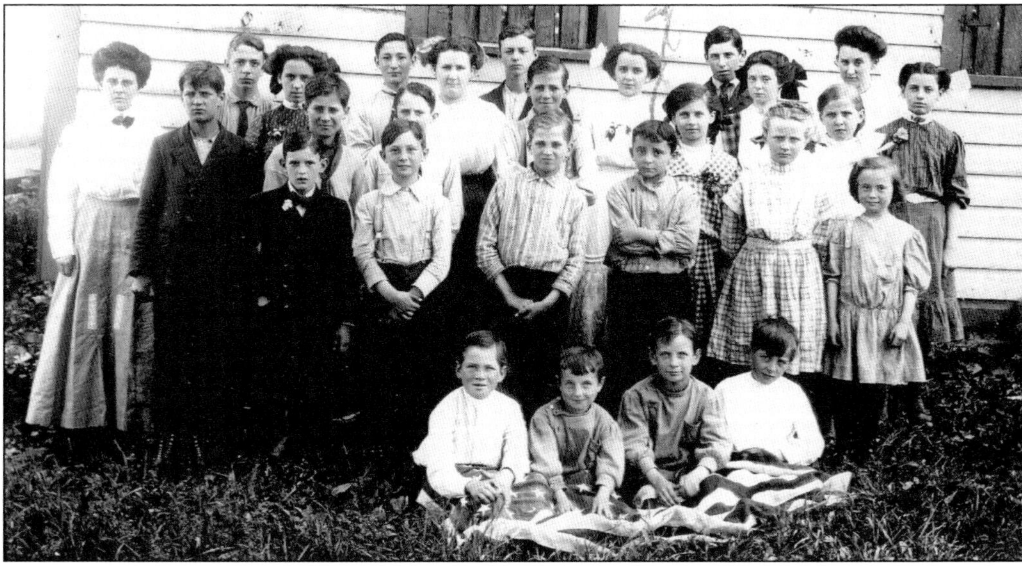

THE OLIN SCHOOL. Pictured here in the early 1900s are the students of the Olin School located on Sykes Morley Road, outside of Canton. This picture was submitted by two people—one from the family of Herb Eggleson, and one from the Dick Meyers family. Dick Meyers's mother was a descendent of the Olins. Their teacher was Lennie Wilcox. Shown here are, from left to right, (first row) S. Aldous, G. Olin, Mark Olin, and ? Aldous; (second row) Clyde McCormick, Herbert Eggleston, C. Aldous, Dick Meyers, Hilda Hart, and Doris Eggleston; (third row) Otis Aldous, Ward Aldous, Leon Galanger, Lela Purvee, Everett Aldous, Harriet Olin, G. Coakley, L. Aldous, and Lucy Place; (fourth row) Harold Matthews, Iona Place, Roy Hale, L. Stiles, C. Matthews, Frank Place, and ? Purvee. (Courtesy of Peggy Eggleston & Joan Meyers.)

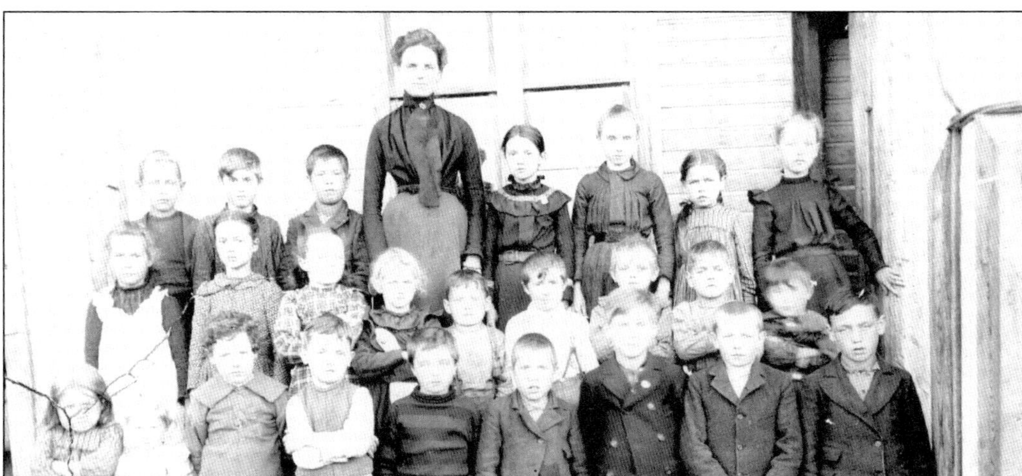

NATURAL DAM SCHOOL. This photograph taken around 1900, shows Eula McKenney, teacher, in the back row. She is the daughter of John and Ida McKenney. Her father was employed at the paper mill in Natural Dam. The family lived in a company cottage next to the Gouverneur Morris Stone Mansion, which, for a time, was used as a schoolhouse. Eula married James F. McCormick of Canton in 1920 and taught piano lessons throughout her life. They had two sons, James and Malcolm. (Courtesy of Malcolm McCormick.)

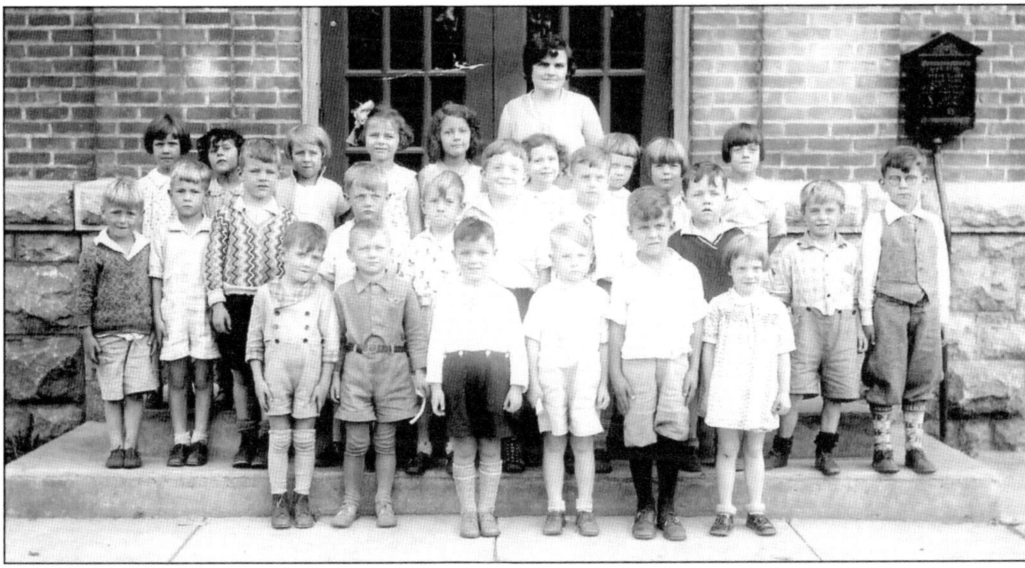

First Grade Is Fun. Pictured here is the first-grade class of the Canton Grammar School in the fall of 1930. With them is their teacher, Margaret Myers, who, in the years to come, taught many of her students' children. This class went on to graduate from high school in 1942. Shortly thereafter many of the boys went off to war. (Courtesy of Harold Wilder.)

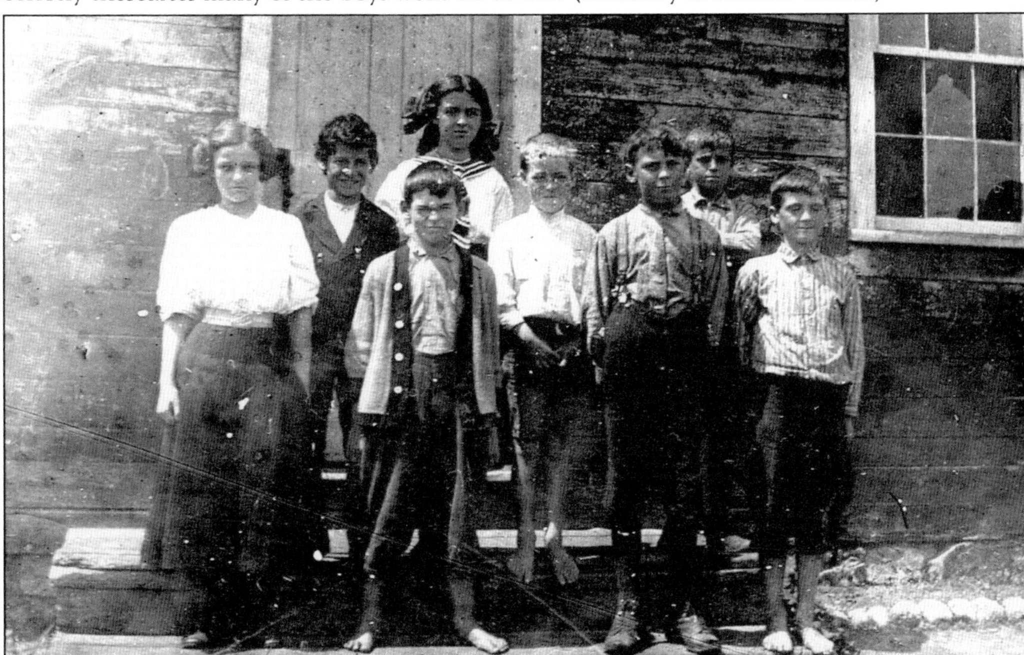

Country School in Pitcairn. Harvey L. Gleason, father of Mary Colton of Canton, is one of the boys pictured here. The date of the photograph is approximately 1909. Many children went to school without shoes in those early days, as noted above. There were about 300 country schools in St. Lawrence County around 1900. If there were enough farms in one area, a school was required. If there were not enough children in the area to warrant a school, the children would be homeschooled. (Courtesy of Mary Colton.)

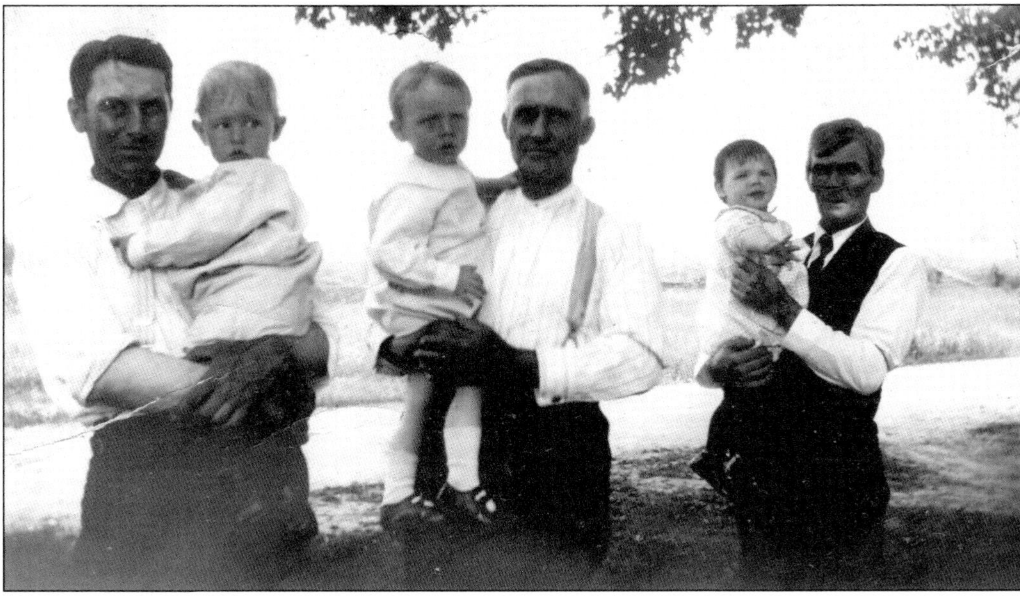

THE FOURTH OF JULY, 1921. Holding their young ones on their shoulders, from left to right, are Grant Porter (with son Lowell), Jake Lyman (with son Oscar), and Leslie Woodside (with daughter Frances). They are celebrating Independence Day at the Porter farm in the town of Lisbon. This was a much-anticipated gathering of the people of the area. It was a day of freedom from work and a day of celebration. The three men were dairy farmers. (Courtesy of Fran Doyle.)

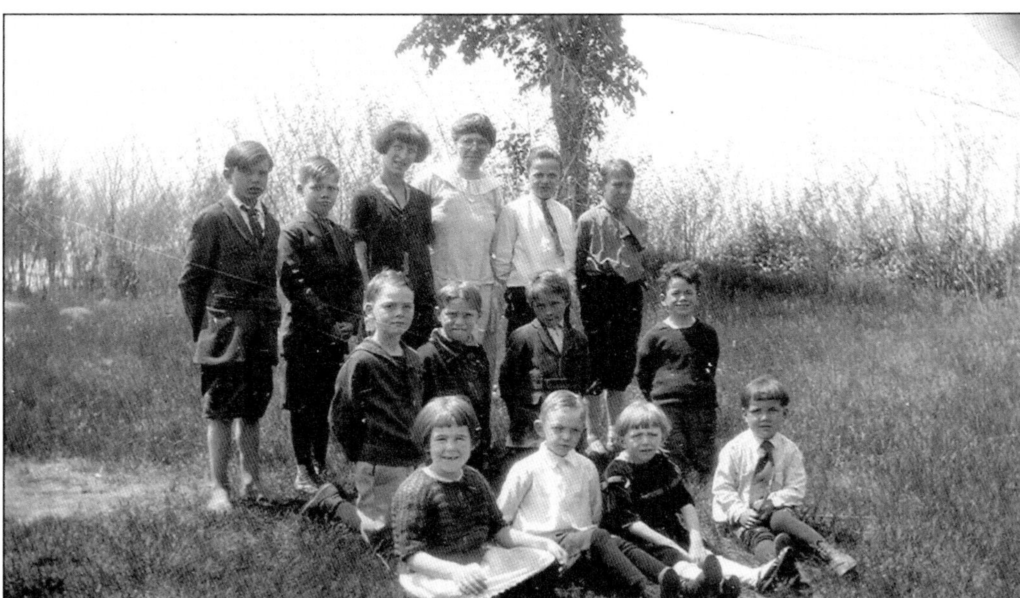

MOTHER AND DAUGHTER AT SCHOOL IN BRASHER FALLS. Eileen Mahoney Fay (first row, left) is enjoying a sunny day with her class at the White School House in Brasher Falls. The teacher (top row center) was her mother, Letitia Mahoney. Eileen loved learning and went on to teach in Tupper Lake and Massena. (Courtesy of Sheila Harrington.)

HIAWATHA. Here is a scene from the production of *Hiawatha* that was kept for posterity in postcard form. This pageant was held at Woodford Farm in Ogdensburg to benefit the homeless children at the United Helpers Home. In the beginning, homeless children were sent to almshouses and poorhouses and cared for by adult paupers. The Ogdensburg City Orphan Asylum was founded in 1885. In 1898, United Helpers led the way in St. Lawrence County in constructing an institution that would offer orphans food, housing, and protection. Today United Helpers Organization operates and manages 29 facilities throughout St. Lawrence County. (Courtesy of United Helpers.)

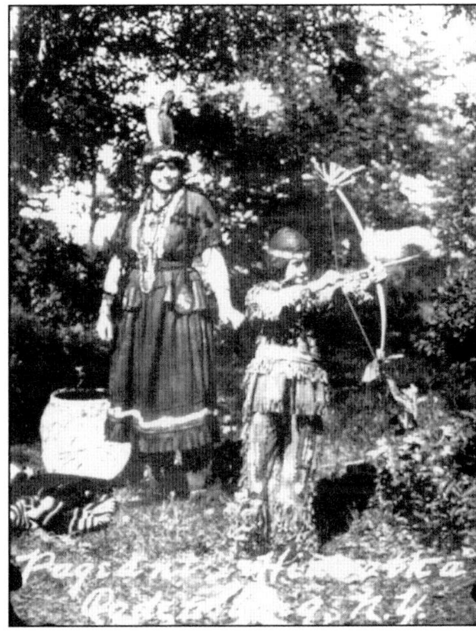

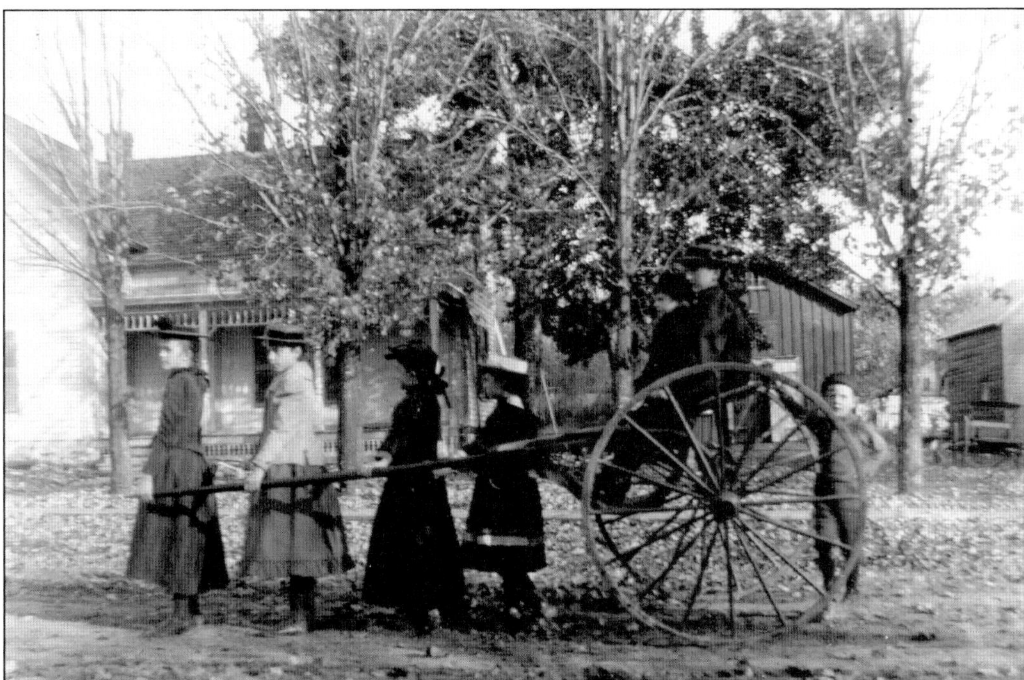

WE'RE GOING PLACES. These children are playing with a buggy at 28 State Street in Canton. The picture was taken using the glass-plate method of photography. The method, invented by an Englishman, Frederick Scott Archer, became public in 1851. The process, called wet-plate method, used a photosensitive liquid combined with collodion and had to be applied at the time that the photograph was taken. In the 1870s, a dry-plate method became available, which meant the plates could be factory-made and stored in a box for future use. Both of these methods dropped in popularity by the 1920s when George Eastman offered his first Kodak camera and flexible roll film. (Courtesy of Kathy Curro.)

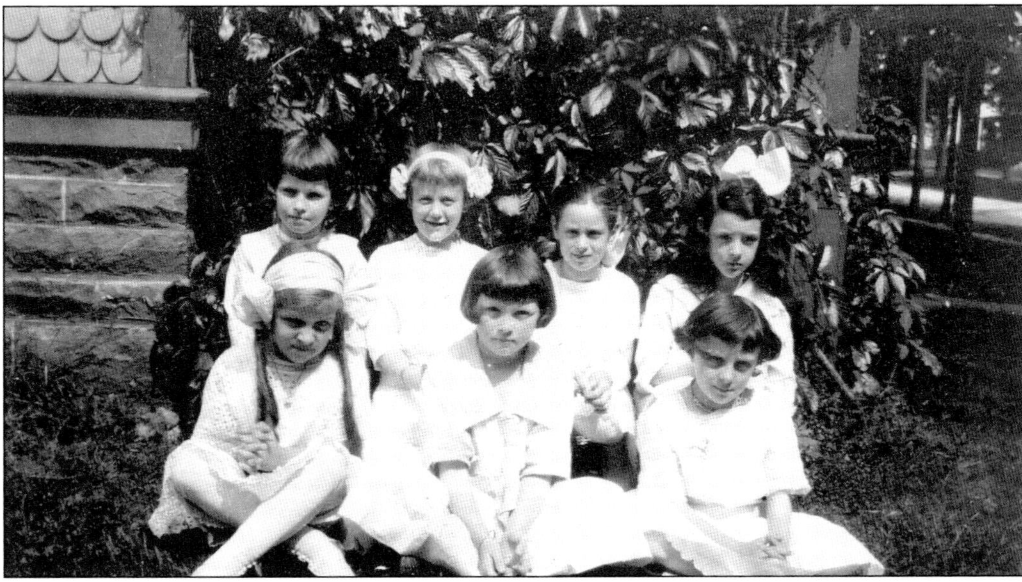

SEVEN CHILDHOOD FRIENDS. Seven little girls gathered at a family home on Main Street in Potsdam on a summer day in the early 1900s. Pictured here, from left to right, are (front row) Marian Butler, Louise Deans, and Elizabeth Fuller; (second row) Sara Clark, Helen Snell, Margaret Fuller, and Elizabeth Cubley. In 2004, both Helen Snell Cheel and Sara Clark Chittenden celebrated their 100th birthdays. (Courtesy of Varick Chittenden.)

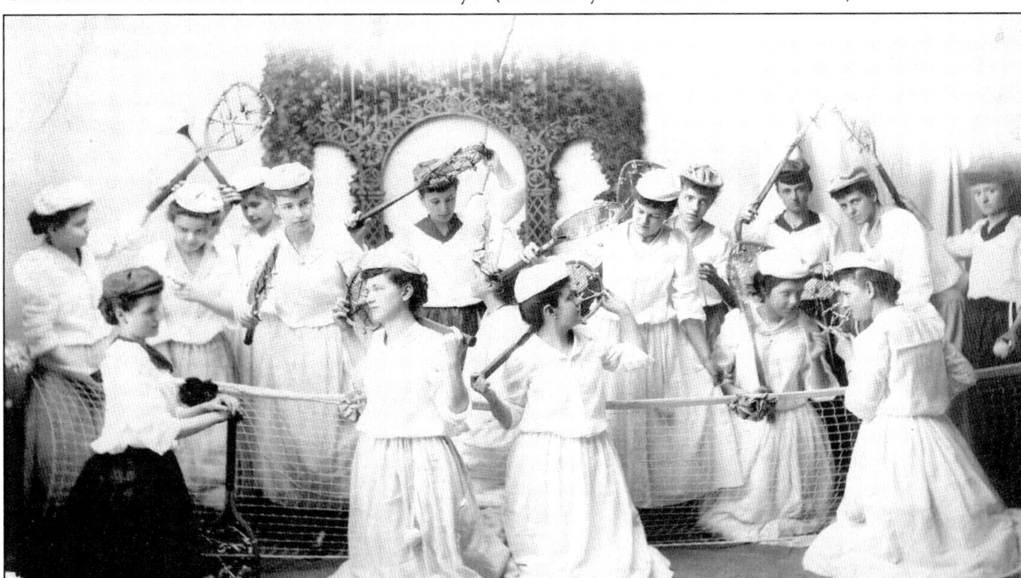

GRACE LYNDE AND FRIENDS ENJOY A GAME OF TENNIS. Grace, (second from left, top row), was the adopted daughter of state senator Delphos S. Lynde and his wife, Esther. Delphos was the president of Canton's First National Bank from 1887 to 1897. In 1905, Grace joined the bank to become assistant cashier, and was active in local causes. It was recorded in the local newspaper that Grace and three other local young ladies sponsored a public dance in Miner Hall to benefit the local library on October 24, 1894. The lovely Lynde home still stands at 43 East Main Street in Canton. (Courtesy of SLCHA.)

TAKE ME OUT TO THE BALL GAME. Here we have four boys ready for baseball practice in the backyard of the Heffernon house, which was located in Canton. The Heffernons lived on Court Street where Community Bank stands today. Young Walter Heffernon took the picture of his buddies. The boy in the center is Dick Wicks. Walter and Dick enlisted in the Army together after World War II was declared. (Courtesy of Rita Heffernon Foote.)

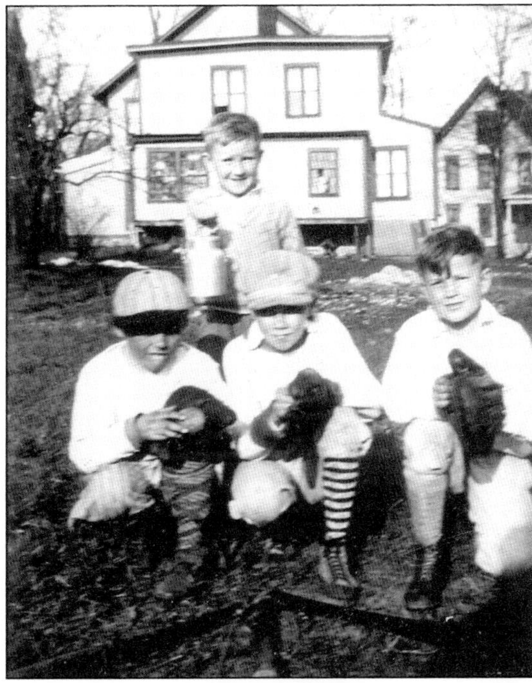

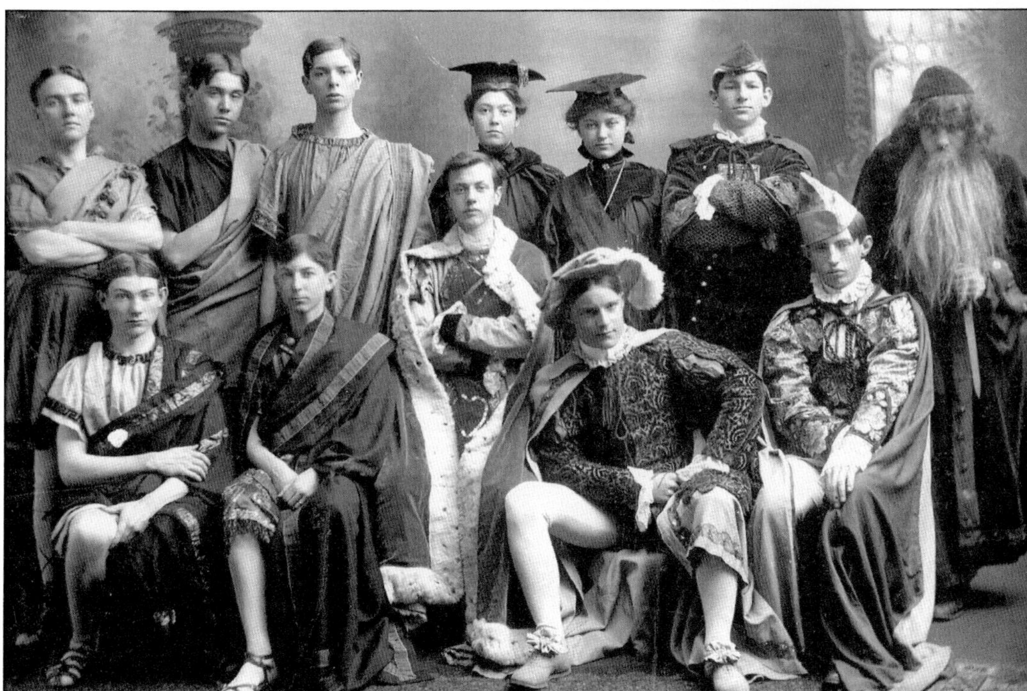

FACING THE SPOTLIGHT. This photograph is of the drama department at Canton High School. The students are preparing an extravagant production of *The Merchant of Venice*. Pictured here are, from left to right, (front row) Norman MacDonald, Ward C. Priest, George Van DeLuider, Clarence Hayden, and unidentified; (second row) Ogden Conkey, Leslie Bailey, Eben Griffiths, Clara Payson, Bessie Farmer, George Terry, and Melford Brown. (Courtesy of SLCHA.)

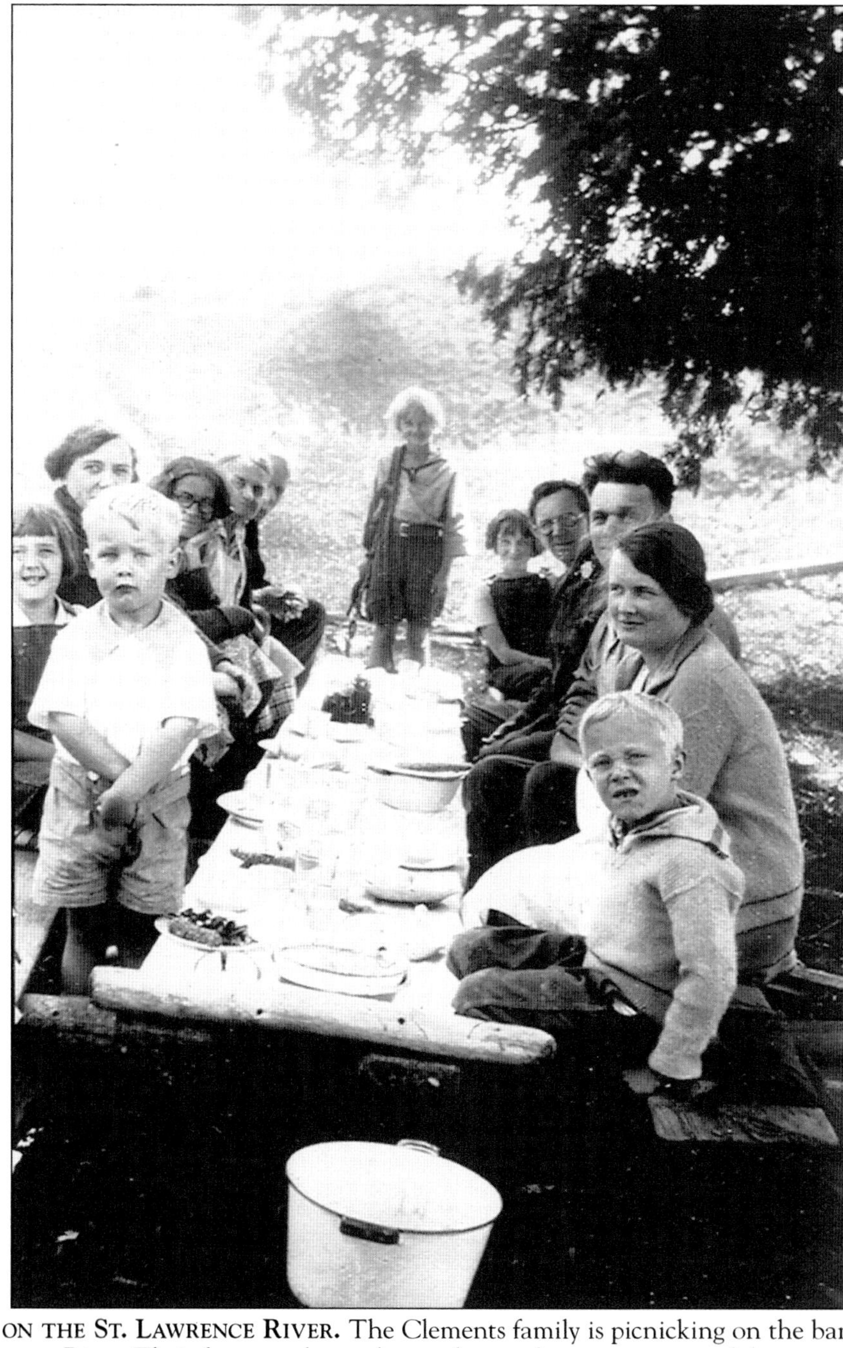

PICNIC ON THE ST. LAWRENCE RIVER. The Clements family is picnicking on the banks of the St. Lawrence River. Their farm was located near the northeastern corner of the town of Lisbon in the area known as Point Rockaway. Abraham and Rhoda (Harvey) Odell were the original owners and had built a stone house that they operated as an inn or halfway house. Samuel and Rhoda (Sharp) Clements purchased the farm in 1877. Many members of the Clements family can be seen here seated around the picnic table. They are, clockwise from bottom left, Paul F., Alice, Fanny (Engert), Estelle, Matilda (Gray), W. Wallace, Georgena (standing in back), Betty, Ralph, George W., E. Dacie (Thompson) and Wallace E. R. (Courtesy of Bill Hull.)